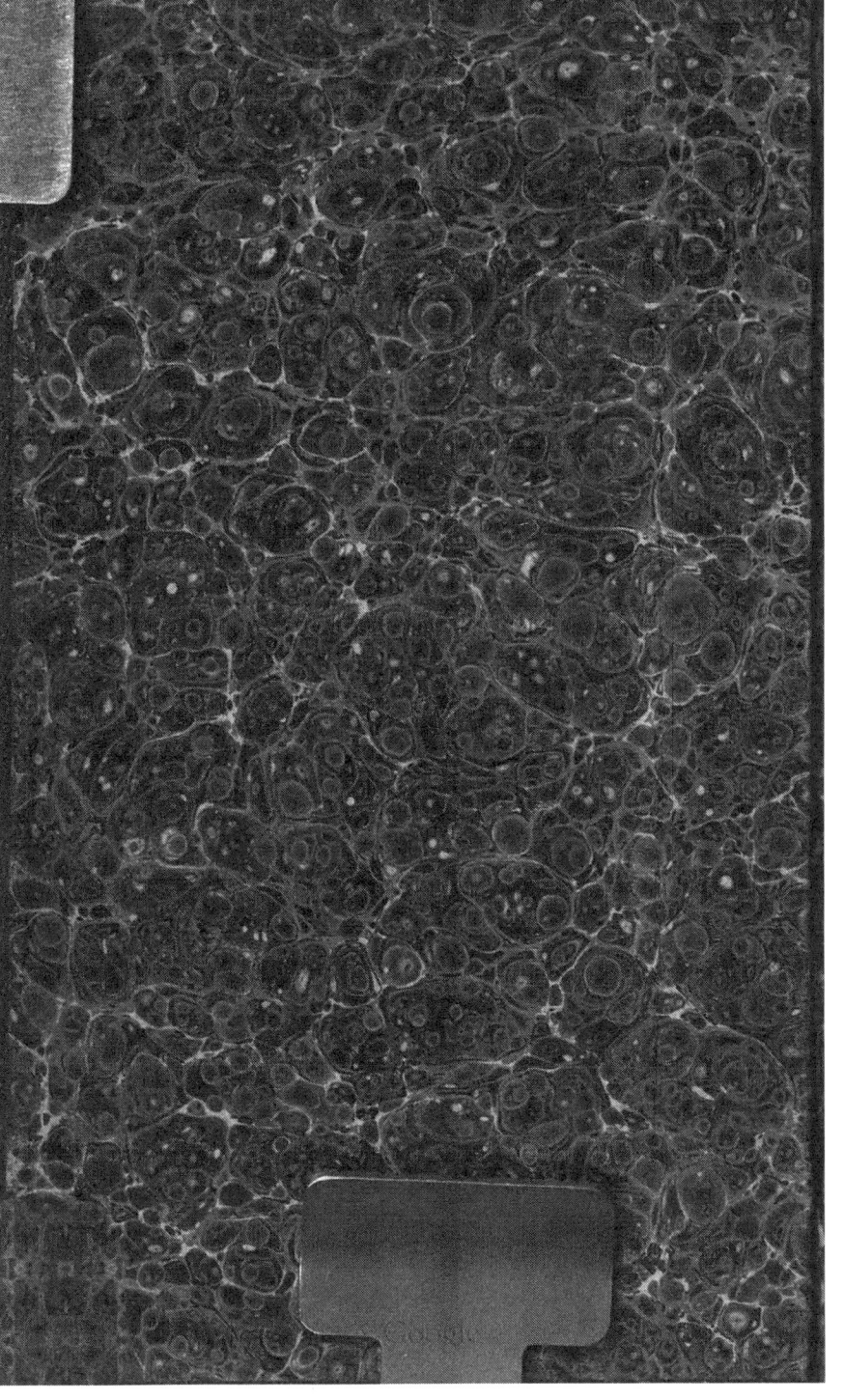

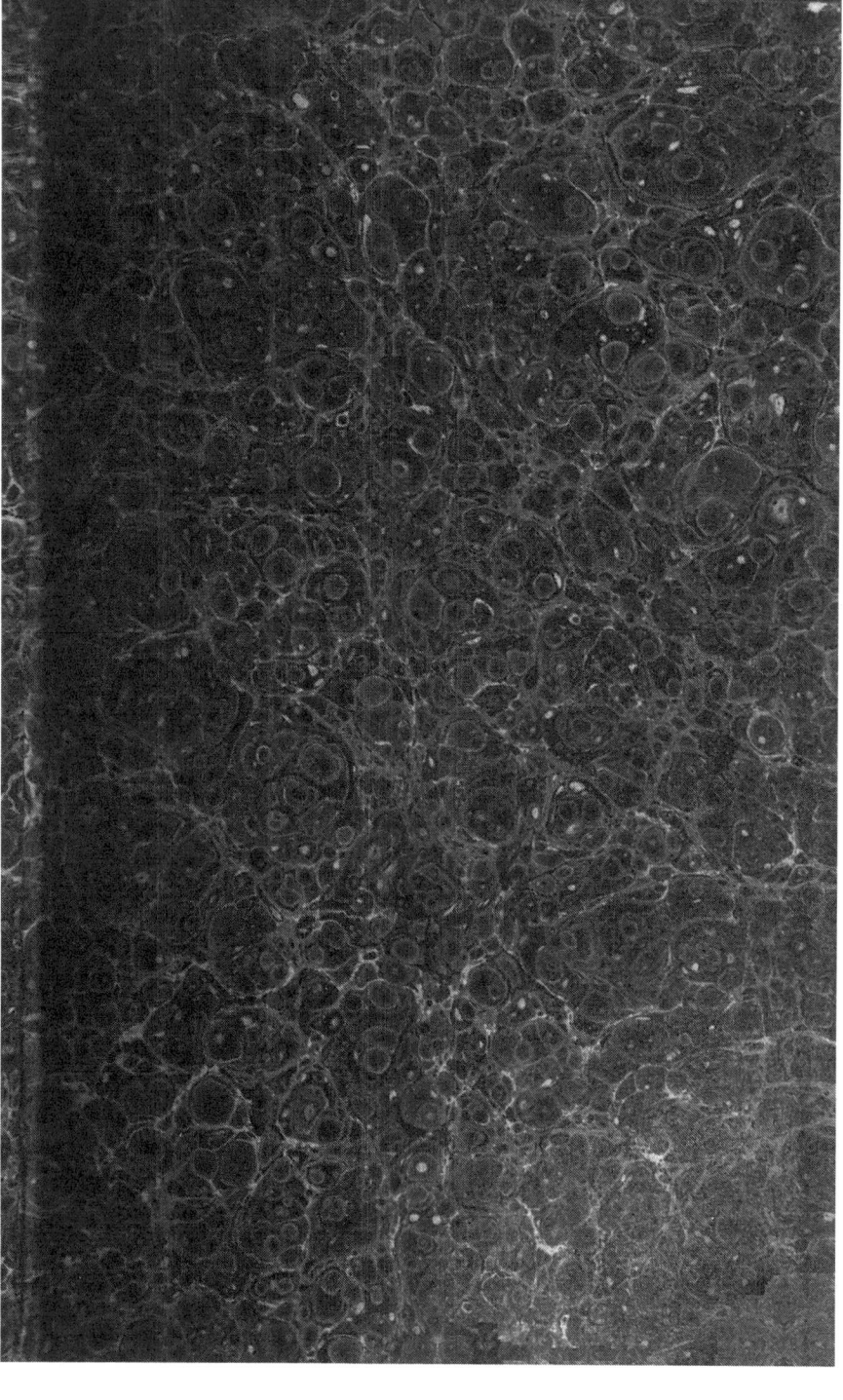

1361. c. 10.

Because thou hast done this thing and hast not withheld thy son thine only son: in blessing I will bless thee.

Genesis XXII. 16. 17.

THE

FOUNDATIONS

OF

The Spiritual Life:

DRAWN FROM THE

BOOK OF THE IMITATION OF JESUS CHRIST.

BY F. SURIN.

TRANSLATED FROM THE FRENCH, AND ADAPTED TO THE USE OF THE ENGLISH CHURCH.

LONDON:
JAMES BURNS, 17, PORTMAN STREET,
PORTMAN SQUARE.

1844.

LONDON:
GILBERT AND RIVINGTON, PRINTERS,
ST. JOHN'S SQUARE.

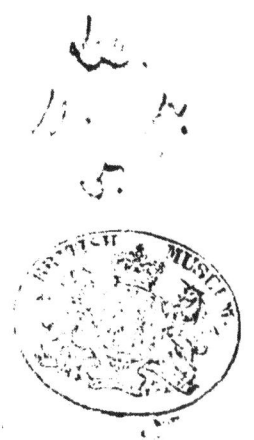

PREFACE.

The following book is founded upon one, long prized among us, "The Imitation of our Lord and Saviour Jesus Christ." It is the application and enforcement of maxims thence derived, circling around the fundamental truth, that "the practice of the doctrine of the Cross is the foundation of the spiritual life." Like all other Catholic teaching, it assumes as its basis the same two truths, which have been strongly, though of late somewhat nakedly, enforced among ourselves as the instrument of conversion to God,—a vivid, penetrating, pervading sense of our own corruption, with the participation of the Cross of Christ. For these, if expanded duly on all sides, must needs contain the whole of our reception of the Gospel. The fervent words of a saint's[a] devotion, "Who art Thou, and who am I?" are a summary of the Gospel, since they comprise Him Who is our End, as He is, and ourselves in relation to Him. The conviction of our own nothingness and God's Infinity, our own

[a] S. Francis of Assisium.

sinfulness and His Holiness, our own boundless misery and His boundless Mercy, is the condition for prayer, the preparation for Sacraments, the ground of penitence, the element of faith, hope, and love. Of course, this must not be understood negatively, (as it too often is,) to the exclusion or disparagement of any truth not distinctly expressed in it, (this were at once heretical,) but as entering into all; not as a distinct confession of faith, but as the outline of it, and the life of all our practice.

Yet, without speaking now of the necessary limitations of such statements, it is hoped that, besides the effect of high maxims and well-tried rules on minds which are striving after "the more excellent way," works like the present may in this way also benefit us, if those who have an earnest perception of certain limited fundamental truths, see the truths about which they are anxious, to be the very foundation of Catholic teaching; that it is proposed to them, not to unlearn any thing they have learnt of positive truth, but to act upon it, carry it out, expand it; receive, it may be, other truths in addition, but to part with nothing which has been a portion of their own spiritual existence. For as such a shock is in all cases perilous, so can it never be needed. Heresy in itself consists in the denial of truth; it is simple poison, and must therefore destroy, not nourish. If then there be any thing in connexion with it which nourishes and preserves life, that is not heresy, but faith, however mingled with misbelief. This, in any case, it is the office of the Church to disengage; to appeal to what people do believe, and engraft the fuller truth upon it; to supply what they have not, not to seem to take away what they have. This St. Paul shows us even in his preaching to the heathen, teaching them Whom they ignorantly worshipped. Much more, when truth, however partially it may at all times have been held, and with whatever negative elements it has of late been unhappily blended, was in its earlier days the instrument of a great moral revival. It was a vivid and energetic, however partial, preaching of the corruption of human nature, and of the Cross, which, by the Providence of God, broke in upon an age of torpor and smooth easy ways in religion. As far as it pressed these truths, it was in warfare with the world, and was derided by it, and prevailed [a]. It may have been that a technical state of things, in which "regeneration" was a *mere* "change of state," bringing men into an external covenant; "conversion" was thought to be a denial of regeneration, and so was itself denied; "sanctification" was little more than "moral amendment;" "Divine

[a] In thus acknowledging what was done for our Church by one earnest section of it, the editor ought to repeat the conviction expressed elsewhere, that the doctrine often found along with their teaching, viz. that "they who believe they are saved, are saved;" that "man's salvation depends on his own personal assurance that he is saved;" that "an act of faith, (as it is called,) conveys in itself the pardon of past sin," are, however qualified or inconsistently held by individuals, deadly heresies. In Wesleyanism, the system thereon founded threatens to be one of the most dreadful scourges with which the Church was ever afflicted, the great antagonist of penitence, as those who have the charge of souls most sorrowfully find.

calls" were rejected as enthusiasm; "communion with God" as mysticism; "Divine grace" was little more than an external help; the very Sacraments were things outward; "mental prayer" was held to be excitement; could not have been broken up, except by some strong antagonist statement;—that holding the shell and skeleton of a true system, some such vehement action was needed to make us aware that it was but a casket deprived of the pearl within, a framework without life or power of motion. Not, of course, that in saying this, one judges those who acted, one must believe, on either side, more truly up to their light[a], than those to whom more has been given, may know that they have done themselves. Nothing controversial is hereby meant; still less to criticise individuals, to all of whom the writer must be inferior. It is rather meant to acknowledge a debt, to indicate the points of contact between the teaching of the last century, which broke through the stagnant state into which we were fast subsiding, and the fuller Catholic teaching; and to suggest that such as hold in earnestness the truths then inculcated, will find more sympathy in the larger system of Catholic truth, than in the stiffening form to which their predecessors found themselves opposed. Both of the systems which were in conflict in the last century were partial, and could not meet together because

[a] There were also, in the worst times, exceptions, and most, perhaps, among those of whom the world knew nothing, who still belonged in spirit to a former century, before sins entailed by the act of 1688 brought this blight over our Church.

they were so. Neither was extensive enough to embrace the other. Each had its strong points and its weak ones; each its own texts; until at last people came tranquilly to divide Holy Scripture between them, leaving as the other's property what they could not master as their own. The true Catholic system is, of course, co-extensive with Holy Scripture. It must embrace all which a partial system cannot grasp. It can reconcile the doctrine of predestination with Sacramental grace, the necessity of the entire conversion of sinners with Baptismal regeneration, deep repentance with Christian joy, the acceptableness of good works with the imperfection of the Christian's best acts. It can combine forms of prayer with the freest and highest mental devotion, spiritual Communion with the intensest devotion for the Sacramental, inspired understanding of Holy Scripture with implicit submission to the Church, the superiority of the teaching of the Holy Spirit with deference for Divine learning. It is absolutely shocking to have to say that the highest eminence of good works leads but to a more implicit reliance on His merits Who gave them; that to holiness such perception is given of its own entire dependence upon Grace whence it sprung, and of the deformity of its remaining imperfections, that it must become the more intensely humble. Living in the Divine light, it gains an insight into its own intrinsic nothingness, which to ordinary men appears exaggerated. But with it every thing is strictly personal. It confesses and abhors, not the short-comings of human nature, but its own. To use the expressive words of St. Francis, after his future glory had been revealed, he still accounted himself the greatest sinner in the world, for, he said^a, "If God had bestowed on the greatest sinner the favours He hath upon me, he would have been more grateful than I am; had He left me to myself, I should have committed greater wickedness."

Whatever signs of decay, then, there may any where be, or however the warfare with worldliness may have been relaxed, we may hope that it is of God, that jealousy for the doctrine of the corruption and helplessness of human nature, and for the preaching of the Cross, has taken such extensive possession of the English mind. The ground-work, we may hope, is laid. Those who hold these truths, such at least as are of the more real sort, will gladly, it is trusted, embrace an expansion of them, when they come to see that the truths they hold are not interfered with, but their reception heightened and deepened. For since the Gospel is "not in word" and confession only, "but in deed," and "is the power of God unto salvation," then these fundamental truths must have practical consequences, extensive in proportion to the position they occupy. Since our

---

[a] Butler's Lives. Words remarkably similar have been transmitted as expressing the habit of mind of a holy Bishop of our own. The Editor would take this opportunity of saying, that nothing was ever further from his intention than criticising any whom he knew to be saints of God. In any thing he ever said, he was following, he hopes, authority, or regarding words only in themselves, or in what seemed their natural or unavoidable effect on ordinary minds, such as his own, quite abstractedly from those who used them.

nature is thus corrupt, then we have need to be guarded against it on all points. Since the flesh rebels, it must be subdued; since the world entices, it must be renounced; since the lust of the eyes captivates, they must be ruled; since "the pride of life" excludes the love of God, it must be tamed; since covetousness is the root of all evil, it must be plucked out; since the praise of men shuts out the praise of God, it must be shunned as a pestilence. But, without giving further instances, what have we already but the value of the Evangelic precepts, of fasting, of large and self-denying almsgiving as a corrective of the danger of riches, of discipline of the body, of detailed vigilance over the senses, of one continuous warfare with our whole selves, of "bearing hardness, like good soldiers of JESUS CHRIST," of living the hidden life in Him?

And, in truth, ascetic practice is not only the natural expression and embodying of our knowledge of "the infection of our nature," but inseparable from any deep sense of it. Feelings live in acts. Can any one be thought to be, in real earnest, persuaded that he bears about him a domestic enemy, ever eager to betray him to Satan and his own destruction, who in act takes no heed to it? If we in earnest believe it, we must feel it as a subtle poison, ever ready to taint all we think, or say, or do, seeking at the time to corrupt, or by after-thought to turn into sin all the good we would do; an active principle, as far as it is unsubdued, craving indulgence, using all our senses as its instruments, our likes or dislikes, our activity or our sloth, our labour or our refreshment, our speech or our silence, our doing or our leaving undone, centering in self as its end, and compassing to make us do all things to ourselves, not to God; to take "His gold and silver, His corn and wine and oil," His gifts of nature, the world, or grace, and offer them to Baal. Can one then really be thought to have any sense of the depth, and extent, and subtle intertwining of this evil, who thinks that its hold over us can be loosened and destroyed, except in detail? that if we cultivate in us certain frames of feeling, things must, as a matter of course, go right, instead of assuredly going wrong? that any mere general desire to love God can, by a compendious method, dispense with the irksome, painful task of plucking up, nipping, weed by weed, what has been sown in us while asleep? Our diligence must surely be co-extensive with the evil; where this is all-pervading, so must be the self-discipline. Since self is in every form our great internal enemy, denial of self, in equal detail, must be our safeguard. A systematic attack at all points cannot be warded off by a mere desultory general defence. Can one really be thought, e. g., to believe in earnest, that "the tongue is an unruly evil, full of deadly poison," "a fire," "a world of iniquity," who yet exerts no reserve in speaking, talks freely of self, relates every unauthenticated tale he hears, disputes fearlessly on sacred subjects, has no rules of silence, criticises freely all he mislikes, or lets his speech run on in an easy careless way, uttering all which occurs, and content if it be not stirred up by some energetic passion, as if there were no Judgment-seat where "idle words" were to be given account of, or no temptations to censoriousness, self-display, evil-speaking, irreverence? Can one be thought to believe deeply in the "deceitfulness of the heart above all things," and its "desperate wickedness," who proposes to go through the trials of the day, with no definite contemplation of his own especial failures, or definite rules to which to appeal, when his besetting temptation offers a bribe to his conscience to judge untruly? It seems quite inconceivable that any should in earnest feel that we have a strong energizing principle within us, "lusting against the Spirit," "warring against the law of our mind," and tempted or set in motion by Satan, and yet think that it is not to be met by an equally energetic series of acts, under the guidance of the Holy Spirit of God. Almost equally inconceivable is it how any can suppose that these acts will (for any considerable time at least, until they have themselves become habitual) be carried on as perseveringly, if left to the disposal of the moment, as if brought under rule. Doubtless the advanced become a rule to themselves, and the Holy Spirit is so present to their souls, that Divine contemplation is the element they breathe, devotion their bodily sustenance; temptations of the flesh absolutely disappear; the very discernment of what they eat or drink is through habitual mortification lost; what is bitter becomes sweet, through memory of "the gall;" suffering with Christ becomes their very craving; humiliation their joy, praise their confusion [a].

[a] The above are in part the characteristics of the saintly character; the love of humiliations and sufferings being found

The mistake has been, not, of course, in exalted thoughts of the all-sufficiency of Divine Grace, but in the unsuspiciousness of human weakness; not as though Divine Grace would not regulate every action of our lives, but as though we, without systematic self-discipline, should not yet more often fail to respond to it; or, still more painfully, whether, when we neglect this, we are really in earnest enough to receive it. Yet something of this sort, some notion that men were setting limits to the free Grace of God, instead of restraining their own ill-regulated freedom, must be at the root of the objection to forms and rules, and systematic self-discipline. But, besides, there is, if it be sifted, a real unsuspiciousness of the deep corruption of human nature, and a vague impression that the whole battle is won, when the soul is once in a state of grace; as though all resistance would

in all, out of desire of conformity to our Lord (*e. g.* witness the saying of St. Theresa, "Suffer or die;" or St. Catherine of Sienna, "I desire, Lord, to live here always conformed unto Thy Passion, and to find pain and suffering my repose and delight;" St. Philip Neri, "Increase my pains, but increase my patience," a prayer also of the Ven. John of Avila). In part they have been special gifts; as temptations of the flesh were suddenly, at once, removed from St. Francis and St. Thomas Aquinas; St. Peter of Alcantara lost the power of distinguishing food; St. Thomas Aquinas often knew not what he had eaten; St. Catherine of Sienna lived for a length of time on no food but the Holy Eucharist. "Can I forget," said St. Francis Borgia, "that Christ drank gall for me upon the Cross?" Five or six hours, again, spent in prayer, appeared to him as a quarter of an hour. St. Antony, after nights of prayer, grieved that sunrise broke in upon their silence, &c.

then be so slight, that the soul would, almost of its own accord, obey the influences of grace, and might be left unbridled, as being sure to obey its Master's Voice. And yet, if self-examination were really used, one can hardly understand how people, day after day, could go on thus; how they could commit the same faults, e.g. be guilty of the same acts and words of vanity, or self-indulgence, or distractions, and not see that there is need for some stricter rule and self-discipline; or, again, how one, who is not very far advanced, can so little account of tendencies to sloth, or distraction, or the absorbing power of duties, occupations, human affections, earthly interests, curiosity, things of sense, or the soul's own heaviness and lassitude and inaptness to things spiritual, as to think that it will spontaneously, as it were, rise of itself to God; that the soul will be equally fixed upon God as if it had regularly recurring hours of prayer through the course of the day, prescribed rules, (as at going out, coming in, entering into society, conversation, in the course of it, pauses of business,) or even conventional occasions, as beholding the sky, natural beauty, the striking of a clock, whereby one may bind the soul to pray. In other words, that if the soul were at regular times forced to pray, it would at others be less with God, than if not thus continually checked and recalled. It really seems a master-piece of Satan's craft, or of man's deceivableness, to persuade men either that the acts of any grace, as prayer, will be more devout when left, so to say, to chance, than if, with the view of guarding against irregularity, or hurry, or weariness, or self-deceit, they are made matter of precaution and forethought; or, as in the use of penitence or humiliation, they either could not, continuously, be done, through God's grace, penitently or humbly, or, if so done, would not enlarge the grace out of which they flowed; or that the grace could long exist without them.

It will be granted probably, that acts of avarice tend to deepen the character of avariciousness, acts of self-display that of pride, acts of cruelty harden the heart and aggravate ferociousness, and so on; that every character of sin is deepened by the continuous acts of the sin which springs from it; and yet it is practically denied either that acts of humiliation can spring from the grace of God, or that so springing, they do not increase the grace of humility. Satan understands the human soul better. He knows how petty, continually renewed acts of evil rivet his chains, and he takes care continually to provide baits and occasions for them, and to suggest thoughts of them, that the soul may at least in will consent. And this in things which are according to the bent of our nature. But where, as all resistance of evil and acts of duty are, it is against and above nature, there it is thought needless to restrain the soul, or do violence to it, or to seek occasions of practising and inuring it to what it shrinks from. When it is a mere natural and easy descent, Satan takes pains to urge the soul downwards; and men think, when it is against nature, that no continued regular effort and holy wisdom are needed to constrain it to follow Him Who calls it upwards. It will be allowed that human love, which never expressed itself in acts, would become torpid;

it would reasonably be questioned whether the feeling had ever existed, or was not a mere phantom: but people doubt not that humility can live without acts of humiliation; they only question whether it can co-exist with them. For to what else do all objections to regular self-discipline, penitence, mortification, fasts, acts of humiliation interior or exterior, come to, than this, either that they cannot proceed out of, or be supported by, the grace of God; or that, so supported, they would not increase that grace of which they were the effect? Either of which, except for profound ignorance, would be nothing short of words of blasphemy against that Holy Being Who gave and sustained them.

One or both of these fundamental errors seem to lie at the root of the practical deficiencies of the popular system of religion. People seem to think, either that acts have nothing to do with forming habits, but that certain feelings will sustain themselves, or be sustained, and issue in action whenever any difficult occasion comes, or that they will be equally performed without any definite purpose of the will binding us to their performance. On the first of these, people seem to act as to the combat with their evil; on the second, as to the practice of what is good: and both arise in an entire ignorance of their own nature, and unsuspiciousness as to the extent of its corruption. Doubtless, were we perfect, feelings might sustain themselves without habitual energy in action, although we know not that they are so sustained in any created beings. Of all the Heavenly hosts, it is said, that they "do His pleasure;" and if the Seraphim live in continual and exclusive adoration, their whole being is one *act* of enkindled contemplation and praise. And if we may in this respect speak reverentially of Him, from Whom all being derives its properties, His Being, when time and creation were not, and there were no beings out of Himself to whom to manifest His Love, was still One Eternal, Unchangeable Love, within Himself, in the Three Co-equal Persons of the Adorable Trinity. For "God is Love." But in this our state of partial restoration, to imagine that any right feeling can abide, or wrong one be subdued, without an habitual effort, co-operating with the inworking grace of God, involves a real denial that we are " not already perfect." For, since we are so miserably imperfect, hold nothing securely even of what, by God's grace, we have gained, it can only be by continual laborious progress that we can ever maintain our ground. This indeed is so elementary a truth, even of Heathen morality, and would in the abstract probably be so readily acknowledged by all, that nothing but a radical failure to perceive the extent and minuteness and subtlety of our temptations, can account for its evident neglect.

It is nothing to say, that, apart from that grace, mere outward acts would become worse than worthless; to doubt of this were Pelagianism; or that, if contemplated and reflected on with self-complacency, they would be Pharisaic and idolatrous. One who could build any thing on this objection would only imply that he had not formed the very idea of self-abnegation. Some, of course, every where will stop short in forms and formulæ, in confessions of sinfulness by word or act, and substitute some more subtle form of self-contemplation, whether of its faith, or works, or feelings, or observances, or phrases, or spirituality, or soundness of confession, or self-renunciation in word or partial deed. Self-abnegation is complete. It relates not (as men picture) to outward actions only, but to the affections, the feelings, the thoughts, the will, our very deepest and most awful hopes and fears. Catholicity prohibits too anxious curiosity or reflection as to its own state. To build upon or to reflect on good deeds, is with our own hands to undo them[a]. By God's grace, the soul, under His teaching, does what it can; it seeks by that grace to love, to repent, to humble itself more; and then it commits itself, its past sins, its penitences, its hopes, its fears, its sufferings, its crosses, its consolations, its present and its to come, to Him Who loved it, and in His love redeemed it, and has borne with it until now.

Self-discipline would indeed be dry and arid, except in union with the Cross; as, conversely, there can be no real loving contemplation of the Cross without self-discipline. Holy Scripture says, "If we suffer with Him, we shall also reign with Him." It speaks of "fellowship with His Sufferings, conformity to His Death." It has been noticed how the preaching of the Cross in Holy Scripture is always accompanied with a mention of the participation of suffering. It

[a] "Would you that God should remember your good deeds, forget them; would you that He should forget your evil, remember them." St. Chrysostom on St. Matthew.

seems a miracle how any can, in the midst of ease, lightness of heart, fulness of bread, abundance of all things, (one would say it reverentially,) sympathize or be in harmony with the Passion; it seems strange how members of the Thorn-crowned Head can live delicately. But it is of the very elements of Catholic teaching, that whosoever would love the Cross must bear it; and whosoever would bear it, must bear it after Him as His Cross, uniting it with His, with Whom he has been united. "He is borne by the Cross that he may bear it;" the Cross he beareth, beareth him.

Self-discipline is never distinct from the doctrine of the Cross; not as, in a modern system, the consciousness of our corruption and sinfulness is to bring us to CHRIST, and therewith its office seems ended. It is the application of His Cross to heal us; it is a cleansing of the soul to receive Him; keeping it clean, through the Virtue of His Cross, that it may retain Him; a chastising what would rebel, and offend His Holy Eyes and grieve His Spirit, through Whom He vouchsafes to be present: it is, in its highest sense, a casting out whatever could usurp His place in the soul, or divide her affections with Him, or distract her from Him. His grace is its commencement and support; His love its consolation; Himself the reward it seeks.

It must, then, be said, not as if in apology, nor yet censoriously, but in charitable warning, that whatsoever difference there may be in the acknowledgment of man's helplessness, or of entire dependence upon our Lord and cleaving to Him, the deficiency is not on the Catholic[a] side. The point of difference is not in the truths believed, but in the mode of carrying them out into life. Happy, at least, is it, if they who think they hold most accurately the corruption of nature, can even understand the language of the self-abhorrence of Saints. Take his, who being asked, "Who were the sheep?" said, "I know not; I only know that I am of the goats[b];" or his who ever prayed that his sins might not bring the vengeance of God on the towns where he preached[c]; or of those who wept for their sins, until sight was impaired[d]; or his, who, having renounced all the riches and glories of this world, habitually accounted

[a] The Editor need perhaps hardly say, that he uses this word of what has ever been the doctrine of the Church, as opposed to the private opinion of individuals, not as though it was found abroad only, to the exclusion of ourselves. The hair-shirt has been concealed under our lawn also; sleep has given way to devotion; grace has endured abstinence above nature, and Bishops have been models of a saintly penitence. With us, too, those who have most borne the Cross, have most loved it. Bp. Taylor, *e. g.* the author of our strictest work on penitence, is the author of the "Life of Christ;" Bp. Andrews, whose own daily manual, which came to us "moistened by his tears," is our most deeply penitential collection of prayer, is, perhaps, also our most fervent and devotional preacher of the mysteries of the Faith.

[b] I think, one of the Eastern Anchorites.

[c] St. Dominic. The like is related of St. Catherine of Sienna, that she thought all the chastisements of Divine justice, which desolated the provinces in her time, to be the miserable effects of her unfaithfulness. Nouet.

[d] St. Francis of Assisium and St. Ignatius Loyola. The largeness of the gift of tears continually recurs in the lives of the Saints.

his only fit dwelling to be hell, or being spit upon all night, counted no place fitter than his own face [a]; or hers who, having followed God's leadings since she heard His Name, confessed, "All my life long has been nothing but darkness, but I will hide myself in the Wounds of JESUS Crucified; I will bathe myself in His Blood, Which will wash off all my sins [b];" or his [c], who, being asked to pray for the continuance of a life spent in winning souls, answered, "I am an unprofitable servant, whom neither God nor His people needeth;" or that which has been the common maxim and first principle of all Saints, that they are to account themselves "the chief of sinners," not professing it only with their lips, but on each occasion acting instantaneously upon it, wishing others to believe it, bearing all reproach patiently, glad to be evil-spoken of untruly, acutely pained at any hint of praise, confounded at the mention of any good in them [d].

[a] St. Francis Borgia. St. Alphonsus Lignori gives this as one of the preparations of any mental prayer (and so of his own), "1. My God, I believe Thee present within me, and I adore Thee from the abyss of my nothingness. 2. Lord, I ought now to be in hell, on account of my sins; I am sorry for having offended Thee; pardon me in Thy mercy." (Quoted by Mr. Ward, p. 350.)

[b] St. Catherine of Sienna.   [c] St. Francis de Sales.

[d] All these tests of deep humility may be verified to any extent in the lives of the Saints, not as the results of reflection, but as part of themselves.

The following instances are given by Nouet, L'homme d'oraison, Conduite dans les voies de Dieu. Ent. xi. St. Francis Borgia having employed much time every day in acquiring knowledge of himself, reduced the principles of

It were strange undoubtedly if, really sinners as most of us are, we do not honestly account all, one by one, superior to ourselves; but in those who

self-knowledge to these. (1.) I was formed from nothing. (2.) I shall return to nothing. (3.) I know not what I am. (4.) If I know any thing, my only knowledge is, that hell is my [fitting] home. (5.) Of myself, I do no good work. St. Theresa being warned one day to take heed of vain-glory, answered, " Vain-glory! I know not why, knowing who I am; it is much for me not to despair:" and in her life, " It seems as if, even would I try to have vain-glory, I could not. For I know clearly through the grace which God giveth me, that of myself I can do nothing. On the contrary, God makes me see my miseries, and discovers to me so many unfaithfulnesses, that whatever time I could employ thereon, I should never see so many truths, as I see of them in an instant. Besides, I know not how I could attribute to myself the good which is in me, seeing that a little while ago I was entirely bare of the virtues I possess, which also are the fruits of the mercy of God, and His free gifts, wherein I am, and can do nothing, no more than a painter's canvass, in that, on my part, I can do no more than receive the grace of God, without rendering Him any service. For certainly I am the most useless person in the world; I am ashamed to see what progress every one makes, except myself who am good for nothing. What I say is not humility, it is truth. I do not believe that there is in the world a creature worse than myself, and when I consider the little profit I make of the graces I receive, I sometimes come to fear that I have been deceived." The B. Angela de Foligny said, with unspeakable ardour, "O unknown nothingness! O unknown nothingness! I tell you in all truth, that the soul can have no richer knowledge than that of its nothingness." And to St. Catherine our Lord said, " Knowest thou well, who I am and who thou art. Happy wilt thou be, if thou understand it well. I am HE who IS, and thou art she who is not." " In this [Divine] light St. Ignatius looked upon himself as an ulcer continually discharging pus; Al-

were really great Saints, it is a very mystery of humility, which one can only explain in that, living in the light of God, their very perception of that lustre they have received is taken from them, and they only see any remaining spot of corruption. Their humility seems a special supernatural gift, to preserve all their other graces, and it has been so accounted. They have not at times understood it themselves, but received it by intuitive inspiration. "All that I can tell you," said " the holy Abbot Zosimus[a]," " is, that

phonso Rodriguez compared himself to graves of dead, putrid carcasses, sewers and sinks of vessels where all defilements collect." [Comp. our own Bp. Andrewes, Morning Devotions, "Despise me not, an unclean worm, a dead dog, a putrid corpse."] "St. Ignatius used to say that he did not believe that another could be found, in whom there was so much ingratitude joined with so many graces and favours which he had received of God; whence he prayed our Lord to deprive him of his spiritual consolations, in chastisement of his unfaithfulnesses, to make him more careful and faithful for the future. St. Francis cried out, from time to time, 'Lord, keep, if it please Thee, the treasure of the graces Thou hast deposited in my soul. For I am a thief who rob Thee of Thy glory.' St. Gertrude thought it one of the greatest miracles that the earth should endure her, seeing there was no one who did not deserve the favours of God better than herself, and did not employ them better." See also St. Vincent Ferrier and St. Catherine of Genoa, below, p. 105. "St. John-of-God, when accused to the Archbishop of Grenada of harbouring dissolute people in his hospital, said, 'The Son of God came to save sinners, and we are bound to labour and pray for their conversion. I am unfaithful to my calling that I neglect this; and I confess that I know no other bad person in my hospital but myself,'" &c. Butler.

[a] Quoted by Rodriguez on humility, c. 34. St. Francis does give an explanation of *his* conviction; see above, p. viii.

I know I speak truth, and that I am very sensible of what I say."

Such is the way in which they have felt the corruption of human nature, who have taken the course of humiliation and self-discipline, because they felt it. Sorrowful indeed is it, that so strange a paradox should have gained possession of people's minds, as that to act upon a truth is the way to efface our conviction of it. Could any thing tear the veil off our eyes, it must be surely that they who did so act believed it in a degree, which is as much above ours as was their practice. At least, if each of us could feel habitually, not only when reflecting upon his past sins, that he is "the chief of sinners," but appreciate vividly at all times, and under all circumstances, that he is a greater sinner than any one whom he sees, miserable as these often are, and take occasion from each of them to humble himself, and is willing to be so accounted, if God sees fit,—as far as this is so with any of us, we may hope that we are in a way to acquire the humility which befits us. And yet, after all, what are we, but what, if we so think, we think ourselves?—and what were not they? The lives of Saints is, alas! a new world to us. Yet had we some portion of their humility, whence all this unloving blame so rife among us, instead of ascribing the evil which is desolating us, each to his own sins?

It is a warning, however, given uniformly by those who guide along this way of humiliation, that the depressing contemplation of our own corruption and infirmity would, alone, prove a snare of Satan, tempting to despondency and sloth. And so, when the foundation of this self-knowledge has been laid, they too (as has been the course among ourselves) bid us go forth out of ourselves, and meditate on the Cross of Christ, contemplate His Sacred Wounds, and bury ourselves and our sins, in their whole weight and number, in those sorrowful and amazing Depths. The language is so far alike. Yet would again, one must say, we who practise not suffering could so lovingly contemplate His Passion as they who do! Would that our trust was as entire and as forgetful of self, that the very idea of " uniting our sufferings with those of our Lord," to be sanctified by His, and blessed to us, were as common among us! Doubtless it is found among very many who know deep bodily or mental pain, and among our simple-minded sufferers who have never unlearnt His truth. To such, suffering itself has been a teacher sent of God. " Blessed is the man whom Thou chastenest, O Lord, and teachest him out of Thy law!" But are fervent books, directing us not to the doctrine, but to contemplate the Blessed Person of our Lord in His Sufferings, common among us? Are helps to such meditation familiar? Does not "the soul upon Calvary" sound to us a beautiful, but mournfully new, title for a solace for all suffering, within or without? But, apart from Christian sufferers who are taught directly in the very school of Christ, and to whom He often imparts the Virtue of His Passion, and makes them to understand It more than in years of our teaching, is habitual contemplation of the Passion a part of the very elements of our devotion? We have not even attempted to replace that form of devotion ordinary in the Roman Church, whereby meditations on the chief mysteries of our Lord are combined with the use of His Divine Prayer, joining meditation on His Incarnation, Passion, and Resurrection, the Mysteries of His Humility, Sorrows, and Glory, with "those words of the Son, in which we may best hope to be heard of the Father," blending (what is so difficult to any beginner) vocal and mental prayer, evolving some portion of the manifold meaning of that Prayer, and habituating the pious mind to find a whole Liturgy[a] in it, so that it should never be at a loss for words, but might gather every longing aspiration, pang, penitence, and want, into its all-comprehensive words, with the affections of a son submitting all to its Father's will, to the Father's glory. On account of one small proportion which we cannot use, we

[a] It may be observed, how, in consequence of this neglect, even valuable persons ceased to understand our own Prayer-book. There was no more frequent complaint among the Church Reformers (one of whom those who knew him must venerate), than the frequency of the repetition of the Lord's Prayer. One is ashamed to say that people counted how often, when "occasional services" occurred, those blessed words were repeated, as if the fact of their often repetition was in itself a decisive proof of the need of a change. Pious minds felt otherwise, as one expressed it, "When I come to the last in the service, I begin to feel what it is." Any one who has tried it, must know how repetitions, either of the whole of our Lord's Prayer, or of single petitions in it, consecutively, add to our perception of its fulness, and our own earnestness of prayer; how, e. g. on a threefold fervent repetition of "Forgive us our trespasses," the mind seems to feel unutterably more than it ever felt before.

b

have, without any apparent consciousness of our loss, willingly or wilfully parted with the whole of that wonderful mode of bringing the contemplation of the mysteries of our Faith home to minds of every capacity or with the narrowest leisure. And now, in our entire ignorance of its very nature, the name of "the Rosary" or "Beads" is associated only with ideas of superstition, even in minds who, if they knew it, would be shocked at their own thoughts. It is painful to think how much superstitious contempt of simple devotion, of the worship of child-like souls among the aged, is virtually involved in the habitual censures of it. This daily, continual memorial of our Lord, in His Life and Death for us, is lost to our very habits, and replaced by nothing [a]. We can see (if it be so) incidental negligences; we have no sense for that worst evil, spiritual dearth.

Again, the very observation of the hours of the Passion, which carry on the mind which uses them devoutly, in reverent sympathy with our Lord, through "the burthen and heat of the day," quelling the sad turmoils of our own thoughts, or recalling them at least continually to Him, and which, the

---

[a] The use of the Lord's Prayer alone at the great hours of the day, in connexion with the memory of the Passion, is a suggestion which our poor will most gratefully receive. One knows not what a source of holy meditation and of enlarged use of that blessed prayer might not thus be opened to them. Their habitual use of the Creed also, in their morning devotions, which has so often been thoughtlessly interfered with, may have been of untold blessing in fixing their thoughts on the mysteries of the Redemption, and might be carried out further.

Fathers tell us, were always "accounted the most solemn times of prayer and Divine Offices in the Church of God," have, after having been reintroduced among us for a time by Bishop Cosins, slept, with slight exceptions, for above a miserable century.

Again, many forms of the devotion upon the Passion, long practised by fervent Christians, would probably, at least on first acquaintance, startle us. We should fear whether we could use them reverentially. Happily, the devotional thought of His wounded Side, as the Fountain of the Sacraments, the Fountain wherein to "wash from sin and uncleanness," the Cleft in the Rock wherein we may be safely hidden, has been perpetuated among us. There is, too, a devotion towards His Sacred Name (however imperfect, and, for lack of austerity and self-discipline, deficient often in reverence), there is a latent sense also of its mystical and sacramental efficacy, which are happy signs of individual love to the Redeemer, and a "feeling after" some fuller contemplation of His Sacred and Suffering Humanity. Love has broken through system, and sits with St. Mary Magdalene, in heart and sight, at the Foot of the Cross. And yet, with this as a testimony to us, I fear, the fuller carrying out of this devotion to CHRIST CRUCIFIED (such as we find universal on the Continent) would seem a strange thing to many of us; we should have at first, almost with doubt, to adapt ourselves to it.

Detailed devotions with reference to each of His Five most precious Wounds, or to the Seven sheddings of His Atoning Blood for us, either with reference to the seven deadly sins, or the seven gifts of the Holy Ghost, or His seven words upon the Cross, or devout adaptations of the petitions of His Prayer to them, or detailed recitations of the events of His Passion, in union with His Sacred Name,—whereby we might plead them, one by one, to Him, and by each, with deepening feeling of His boundless love, and our boundless thanklessness, pray Him to have mercy upon us—or, the manifold repetition of that Saving Name (as in the Litanies of the Passion [a]), have not been the product of our own practical system. They find response enough among us not to create undue or over-anxious misgiving; our own Litany contains a precious witness to them. And yet how little have we developed its meaning, how foreign mostly (it is to be feared) the very thought of the Circumcision [b] as a great mystery, or of that Blood-shedding as a meritorious prelude of the outpouring of all His Blood upon the Cross. One ought not, of course, to lay too great or too painful a stress on the absence of any particular form of devotion. But we should bear in mind, that these were part of our ancient

---

[a] Such litanies have, of late, been reprinted for our poor under the title, "Short Meditations for the Sick," containing the Litany of our Lord Jesus Christ, the Golden Litany of the Passion, Litany of the Blessed Sacrament, and for a happy death, with the Jesus Psalter. The latter was here and there altered for our own use. The same collection contains fourteen brief meditations on the Passion, from the Abbé Landrieu.

[b] It is observable how the first herald of restored Catholic teaching brought back the reverence for its mystery. See The Christian Year, Feast of the Circumcision.

inheritance; and they flow so naturally from the contemplation of our Blessed Lord's Humanity and Passion, that we must have misgivings whether we should ever have lost them, or be now to such an extent without them, had our Devotion to the Person of our Suffering Redeemer been what it ought. There are but too many indications (little as we have suspected it) that the way in which the doctrine of "justification by faith" (relatively to ourselves) has been made to take the place of contemplation of our Lord in Himself, has very injuriously affected, not only the completeness, but the soundness of the faith of many. Had it been deeply impressed upon us that He is "Very God and Very Man," and that every thing that He wrought or suffered for us had therefore an Infinite Value, or had we contemplated His Sacred Humanity as they only may venture who think habitually of His Human Nature as wholly taken into God, we could hardly have ceased to have dwelt reverentially on each single act and moment of His Life and Passion.

It is almost the inevitable consequence of such compendious or arbitrary selections or substitutions of doctrine, as of "justification by faith," or even "the Atonement" for "Christ Crucified," that in the end they contract men's faith, risk its forfeiture, and banish contemplation of the Object. The selection of one doctrine overshadows others; the habitual abstract statement of it turns away from meditations of its detail. The very emblems in our older churches show how reverentially the thoughts of our forefathers dwelt, one by one, on the

> "Thorns[a], and Cross, and nails, and lance,
> Wounds, our treasure that enhance,
> Vinegar, and gall, and reed,——"

How they

> —— "stored deep in heart's recess,
> All the shame and bitterness."

Such is the real contemplation of love. Think we not that such must it have been to those who were on Calvary, love riveting them, while each awful infliction pierced the soul with a sword, and upholding them to endure the pain it gave? But since His love comprehended us, as though we were there, and He beheld us, one by one, from the Cross, and loved us, and shed that Precious Blood for us, and each pang was a part of the price of our Redemption, how must not a living faith, "the evidence of things unseen," be present with Him, and behold the Crucifixion, not "afar off," but as brought by the Holy Gospels to the very foot of the Cross, and, if not standing there with His Blessed Mother and the beloved Disciple, yet kneeling at least with the penitent who embraces It? To love, nothing is of small account. Human love finds a separate ground of love, a separate meaning and expression of that inward holy loveliness which wins it, impressed on every part even of the pure visible frame of what it loves. Grief loves to recall each separate action, and token of love or holiness, and muses upon them, and revolves them on all sides, to discover the varied bearings of what yet is finite. How much more when the Object of

---

[a] Devotions on the Passion, Hymn at Matins.

Contemplation is Infinite, and that of love! When the Passion was "the book of the Saints [a]," they contemplated it letter by letter, and combined Its meanings, and explored Its unfathomable depths, the depths of the riches of the mercy and loving-kindness of God; each Wound had Its own treasure-house of the depths of Divine Mercy, its own antidote to sin. They, in spirit, "reached forth their finger, and beheld His Hands," mightier to aid, because bound to the tree; they felt themselves encircled within the outstretched all-encompassing Arms of His Mercy; they fell at his wearied and stiffened Knees, and their own "feeble knees" were strengthened; they bathed with tears His transfixed Feet, that so He might forgive the mournful liberty and wanderings wherewith their own had gone astray; but chiefly were they ever drawn to the very Abyss of His unsearchable Love, His pierced Side and His opened Heart, there to "draw of the fountains of salvation," to "drink that water after which they should never thirst" for aught beside, there reverently to "enter, and to penetrate to the inmost recesses of His boundless Charity [b]," to "enter into Its Chambers, and

---

[a] This is said, e. g. of St. Francis, who "wished to open no other book than the Four Gospels." From him St. Bonaventure inherited it, who, when St. Thomas Aquinas asked him where were his books, showed him his crucifix; and generally St. Francis is said to have transmitted the love of the Cross as a sort of inheritance and patrimony to his order. Nouet Conduite, iv. 4. "The Passion of Christ was the book" also of the venerable John of Avila, "the father of so many eminent saints of Spain," and one of their most eminent devotional writers. [b] St. Bonaventure.

close Its doors about them," there to "hide them in the secret of His Presence" from the wrath to come. They wearied not of contemplating His Wounds, His healing Stripes, His Words, because the unutterable love, of which they were the tokens, being Infinite, there issues from them an Infinite attractiveness of love. How can we be thought to love, if we linger not there, now we may bear to behold It, since we see not the Pain, but only the Love which sustained it? Can we conceive but that the Magdalene, to whom alone in that blessed company we could be like (would that we were!), must, when His Holy Body was removed from the Cross, have gazed with unutterable amazement of love, one by one, on the Sacred Wounds, and have found even a special miracle of sorrowful comfort in touching the pierced Feet " at which she had found mercy [a]?" Can we think it was not grief to her to part with Them out of sight? Or that, when the time came, even amid that bewildering perplexity, the memory of them remained not impressed upon her soul? Think we not that she beheld, as far as she could bear, each of those awful "Stripes" by which "we are healed," and through which, "from the sole of the Foot even unto the Head," all was " wound and bruise?" and how have we the blessing of those who have "not seen and yet have believed," if we cannot behold them with her, or are not touched with sorrow at the sight, or in that mirror shrink not at " the wounds and bruises and putrifying sores," wherewith our whole

[a] St. Bonaventure, Life of Christ.

selves have been ulcerated, and which were the Thorns, and Nails, and Stripes, which tore His All-Holy Body to heal the unholiness of ours? And that the more, since we may now behold those Wounds, not merely in their extreme humility and painfulness, but glorified; and Tabor and Calvary are united, and "the lifting up from the earth" has been the Ascension to glory, and His Sacred Wounds have of the capacity of His Godhead; and His Heart, Which is ever open to receive us, can contain the sorrows, and hide and heal the sins of the whole human race.

"Oh the blindness of the sons of Adam," exclaims a Saint[a], "who know not how to enter into JESUS CHRIST through these Wounds! They toil in vanity above their strength, and the doors to repose are open. Know ye not that CHRIST is the joy of the Blessed? Why, then, delay to enter into that joy through the openings in His Body? Why so mad, when the bliss of Angels is open, and the Wall which encompassed it broken through, ye neglect to enter? Wait ye, then, that your body may be dissolved, not thinking that the soul can even now be soothed to CHRIST ? But, believe me, O man, if thou wouldst enter into Him by these narrow Openings, not thy soul only, but thy body also, shall find therein a wonderful repose and sweetness. What in you is earthly, and tends to earthly things, shall become so spiritual by the entrance into those Wounds, that thou wilt esteem all other pleasures as nothing, save those which it tastes there.

[a] St. Bonaventura, stim. amor. par. c. 1. cir. med. [Opp. t. vi. p. 194] quoted by Nouet.

Yea, it may be, at times, the soul shall oft repeat, that for duty or some good end, thou must depart thence, and the flesh, won by that sweetness, will say, it must linger there. And if it shall be thus with the body, what sweetness, thinkest thou, will the heart enjoy, which, through those openings, is joined with the Heart of Christ! In truth, I cannot express it to thee; thyself essay it, and quickly. Lo! a store is open to thee, full of sweet spices, and in medicines rich. Enter thou then through the windows of those Wounds, and receive a medicine, healing, restorative, preservative. Take what kind thou wilt. Whatever tender healing thou wouldest desire, take it there. Or wouldest thou be softened by the sweetest ointments, delay not to enter through those Wounds. Lo, open is the gate of Paradise; the flaming sword removed by the soldier's lance! Lo, the Tree of Life pierced in its trunk and in its branches! if thou puttest not thy feet, *i. e.* thy affections, in Its openings, thou canst not gather Its fruits! Lo, open is the Treasure of Divine Wisdom and Eternal Charity! Enter then through the aperture of the Wounds; with light thou wilt find delights. O blessed lance and blessed nails, to whom it was vouchsafed to make this opening. O had I been in the place of that lance, loth had I been to go forth out of the Side of Christ; I would have said, 'Here is my rest for ever; here will I dwell, for I have a delight therein.' 'O fools and slow of heart' who, to possess some vanity, trust yourselves to enter perilous and doubtful openings, whence ye often cannot go forth; but to possess the Son of God, the

Sovereign Good, the Eternal Purity and Brightness, enter not by the open gates of His Wounds! Soul, created in the image of God, how canst thou contain thyself? Lo, thy most sweet Spouse, wounded for thee, and now All-glorious, longeth to embrace thee, and give thee the Kiss of Infinite sweetness; and thou neglectest to go to Him speedily!"

"He through exceeding love hath opened for thee His Side, to give thee His Heart; He hath willed that His Hands and His Feet should be pierced, that, when thou comest to Him, thy hands should so enter into His Hands, and thy feet into His Feet, that thou shouldest be indissolubly united with Him. Make trial, I pray thee, as the Apostle says, 'Prove all things, hold fast that which is good;' and, if thou findest thyself well there, go not forth again: I doubt not that, when thou hast essayed it, thou wilt account all things, except Himself, bitterness. After thou hast entered there, thou wilt desire with thy full heart that the doors of His Wounds should be so closed, that thou couldest not go forth. Amazed exceedingly wilt thou be at thine own and others' blindness. Yet thou wilt joy in such exceeding sweetness, and thy heart will be so kindled, that it will be as though thy struggling spirit would burst from thy body, to dwell, as in its own home, in the Wounds of CHRIST. And the soul shall be inebriated with such sweetness, that scarcely shalt thou be able to turn it away to aught besides. O Wounds, wounding hearts of stone, kindling souls of ice, melting with love affections harder than adamant!"

"What more marvellous," says St. Bonaventura

again, "than that Death gives us life, Wounds heal us, Blood makes whole and cleanses the inward parts, an excess of sorrow gives an exceeding joy, the opening of the Side unites heart to Heart? Yet cease not to be amazed; for the sun when eclipsed enlightens the more, fire when extinguished gives the greater heat, the ignominy of the Passion glorifies us; and truly wondrous is it that Christ, when thirsting on the Cross, inebriates us; naked, He arrays us with the ornaments of grace; His Hands nailed to the Wood set us at liberty; His pierced Feet make us run; expiring, He gives us life; dying on the Tree, He calls us to the things of heaven."

It is indeed so intense a paradox, that to act on a belief weakens it; that the unwearied effort to tame and chasten the rebellions of nature makes men less alive to its rebelliousness; that to call the flesh an enemy and to treat it as a friend, impresses the sense of its enmity, more than to act towards it as we believe it to be; that to bear the Cross after Him hinders the belief in It; that conformity—in whatever degree His Saints might through Him attain—to His Holy Poverty, or Watchings, or Fastings, or Stripes, would make men forget Him Whom they sought to imitate, and out of love and penitence to express in their lives; that one would hope it cannot stand for a moment in the presence of realities. On the contrary, with the amazingness of love in those Saints who were most penetrated with love, there was a proportionate intensity of love for conformity with Him Whom they loved, in suffering. We can, for the most part, would we be true to ourselves, as little understand the one as the other, and may thereby the more come to suspect that mysterious connexion which Holy Scripture itself points out between the love of Christ and of His Suffering. Indeed, as has been already said, the contrary, as it is unscriptural, would seem in the highest degree unnatural—a very paradox of unreality—how people could indeed love that to which they are wholly unlike,—how, any way, appreciate that, which they never in any degree felt, and which it is a very pain to think of, until the pain itself, by paining, give pleasure. "Suffering is the livery of Christ Crucified."

"The Passion of the Saviour," says St. Bonaventura[a], "must be the rule of our life; and the degree of the consolation we derive from this is the measure of our conformity with Christ, while the absence of this consolation is the evidence of our departure from this rule and example. We must long, as far as in us lies, to be, like Him, trampled under foot, rejected, despised, mocked, persecuted, beaten, and, in the exercise of holy duties, to be reprobated by all the world. Be it ours to be naked like Him Who was bared of all things, and desire to possess nothing; nay, to hold it our greatest punishment and sorrow to possess anything, our greatest joy to have nothing. Be it ours to abhor all the pleasures and delights of the earth, and wish that all in the world had for us the taste only of gall and wormwood; thereby to imitate Jesus Christ, Who in His extreme thirst had only a draught of vinegar and gall." . . . "Then truly

[a] l. 2. c. 4.

is the whole man changed into Christ, when detached from himself, and rising above all creatures, he is so wholly transformed into his Suffering Lord as to see nothing and to feel nothing but Christ Crucified, mocked, railed at, and suffering for us."

There is a danger in even imagining that, with any thing like our usual practice, we can even understand, or any way make our own, the language of the exceeding love of the Saints. Miracles seem far less amazing than their superhuman love. We hear of outward manifestations of it, as that the very mention of the Passion would melt persons into abundant, overflowing tears, or cast them into ecstasy, so that they became insensible to the external world, or It filled them with holy raptures, so that the very face beamed with the light and joy within,— not to speak of higher yet certain instances, in which the Holy Spirit within so acted upon the outward frame, that it ceased for the time to be subject to earthly laws— at the Holy Eucharist, the utterance of Priests, for excess of devotion, was habitually interrupted by streams of tears [a]; "the grace of tears" was a gift to sanctity.

Yet even these outward signs [b] are as nothing to

[a] The above instances are frequent in the lives of the Saints.

[b] Or if any look to visible fruits only, would that our Sermons in Passion-tide yielded the same fruits as theirs, in the conversion of sinners; would that we could so melt stony hearts; or (which, it is to be feared, is at the root) that our own hearts were so kindled at the thoughts of the Passion, as those in the Continental Churches have so often been. "Brother Bernardin" (it was said to an eminent preacher,

that ineffable nearness to our Lord, that close and supernatural union with Him, which exhibit to us as visible realities what we know by faith, that Christ dwelleth in His Elect, and they in Him.

The present volume lays, as it claims, but " the foundations of the spiritual life;" yet with an entireness of self-abnegation, whose extent will almost startle us, a sense of oppression from any remnant of self-love, a complete baring of the soul from all self-will, " that Jesus may fill it all, be its only support, and His Cross its sole dependence;" there are almost overpowering hints of the amazing overflowing of His Love[a], which He pours upon the soul which follows this course faithfully. They are hints only, for, as the words which St. Paul heard were "unspeakable," so all the Saints say (in the words of St. Bernard),

> No tongue of man hath power to tell,
> No written words can prove;
> But he who loveth, knoweth well
> What Jesus 'tis to love.

Indeed, the Author knew in its inmost depths, what is self-abnegation, and what " the abundance of the consolations" of Christ. This book, like so many others [b], was the direct fruit of the Cross. "We are,"

---

who asked why his sermons did not produce the same fruit) " is a fiery glowing coal. What is only warm hath not the power of kindling fire in others, like the burning coal."

[a] See especially pp. 225, 226, but also up and down the work, as pp. 85. 93. 128. sqq. 150. 158. 171, 172, &c. 192. 196. 198. 216.

[b] As those of Boudon, of whose life, thus far, a notice will be shortly given; Scupoli, whose " Spiritual Combat" was written when yielding to an atrocious calumny; F. Tho-

he says, towards the close of life ª, " grown old insensibly, and have passed the vigour of our age in suffering." He adds, " God maketh us feel that He is so good a Master, that one could not complain of Him. He changes so blessedly evils into good, that the soul would not wish to be otherwise dealt with. He gives happiness in proportion to the miseries which any has suffered, and the slightest pain is so richly recompensed, that it is a loving-kindness to be miserable under His Guidance." So God conducts souls; to one He assigns severe bodily pain; to others, mental; some He guides by that special token of His favour, a likeness to our Lord in undeserved and shocking calumnies. Surin He led by what in later times has been a yet rarer way,—direct visible conflict, as it seems, with Satan. He was brought into the trial in the way of duty, as sent by his superiors, to succour Religious, over whose bodies God had allowed Satan to have power. His office was, by God's grace, accomplished; and after nearly three years (with one interval of absence) all ᵇ the Religious were set free. During the period of his ministry at the convent, he retained his full powers of body and mind, but seems to have suffered in some way which they only may

mas, who wrote " The Sufferings of Christ," in a Moorish prison, exhorting his fellow-prisoners when tempted to apostasy; St. John of the Cross wrote his mystical treatises, having learnt " a love for sufferings, and a high idea of heir value, in the prison of Toledo," and then again in solitude and disgrace.

ª Lettres Spirituelles, end.

ᵇ A letter, I think, in 1637, mentions that some were already freed.

understand, who, themselves holy, have been brought into contact with ("have," in his own words, "touched") the Evil One.

The subjoined notice, to which alone the Editor had access, gives no intimation of the nature of his subsequent sufferings[a]. Sufferings, resulting from conflict with Satan, could probably no more be described than the consolations which turned them in the end to gain. Yet, to take the outward circumstances only, a period of twenty years, during which he had full possession of his faculties, but was, for the most part, wholly[b] cut off from all communication with the outer world; with intense suffering within, both spiritual and bodily,

[a] The letter to the P. d'Attichy, in which the author of the notice in the Biographie Univ. says that he "describes" them, must have been in MS. Those to that Father, in the Lettres Spirituelles (6—9) are all of an early date. In his printed letters he speaks of his sufferings generally; "My great sufferings" (Lett. 51. 56); "My great infirmities" (Lett. 102); "Strange sufferings and exceeding crosses," without any nearer description.

[b] He lost the power of writing for the whole twenty years (Lett. 15), and probably all power of communication (see note in p. lxvi). He wrote in some way at the close of 1656, and resumed his correspondence early in 1657 (ib. fin. and 123); but if the dates be correctly printed, he must have lost it again that year, for at the end of August he says (Ep. 17), "When it shall please the Lord to give me the power of writing, I shall use it with extreme joy to communicate with you, and unfold my thoughts from the bottom of my heart." Of his then state he says, "To say a word of my present condition, I find more facility and more freedom for the functions of the mind; but I have need, if our Lord will to loose (délier) me entirely, that you entreat Him for this by your holy Sacrifices."

yet unable to communicate the very nature of his sufferings, and so almost wholly cut off from all sympathy or counsel; with power of thinking for those he loved [a], yet of expressing nothing; accounted and confined as one insane; unrefreshed and unrelieved even by sleep [b], and so living an un-

[a] " Not that I did not often remember you in my great sufferings, but now I wish to give you marks of my remembrance of you, and to recal to you that of old." (Lett. 56.) " I never forgot you in my great sufferings, and I always had the same affection for you, and the same zeal for your good and your progress in the love of the Lord." (Lett. 51 to another.) He speaks in other places of the charity of those who wrote to him. (Lett. 102, 123.)

[b] This is implied by his mention of the contrary as something new after his recovery. The whole passage, in which he seems carried on, by very thankfulness, to speak of himself in a way quite unusual to him, gives such a picture of his childlike mind, that it is valuable, amid the slight notices open to us:—
" My natural strength, by the grace of God, is so renewed, that I have almost forgotten past sufferings; and this, which is the sixty-second year of my age, seems to me to be joined on immediately with my eighth. I recollect how I was enjoying peacefully the joy God gives to children. This autumn, which has been so beautiful, I have passed entirely in the country. I am but just come from it, and expect to return again till Advent. For some time past I have slept the whole night through, a peaceful and unbroken sleep. In all truth, it seems that I am as a child in the arms of our Lord, with as little care as at eight years old. I have no longer any Cross but the sight of the miseries of my neighbour, and the extreme poverty of the people, which I cannot see without sorrow. This is to tell you that our youth is sometimes renewed as the eagle's, after ills which would have been thought remediless. Pray our Lord that He will give me grace to take to me no stay in this world, but always to live on earth

broken intense existence,—this was a life of isolation from all but God, a vivid ever-present separation from all created things with which he was yet continually encompassed, such as is but rarely vouchsafed. Still more wonderful is it, yet not unexampled, even to this extent, in the history of those near to God, if for almost this whole period he had to abandon all sensible consolations, having for eighteen years that fulfilled in himself, which he had ever taught, "that man must seek God for Himself Alone," in abnegation of his whole self, "remaining [a] tranquilly under His good pleasure and Almighty Hand, sacrificing to Him all the motions of the heart, holding it in expectation of His orders, abiding and lost in God, awaiting His Light." He speaks, at least, in one place, to an intimate friend, as though the first eighteen years had been passed in suffering, unmitigated by any sensible Divine comfort; certainly that fulness of joy, which he every where speaks of as bestowed upon those who "give all for All," came not upon him until those eighteen years of fiery, purifying, trial were closed. "For twenty years," his words are [b], "I have been in

as a stranger, who is only occupied with the thought and desire of his home."

[a] Letter 93.
[b] Letter 15. In Lett. 123, he writes (Feb. 16, 1657), "To fulfil your wish to hear of my state, I will say, that *after* twenty years of no slight sufferings, our Lord has given me much peace, and has restored to me the power of writing; but I have not yet free use of my limbs. I seldom leave my room; I cannot say mass, and can perform but very few of the outward actions, which my profession would require of

strange sufferings and exceeding crosses. For two years our Lord has begun to re-establish me in peace, and to overwhelm me with joy." It is also the more marvellous, that this state of suffering isolation came as an answer to his early longings, yet was brought about directly by God's Hand, without any co-operation of his own, and in a way apparently the most opposite to the end. On a period of intense occupation of mind, in which all his spiritual skill and wisdom were called forth in direct conflict with the spiritual cunning of the Evil One, there followed this dreary stillness. Not the mind, as might have been expected, but the body, was allowed to give way; yet this too in such sort as to impair no power of the mind, even while its every outward function was absolutely suspended. It had not even such mitigation of pain as exhaustion mostly gives to intense suffering. With full powers of reflection, conscious of all around, within, and against it, his mind was imprisoned in a body over which he had no control,—a living soul within a body, as it were, already dead, except so far as it was allowed to be Satan's instrument for the infliction of suffering. Thus was he marvellously brought into the state for which, following God's leadings, he had first prepared himself, and then ardently longed,—a state like our Lord's, wherein he was deprived of all, and our Lord his only portion. He says, in one of the earliest of his published letters [a] (he was then thirty-four):

me, or which I would, though, to say truth, I have no longer any will but what God wills."

[a] Letter 6.

"I own frankly that it has been so beneficial to me, for the amendment of my life, to break off all intercourse with all sorts of persons, and even with my most intimate friends; and to efface from my memory, as much as I possibly could, all objects except Him Who Alone is essential, that the benefit which I have derived from this loneliness leads me to abstain from many actions which might seem very lawful. I even doubt whether the great good which I find in this general detachment from all things, will not oblige me hereafter to keep a continual silence." And—"In order that Jesus Christ should take the place of all things, we must forsake much; and if any ask me what we must forsake, I should answer, 'All things, great and small, without reserve and without ceasing, at all moments of our life.'"

In another letter of the same date[a], he seems almost to describe by anticipation his subsequent condition. It may be well to premise, in his own words, the tenor of his thoughts. "My taste is changed extremely. Would to God my life were also! I can prize and take pleasure in nothing but that affectionate simplicity which carries the heart to God and things Divine. All besides wearies and pains me. The object which occupies me above all others, is the ineffable Gift which God has bestowed on the world in giving it His Son, the humble and gentle JESUS,—a Gift so great and so precious, that

---

[a] Letter 8. The date 1654 must be a misprint for 1634, to which internal evidence assigns it. In 1654 the power of writing had not been restored to him. Madeleine Boinet, referred to as living, died in 1650. Lett. 129. t. ii. p. 106.

the feeling of such a mercy ought to absorb all the powers of man, leaving him unable to recollect aught save JESUS, to esteem or have pleasure in aught save JESUS. It seems even as if, at sight of JESUS, all which is of nature is lost; the mind becomes stupid with amazement, through the desire it hath of being consumed by love of an Object so Lovely; it has only strength enough to sink itself in an awestricken gratitude before an Incarnate God."

The words immediately describing that state of severance from all created things which was so soon to be his, are written on occasion of one, by birth a peasant, but whose high spiritual gifts had placed her as instructress in a family, of whom Surin had the spiritual charge. Of her he says:—" I should never have thought, and had never yet known, how God would bare us of all things, to what a desert He would lead us, to bring us up to the purity of His grace. In a word, the soul must feel nothing of the things of this life, nor its own operations; it must not feel itself; it must live in an obedience which turneth upside down all its movements, good[a], bad, and indifferent; in a poverty which leaves it not the free use of its own faculties; in a purity which does not allow it to take pleasure in any created thing; that thus, bared of all, and become, as it were, a 'wild man' in this wilderness, it may be capable of being tamed to God, and becoming familiar with Him; that, returning into the simplicity of its first origin, having gained a new birth, it be recog-

[a] The context limits this to motions of nature, as distinct from those of grace.

nized no more, either by itself or others, having no longer life or motions, save to adore and serve Him, the Man-God, the Saviour of men, to Whom all men owe their adoration, and Whom most know not; Whom even they who adore oppose by a conduct the entire reverse of His."

"Here it is that God seems to me to have appointed us a great and trying exercise, commanding us to imitate His Son, and to lead a life wholly opposed to that of the world. For since we cannot possibly live thus, without giving a shock to those with whom we live, by sentiments and maxims contrary to theirs, it cannot be but that they will rebut us, treat us as fools and extravagants, God so permitting, by a wise guidance of His Providence, that, rejected by creatures, and deprived of all the consolations of the earth, we may be constrained to have recourse to Him, and to seek in Him our consolation and our stay."

"In this state the soul is strengthened, established, inrooted in God. She lives by faith and hope, feeding on the truths she believes, and the Sovereign Good she hopes for; she dwells in a void where she sees nothing sensible; suspended, as it were, in air, without any distinct object; plunged into the abyss of faith, and, as it were, wholly lost in the darkness wherein God dwelleth; seeking neither to experience nor to enjoy aught, reserving for the future all her joys. Yet love occupies, fills, frees her from all care, thinks not whether she be ridiculed or censured. If stricken, she feels it not; if caressed, they cannot gain her. Neither promises nor threats can bend her; nothing is capable of moving her, because she takes no account of what is done to her, nor of what is passing around her, ever hanging on the Object of her love, and thinking but of Him."

It may complete this picture to show from another letter of uncertain date[a] wherein it centered; the meditation on the Passion of our Lord.

"The third disposition which binds us immediately to our Lord, and which makes us enjoy the closest embrace of His love, is that which St. Ignatius so much recommends, and which he calls a precious step in the spiritual life, viz. to desire with our whole might that condition wherein Jesus Christ appeared in the prætorium, when Pilate showed Him to the people, His Body all torn with scourgings, His Head covered with thorns, His Face all marred, a reed in His Hand, an old purple mantle on His Shoulders, compared with Barabbas, set below that accursed criminal, and judged more worthy of death than he. This condition, which the Son of God chose for love of us, and to give us an example, was one universal loss of all which could give credit in the eyes of men,—honour, reputation, credit, authority, comfort, peace, life; a state of hatred, rejection, contempt, abandonment; a state wherein He re-

[a] Letter 10 au Père L. Frison. Letter 11, which is connected with it, in the printed edition bears date 1661; the date of the third, 1694, ought perhaps to be 1664, as he died in 1665. This throws some doubt whether the state of mind was the fruit of his experience in suffering, or a preparation for it. The Editor feels incompetent to decide the date on internal evidence.

tained as His own nought save His Father's will and perfect obedience; a state which He has so ennobled, that we ought to love and desire it, as men ordinarily desire a marshal's staff, a cardinal's hat, and the highest offices and dignities of the world, wherein, when they have arrived at them, they rest complacently as the centre of their being.

"True, that to arrive at this, costs nature much; but one is well recompensed for the labour and the pain, for one finds one's-self forthwith brought within the inmost Friendship of Jesus Christ; one embraces Him closely, possesses Him fully, tastes His Spirit, has an amazing familiarity with Him; one feels a strength and power for all sorts of good, a noble determination towards all Apostolic employments, a most pure desire of His Glory alone, an ardent zeal for the love of souls; one leads on earth the life of Heaven, and is overflowed with those Divine consolations, the excess of which forced St. Xavier to cry out, 'Enough, Lord, enough.'"

Strange (if this too were written before that period of trial) that he should have been allowed so wonderfully to anticipate in longing, and by a deep feeling of necessity for his soul, the state into which He was brought by the immediate Hand of God, to crave for it, as a hungry man for his food, and have a foretaste of it, and with what sweetness he should be satisfied; to sketch out what God, in His secret purpose, had willed to do with him, while yet it was wholly hidden from him what he himself should do. For God did indeed "bring" him "into the wilderness," (Hos. ii. 14,) and there in the inmost solitude which thought can conceive, bared of all things without and within, "without pleasure in any created thing," and "in a poverty which did not leave it the free use of its own faculties," He "spake to" his "heart;" but the fruit of all seems to have been rather in what He made himself, than in forming him for "Apostolic employments," or giving him "strength and power for all sorts of good," at whose thought his heart had kindled. For when his health was restored, his bodily strength was well-nigh gone[a]; his great achievement[b] (so to speak) seems to have been, at the outset, the visible triumphs over Satan at Loudun; after his twenty years of suffering, his chief office seems to have been to tell others the blessedness of privation, and to exhort those under his guidance to attach themselves to God Alone; even to those whom he had in earlier years guided, he writes almost as one returned from another world, ignorant of all that which had passed in the fulness of twenty years of religious life; nor was he ever permitted to revisit them. He had, it seems, for his few remaining years, chiefly the high but simple office of gaining to Christ the poor villagers near Bordeaux, among whom he preached, and in whom he did indeed reap an "abundant harvest[c]."

So far other must God's thoughts be from ours,

[a] Letter 50. Towards the end of 1658, he writes to the Marquise d'Ars:—"Yet I am more incapable than ever of serving you, and can only see you by letters."

[b] He speaks of it, in a letter to one of the community, as the chief office of his life.

[c] His own expression in a letter.

that He broke, so to say, His own instrument in two, in the vigour of his age; and when, by destroying it, He had perfected it, employed it for nothing outwardly great in His kingdom. For twenty years He tempered and polished and refined this sharp sword, and then laid him up in His everlasting armoury, for what ends in the world invisible we know not, but here chiefly, as a memorable specimen how His weapons of proof are formed and tried in the fire. Like Isaac, his one great office seems to have been to yield himself meekly to suffering, and therein to be a type of blessings, and transmit them. God employed chiefly not his active service, but himself.

He is a very ideal of the blessedness of privation; a witness, with what awful marvellousness of mercy God will accept the ardent longings which willing souls receive from Him, "calling them to His Feet," and "leading them safely by a way that they know not," the path of the Sufferings of their Lord. He is a living witness and picture of the truth of the great sayings which he early learnt, "Bare [a] thyself of all, and thou shalt have All;" "Empty thyself of all creatures, and Christ will dwell with thee;" "To forsake himself inwardly, joineth man to God." God set His seal upon him, and in that He fulfilled those intense longings in His own way, while He accepted His servant, bore witness to the good part which he had chosen. The value of sufferings and privations and mortifications, which the Saints have chosen, is no dream, since He has poured in upon them such

[a] Thomas a Kempis.

abundance of His love, has moulded minds, within and without, for suffering, and through that suffering purified them for closer union with Himself, and the fuller reception of His love.

"Good courage," writes Surin in an early letter to a Religious, "in poverty, my very dear daughter, it will bring you riches; full discharge of ourselves on God; large abandonment to His love, confidence in that love which will draw the poor out of his misery, and make no difficulty about losing every thing except grace and eternal bliss. The more you shall lose, the more God will gain in you. Remain absolutely exposed, forsaken, despoiled of all which you ever possessed. Prepare yourself to see new worlds, and to experience all diversities at the will of God. So shalt thou be brought under the power of love. Be for ever His spoil and His captive, and praise His mercy."

It is hardly to be expected in our times, that that deep and universal love of the Cross, which this book implies, will be at once vouchsafed. We have neither patterns to follow, nor have the very ideal of it before us, nor have been brought up in sympathy with the Saints who practised it, nor (except one, perhaps) have spiritual guides along it; and too often are clogged by the chain of past sins, which leaves us no strength to follow it. Yet if we cannot hope that such large grace should be vouchsafed to us, at least the commencement, as it is necessary to salvation, so it is open to us. And for this too, besides the general tenor of the volume, many very valuable suggestions and definite practical rules will be found up and down in it. *Est quadam prodire tenus, si non datur ultra.* If, in dependence upon God's grace, the foot be once set in the course of self-discipline, and any can, in simplicity and sincerity of heart, say, "Give what Thou commandest, and command what Thou wilt," who knows whither the heart which so yields itself to God's Hand, may not be carried?

But, in emerging from our state of sloth and self-indulgence, (if such as the Editor may in any degree judge,) humble beginnings are for the most part most fitted for us. A deep and searching examination into the whole past life, with prayer to God to unfold its recesses, is obviously indispensable to any course of amendment or self-discipline. There is indeed a more awful knowledge of self, which God has from time to time vouchsafed, when He has upon prayer revealed the soul to itself, as it is; but if this be asked for, there needs, even in purer souls, much grace, and strength, and sense of His mercy to endure the sight[a]. Yet, short of

[a] "After the use of the Exercitia Spiritualia of St. Ignatius had been introduced into Portugal (among other countries) with a wonderful change of life, it was reported in Coimbra that those who made these holy retreats had strange visions, which led them to extraordinary fervour. One, employed by Card. Henri, Inquisitor-general, to ascertain the truth, applied, among others, to a good Religious, whose sincerity he knew, who told him in all simplicity that he had had a terrific vision during those exercises. On being pressed further what was this strange sight he had seen, he said, "I saw my-

this, that insight which He will bestow upon a faithful, painful, search into memory, recalling periods of life, scenes, persons, local circumstances, conversations, every thing which aids its associations, and, above all, not shrinking from gazing on any the faintest trace of a forgotten sin, until what we wish had never been, or have "hid from our own memories," gradually takes a distinctive shape, and we see a self we would fain have turned from; such insights will both set a person upon a truer penitence, and give him the groundwork of real well-directed self-denial. Books developing the Ten Commandments, the seven deadly sins, the abuses of the senses, are of use in this search; but if these be not at hand, "the best book," says a very eminent Confessor[a], "is the book of conscience." This discovery of self must be the ground of our continual repentance, the guide of our habitual self-examination, the basis of self-discipline, the substance of continual confession to God, if confession to man is not open to any. Continual confession will, by God's grace, fix and deepen repentance: rules founded on that knowledge will help on the narrow road of self-discipline. Well is it, if the mind can bring itself to the

self, which I never had before! O horrible monster! I assure you I never saw any thing more deformed, or which more terrified me." Nouet, l. c. It is related of two Saints, that, having prayed to God to show them themselves, they were obliged, when heard, to pray that the sight might be removed from them. And if so with them, how inexpressibly more with us!

[a] B. Leonard, Traité de la Confession Générale, in the Manuel des Confesseurs, § 424, p. 434.

solemn task of discharging the heavy load, of which it will too often become conscious, under the sacred seal of confession to God's Priest; for the Absolution so solemnly bestowed has often been, among us, the source of new life. And little as we of the Clergy (as far as the Editor may speak of an Order in which he is of the last) may be fitted as yet for Confessors, and still less as spiritual guides[a], to lead

[a] The Editor is glad to take this occasion of expressing his sense of the considerateness of the article on Confession in the British Critic (No. 66), and of the great value of the practical hints and temperate and thoughtful cautions, in Mr. Ward's recent book, in the chapters vi. vii. "on our existing practical corruptions," and "additional suggestions by way of remedy," which are most seasonable to those who are in earnest about the amendment of the deep practical evils and sins of omission in our Church. Of course, in making such a statement, any one must include himself as the guiltiest. It does not become such an one as the Editor to speak at all, and he has hitherto avoided it, having no office in the Church which any way entitles him to do so. Perhaps what has been said about himself (not in Mr. W.'s book) may excuse his now saying, that, however there were in the British Critic statements which he could not go along with, or which at times (as he understood them) gave him pain, he could not but see that there was a moral depth about the writers of the articles which gave most offence, to which he had himself no claim; he could not but, on that ground, feel more sympathy with their writings generally, than with those of others, with whom negatively, as to one extensive practice in the Roman Church, he was more agreed; he could not but respect them deeply as much superior to himself; and he felt satisfied, that they were an important element in the present restoration of our Church, and an instrument in the Hands of its Lord. To Him, therefore, Who Alone can guide her amid her present perils, he cheerfully committed the result,

on others, yet we cannot think that He, Who is so putting into the hearts of the children of our Church the longing to disburthen their hearts, and for individual guidance, will fail either her or them. The very emergency calls on us to use fervent prayer, self-discipline, to deepen the solemn sense of our responsibility, and to supply by study [a] what we want in experience; so may we, even if little fit for the office of leading on others, yet obtain grace to discern God's guiding of a soul, and ourselves follow it.

and would rather, to any extent, have been misunderstood in the one way, than have been supposed to undervalue what, amid whatever differences, he highly estimated. Especially we seem very mainly indebted to those writers for a more humble tone as to our own Church, which must be the very condition and basis of all solid restoration. Only that our humility must ever be personal; for who knows how much of our present sad confusion may not be owing to his own sins? On the other hand, the vivid sensibility to any thing on the one side, while a document, full of miserable heresy, put out without any religious earnestness, and largely signed, elicits no protest, is no good token of our religious temper, or of our sense of the sacredness of God's truth.

[a] The Manuel des Confesseurs is a most valuable digest of the judgments of some of the most experienced Confessors of the Church, and of the greatest use, whether in the receiving of Confessions, or the more ordinary spiritual ministrations. Mr. Newman's Sermons furnish a most wonderful body of instruction to any who have to guide souls, as they would go very far to supply the absence of individual direction. Every body may find himself in them, and what he needs. But chiefly we must be impressed, that the first element in guiding others is self-discipline. Without earnest care for our own sanctification, we should most miserably be "blind leaders of the blind."

Nor is this any slight help. It is no little relief in perplexity, and no little safeguard against waywardness, to have our own judgments or half-judgments of what is best for us, confirmed by an authority from without. At the last, our All-merciful God never will be wanting to those who are His. Let any one really desire to do His Will, pray for guidance and a guide, and God will either provide him one, or will Himself guide him.

It is not, I hope, through sluggishness, or inexperience in the ways of God, that I have ventured to recommend to any gentle steps; if any are led by giant strides, happy are they. I am speaking only of the ordinary preparation of heart, until persons know themselves, and whereto God calls them. Let any one give himself up without reserve to God, and He will either send him crosses, or guide him directly or through others what to lay upon himself. "I have received," Surin writes to a Religious [a], who became "one of the most perfect of her day," "some of your letters, wherein I see your condition of poverty and suffering. I see, my very dear sister, what it is to abandon one's-self to God. When a soul has had the courage to resign itself entirely into His Hands, He fails not to purify it by severities, and to conduct it by this way of entire privation to the great goods which He will give it, as a recompense for having abandoned to Him its interests and itself."

But I suppose it is the most ordinary way, that God leads people step by step. It may be because

[a] Letter 98 to La Mère Angelique de St. François.

they have not great fervor, perhaps because previous unfaithfulness makes it unfitting to bestow more grace at once, and to preserve penitence and humility. "Perfect service," says Surin[a], "comes not all at once. It is attained little by little with patience, retaining constantly the good purpose to stretch towards God in the most perfect way, often renewing it on occasions in which it might be relaxed, permitting no disorder of the senses or the mind, holding up vigorously against that heaviness into which one falls unceasingly through the weight of nature, never discouraged by falls or unfaithfulnesses; lastly, ever keeping one's-self united to Jesus Christ by a lively faith, a tender love, a continual remembrance of His Life and Death, and endeavouring to taste His Sorrows." "The good I wish for her," he says to another[b], " and the grace which I ask without ceasing for her, is, that Jesus Christ in His glory, His greatness, and His victory, will overthrow and destroy in her all which would resist His purposes, and cast into her soul such fire and flames, that her heart should become a furnace, wherein she should be blessedly consumed with the burning glow of the Seraphim. This is not so impossible as we often imagine it. Step by step, by a scrupulous faithfulness, and a constant attention in watching over our inward selves, we carry at last what seemed to us at first inaccessible, and accomplish things the very idea of which seemed to exhaust our whole strength."

But if one might select one maxim as of import-

[a] Letter 48 to the Marquise d'Ars.
[b] Letter 23.

ance to beginners, it is, that there are no little things in religion. As " he who despises little things shall fall by little and little," so, too, little steps in faithfulness carry a great way. Little self-indulgences, slight evil-speaking, petty self-praise, unceasing slight distractions, trivial self-reflection, are the countless cords of vanity which wind around the whole man, and bind him fast, so that he can no way move freely, or go straight to God. No one, until he have tried, will have any thought how much occupation the cutting off of these petty things will give him, or how it will open the heart to Divine grace. It is a first principle, that nothing is indifferent. Every thing, we know from Holy Scripture, ought to be done to "the glory of God;" and at every turn self thrusts itself in and takes the place of God. Every sense is an avenue of distraction, or an instrument of self-gratification. We are by nature scattered abroad amid the manifoldness of outward things; by Grace we must be gathered up and collected into God. Not a glance of the eye, not a resting of a thought, not an attitude of our bodily frame, but may have some connexion with the infirmities which keep the mind on the ground. Nor is there any sacrifice ever so slight, made out of love to God, which He does not almost instantly reward. "To one[a] who wishes to know what relates to his spiritual progress, I would say, 'Enter into thy inner self; shut the doors of thy senses; flee all sorts of pleasures; do no useless action; receive no impression

[a] Letter 7.

from any objects needlessly; empty thy heart continually of all things, and seek God unceasingly in the depth of thy soul. Thus thou wilt know what hinders thee from uniting thyself with the Sovereign Good; thou wilt discern the very smallest atoms; thou wilt see that the slightest pleasure retained habitually, even if not of set purpose but by connivance only, curiosity in little things, familiarity with outward persons, a glance of the eyes cast on some object needlessly, every superfluous care, are obstacles to union with God."

And if the Editor might allude to the higher uses of this book to such as may profit by it, to a degree he dare not hope himself, it may, he trusts, have come providentially into his hands, as a sympathizing voice speaking to those who are now lying under a degree of suspicion and obloquy, and (it is to be feared) often more angry and un-Christian tempers, of which he himself is not worthy to be the object. Such had been the special suffering of the Author, and there is hardly any point of self-abnegation on which he lays so much stress as the love of contempt and reproaches. It seems the crowning gift of the Cross, likening them most to their Lord, and tending to form in them "the same mind which was in CHRIST JESUS." Such indeed is the one voice of the Saints. Since then our Lord has vouchsafed now these many years to turn that to chiefest good to our Church, from which "flesh and blood" and human calculation would most have shrunk; so now this Cross of shame and reproach, " the livery of CHRIST JESUS," is, we may trust, a gracious vouchsafement and a special token of His Presence, to those to whom it is in any real measure granted; and since our individual character is of far more importance to the well-being of the Church than even our labours for her, they who, through the unhappy circumstances of our times, are hindered from serving her as they would, may, by the blessing of Almighty God, in the more secret life of self-abnegation to which they are called, yield her higher service, than they might perhaps, had their most devoted labours been accepted of their hands.

E. B. P.

Vigil of St. James, 1844.

"Grant, O merciful God, that as thine holy Apostle Saint James, leaving his father and all that he had, without delay was obedient unto the calling of thy Son Jesus Christ, and followed him; so we, forsaking all worldly and carnal affections, may be evermore ready to follow thy holy Commandments, through Jesus Christ our Lord. Amen."

NOTICE OF SURIN.

(FROM THE BIOGRAPHIE UNIVERSELLE.)

Surin, an ascetic writer, born at Bordeaux in 1600[a], was the son of a parliamentary councillor of that city. He was of exalted piety, and at the age of fifteen, his father yielding to his importunity, he entered among the Jesuits. He made his novitiate at Bordeaux, and was sent to La Flèche and Rouen to continue his studies. His taste inclined him to solitude and the contemplative life, while his piety fitted him for the direction of consciences. From the age of thirty he was regarded as a good guide in the paths of perfection, and we learn from his letters that many pious persons sought after his counsels. He also gave himself to preaching; and from Marennes, where he resided, he visited the towns and country around, applying himself to all the functions of his ministry,

[a] If the date of Letter 47, in the printed editions (1664), is correct, he was born in 1602, since he was then "in his 62nd year." This would be so far interesting, as placing the great maturity of mind, evinced in his earliest letters, somewhat younger. But if the letter is placed chronologically, it should be 1662, which agrees with the above.—[Ed.]

and by his teaching and example leading others to love God. His great excellencies and skill in the ways of the inner life induced his superiors to confide to him an undertaking delicate and perilous; they sent him to Loudun, to direct the convent of Ursulines, who were thought[a] to be possessed by the

[a] Only half of the convent, with the superior, was so possessed. (Surin, Letters, t. ii. p. 405.) It is specified that the Préfète was exempt. (Ibid.) Surin speaks of it undoubtingly as a real possession. Thus he writes to the Mère Jeanne des Anges herself in 1662:—" I would that as the demons aforetime put forth their rage in your house, our Lord would now the workings of His grace.—God has given you many new members, who have no idea of your past condition, nor the experience which the elders have had of the malignant operations of demons, or of what God has done to deliver you from their oppression.—As St. John says, ' The Word of Life, Who was from the beginning, Whom we have heard, Whom we have seen with our eyes, Whom we have looked upon, and our hands have handled, we declare unto you;'—so the elder sisters of your house can say to the younger, What we have seen and experienced, and almost touched with the finger, of the misery of those who are condemned and rejected of God, we declare to you; and we say to you, it is a miserable condition to be an enemy of God, and to have fallen from His grace. We have seen the disorders and the sufferings of spirits damned and cast away by God, and thereby we have learnt and seen plainly, of what moment it is, not to separate from Him, and fall into the darkness and disorders wherein the wretched demons live. For my own part, I assure you that in the employment which the Lord has given me to preach to the country people—I find nothing better to tell them than that, after so many infirmities in which I was so long plunged, God has, in some sort, given me back life, to impart my experience to those who are under the ordinary dispensation of faith; that He would, that, to recall them from

devil. We must not here enter into the details of a history which made so much noise, and on which

their sins and bring them back to Him, I should communicate the knowledge which I have received out of the usual course, as to the truths whereon the salvation of souls depends; and that, discovering to them the fearful condition of demons, as one knows it, when, by a possession they have fallen under the power of the Church, and by her exorcisms she holds them as her slaves, they may escape the same misery, and keep themselves from the snares which these invisible enemies continually lay for them." (Lett. 72.) Surin, also, in several letters, notices some signal triumphs over Satan. To another (Lett. 85), "And why, think you, did our Lord so many things out of the ordinary course, in your house? Why so many marvellous protections? Why has He given poor maidens, despised and abandoned by the world, so signal a victory over the powers of darkness? Why so many prodigies of grace, which, so to say, put out your eyes?" &c. To another (Lett. 100), "I long greatly that the grace which He has shown your community in restoring it peace, and delivering it from the attacks of hell, may have its full effect by subjecting your hearts to the empire of Jesus Christ. You cannot, without extreme ingratitude, be satisfied with any slight excellence." (Lett. 101), "Where are now the marvels of God? Where is the God of Israel? That God of Goodness, Who manifested so gloriously His power to succour poor maidens, weak, abandoned, and become, in their misery, outcasts of the world? After so many favours, must He be served poorly, my dear sisters?" (Lett. 72), "Such is the fruit which Jesus Christ looks for from the good seed which He has sown in your field by so many extraordinary assistances of His grace, which He had made to triumph so signally among you over the powers of hell." He notices in the same letter (1662 or 1663), "I observe not without amazement, that He has preserved the lives of almost all the religious of that period. Only three are dead." (About twenty-six years afterwards.) [ED.]

different judgments have been passed; we will only remark, that Surin was not sent to Loudun till after the death of Grandier, and that consequently he had no share in the unhappy end of that curé. On December 7, 1634, he set out from Marennes to fulfil his mission, and was specially charged to direct La Mère Jeanne des Anges, prioress of the convent of Ursulines. That daughter, who had no less prudence than piety, was at that time encompassed with trials as singular as they were difficult; Father Surin applied himself especially to form in her the inward life, and to inspire her with an entire detachment from all earthly things, and a deep humility.

A manuscript now before us relates very circumstantially the means he took to comfort and strengthen the prioress. He himself was not permitted to escape the torments which she endured. On Good Friday of 1635, he also fell into a most extraordinary state, as he himself relates in a letter to the Père d'Attichy. Nearly two years were passed in an alternation of conflicts and calm: some pitied his being subjected to so hard a trial; others blamed him for neglecting exorcisms[a], in order to apply himself more to regulate the inward conduct of the religious. At the end of 1636 his superiors ordered him to quit Loudun; he obeyed at once, and after his return to Bordeaux, gave himself up anew to the ministry of the pulpit. About this time his father died, and the widow, by her son's advice, entered among the Carmelites, where her daughter had already professed. Still many de-

[a] This, if so, relates to an early period, for he himself speaks of the use and effect of exorcisms. See preceding note. [ED.]

manded that P. Surin should go back to Loudun to finish what he had there begun; his superiors, therefore, again sent him there in 1637, and the prioress was set completely free on the 15th of October in that year, in consequence of a vow she had made to go with Father Surin to the tomb of St. François de Sales, who had died in the odour of sanctity fifteen years previously. They travelled separately in 1638, and were received at Anneçi by La Mère de Chantal, who was then living. On his return to Bordeaux, Surin found himself in an almost indescribable state, in the entire enjoyment of his reason, and yet deprived of the outward exercise of his faculties; he could neither walk, talk, nor write, and was continually assailed by violent temptations. In this humiliating condition it was thought necessary to his safety to keep him in confinement. Object of the scorn of some and of the anxiety of others, he had strength enough to offer to God his troubles; and it was during this very period of sorrows of every kind that he composed his "Catéchisme Spirituel" and the "Fondemens de la Vie Spirituelle," which were written [a] under his dictation as soon as he

[a] The following account of his "Catéchisme Spirituel" and his "Dialogues Spirituels" occurs in a letter of Aug. 1657:—"In conclusion, I thank you for the pains you have kindly bestowed on the printing of the 'Spiritual Catechism.' That book only escaped me through my facility in giving copies of it to some persons of piety, who have put it in the condition in which you have seen it. The other parts of this work are at Loudun, in the hands of La Mère Jeanne-des-Anges. I am now engaged in writing another, as an useful occupation to myself. Its style is much the same as that of the Catechism, but

was able to speak. At the end of more than twenty years, this violent state subsided by degrees; Surin recovered, in 1658, the use of his faculties, and resumed his correspondence after a long interruption. We have a great number of letters of spiritual direction which he wrote to different people, and in which he speaks with simplicity of the state in which he had languished during so many years. The Prince de Conti, whose conversion had been so famed, esteemed Father Surin, and they were in habitual correspondence. This prince made him publish the "Catéchisme Spirituel." Father Surin also kept up a correspondence with persons of distinction in the world and at court; he resumed the exercise of the ministry, and he loved,

the form a little different. In it I treat of the ways of perfection, beginning with the desire one ought to feel for it." (Lett. 17.) I have not been able, in the published letters, to see any trace of the period of partial restoration implied in the text, unless, in Lett. 15, he means by "writing," in the first place, "composing" only, which would agree with the date in Lett. 103, in which he says, "For twenty years I have been unable to write. Within these few days God has restored me the power." His words in Lett. 15 are—"My strength is returning, and I hope it will serve me to do service to God. My outward frame, however, is still cramped, and I have no power to exert myself for any thing, except in my room. I have written much during the last three months, but I have only set myself to write letters within the last fortnight or three weeks." (Feb. 6, 1657, Lett. 15.) From these passages it would seem that the Catechism was the first occupation of his restored strength, and was written in the first three months of his recovery, from the beginning of Advent, 1656. If this be so, it would appear that the power even of "dictation" was only restored to him about the end of the period.

above all, to make himself useful to the humbler ranks, to visit the poor in town and country, and suit his instructions to their capacity. He gave his care most cheerfully to the sick most despaired of. It had been his wish to return to Loudun to visit those whom he had once directed, but his superiors judged it not fitting to permit him. La Mère Jeanne des Anges died at Loudun towards the end of January, 1665. There are a large number of Father Surin's letters addressed to that daughter. He survived her a short time, and died April 21, 1665.

CONTENTS.

BOOK I.

PAGE

CHAPTER I.—To walk inwardly with God, and not to be kept abroad by any outward affection, is the state of a spiritual man. B. ii. c. 6. 1

CHAPTER II.—If thou attain to the full contempt of thyself, know that thou shalt then enjoy abundance of peace. B. iii. c. 25. 6

CHAPTER III.—All things are comprised in these few words : Forsake all, and thou shalt find all. B. iii. c. 32. 14

CHAPTER IV.—The more thou withdrawest thyself from solace of creatures, the more will I heap upon thee spiritual joys. Book iii. c. 12. 19

CHAPTER V.—Rejoice to be thought guilty, that you may be innocent in the sight of God 26

CHAPTER VI.—Set thyself always in the lowest place, and the highest shall be given thee. B. ii. c. 10. 32

CHAPTER VII.—I cause all devout persons to pass through severe trials...................................... 37

CHAPTER VIII.—It is matter of great skill to know to hold converse with Jesus ; and to know how to keep Jesus, a point of great wisdom. B. ii. c. 8. 43

CHAPTER IX.—A certain person, by loving Me entirely, learned divine things, and spake that which was admirable. He profited more by forsaking all things, than in studying subtleties. Book iii. c. 43. 48

BOOK II.

CHAPTER I.—Learn to despise outward things, and to give thyself to things inward, and thou shalt perceive the kingdom of God to come in thee. B. ii. c. 1. 52

CHAPTER II.—He that judgeth of all things as they are, and not as they are said, or esteemed to be, is truly wise, and taught rather of God than men. B. ii. c. 1. 57

	PAGE
CHAPTER III.—The more holy violence thou usest against thyself, the greater shall be thy spiritual profiting. B. i. c. 25................................	62
CHAPTER IV.—Presume not upon thyself. B. i. c. 7....	67
CHAPTER V.—False freedom of mind, and great confidence in ourselves, are very contrary to heavenly visitations. B. ii. c. 10.	71
CHAPTER VI.—In whatever instance a person seeketh himself, then he falleth from love. B. iii. c. 5.	77
CHAPTER VII.—Simplicity doth tend towards God; Purity doth apprehend and, as it were, taste Him. B. ii. c. 4.	82
CHAPTER VIII.—He that can best tell how to suffer, will best keep himself in peace. B. ii. c. 7...............	88
CHAPTER IX.—What is not savoury unto him, to whom Thou art pleasing? B. iii. c. 34.	93

BOOK III.

CHAPTER I.—Wheresoever thou findest thyself, renounce thyself	98
CHAPTER II.—It is, therefore, no small matter for a man to forsake himself even in the smallest things. B. iii. c. 39...	101
CHAPTER III.—That I may not feel myself. B. iii. c. 21.	104
CHAPTER IV.—If thou wouldst perfectly empty thyself from all creatures, Jesus would willingly dwell with thee. B. ii. c. 7.................................	107
CHAPTER V.—Where shall one be found who is willing to serve God for nought? B. ii. c. 2................	111
CHAPTER VI.—If thou seekest thyself, thou shalt also find thyself. B. ii. c. 7..............................	115
CHAPTER VII.—If thou dost more rely upon thine own reason or industry, than upon that power which brings thee under the obedience of Jesus Christ, it will be long before thou become illuminated. B. i. c. 14.....	119
CHAPTER VIII.—A true lover of Christ, and a diligent follower of virtue, does not fall back on comforts, nor seek such sensible sweetnesses. B. ii. c. 9...........	124
CHAPTER IX.—O happy minds and blessed souls, who have the privilege of receiving Thee, their Lord God, with devout affection, and in so receiving Thee are	

permitted to be full of spiritual joy! O how great a Lord do they entertain! how beloved a Guest do they harbour! how delightful a Companion do they receive! how faithful a Friend do they welcome! how lovely and noble a Spouse do they embrace. B. iv. c. 3..... 127

BOOK IV.

CHAPTER I.—For a long while shall he be small, and lie grovelling below, whoever he be, that esteemeth any thing great but the One only Infinite Eternal Good. B. iii. c. 31. 134
CHAPTER II.—If thou dost walk spiritually, thou wilt not much weigh fleeting words. B. iii. c. 28............ 139
CHAPTER III.—For that is the cause why there are so few contemplative men to be found, for that few can wholly withdraw themselves from things created and perishing. B. iii. c. 31. 143
CHAPTER IV.—As to be void of all desire of external things produceth inward peace, so the forsaking of ourselves inwardly, joineth us unto God. B. iii. c. 56..... 147
CHAPTER V.—He that loveth with all his heart, is neither afraid of death, nor punishment, nor of judgment, nor of hell. B. i. c. 24. 153
CHAPTER VI.—Give all for all; seek nothing; require back nothing; abide purely and with a firm confidence in Me, and thou shalt possess Me. B. iii. c. 37....... 158
CHAPTER VII.—He to whom the Eternal Word speaketh, is delivered from a world of unnecessary conceptions. B. i. c. 3. 162
CHAPTER VIII.—If it were well with thee, and thou wert well purified from sin, all things would fall out to thee for good, and to thy advancement in holiness. B. ii. c. 1. 166
CHAPTER IX.—A perfect contempt of the world .. will give us great confidence we shall die happily. B. l. c. 23... 169

BOOK V.

CHAPTER I.—Desire to be unknown. B. l. c. 2......... 174
CHAPTER II.—From that One Word are all things, and all speak that One. B. i. c. 3. 177
CHAPTER III.—Thou oughtest to give all for all, and to retain nothing of thyself. B. iii. c. 27. 179

	PAGE
CHAPTER IV.—The more thou canst go out of thyself, so much the more wilt thou be able to enter into Me. B. iii. c. 56.	181
CHAPTER V.—He that endeavours to withdraw himself from obedience, withdraweth himself from Grace; and he who seeketh for himself private benefits, loseth those which are common. B. iii. c. 13.	184
CHAPTER VI —There is great difference between the wisdom of an illuminated and devout man, and the knowledge of a learned and studious clerk. B. iii. c. 31.	188
CHAPTER VII.—If thou hadst but once perfectly entered into the secrets of the Lord Jesus, and tasted a little of His ardent love, &c. Book ii. c. 1.	191
CHAPTER VIII.—Drink of the Lord's cup heartily..As for comforts, leave them to God. B. ii. c. 12.	194
CHAPTER IX.—God will have us perfectly subject unto Him, that being inflamed with his love, we may transcend the narrow limits of human reason. B. i. c. 14.	197
CHAPTER X.—He is truly learned, that doeth the will of God. B. i. c. 14.	201

OF THE FOUNDATION OF THE WHOLE SPIRITUAL LIFE, WHICH IS HUMILITY.

CHAPTER XI.—A man's worthiness is not to be estimated by the number of visions and comforts which he may have, or by his skill in the Scriptures, or by his being placed in a higher station than others; but the proof is, if he be grounded in true humility. B. iii. c. 7.	207

OF THE PERFECT USE OF FAITH.

CHAPTER XII.—Endeavour to withdraw thy heart from the love of visible things, and to turn thyself to the invisible. B. i. c. 1.	213

OF THE REMEMBRANCE OF THE PASSION OF OUR LORD.

CHAPTER XIII.—If thou canst not contemplate high and heavenly things, rest thyself in the passion of Christ, and dwell willingly in His sacred wounds. B. ii. c. 1.	217

OF THE GOOD THINGS, FOR WHICH THOSE WHO EMBRACE VIRTUE MAY HOPE IN THIS LIFE.

CHAPTER XIV.—Great grace shall be given to those who shall have willingly subjected themselves to Thy most holy service. They who for thy love shall have renounced all carnal delights, shall find the sweetest consolations of the Holy Ghost. B. iii. c. 10.	220
A spiritual letter to a lady of rank	227

THE

FOUNDATIONS OF SPIRITUAL LIFE.

BOOK I.

CHAPTER I.

(On these words)—"To walk inwardly with God, and not to be kept abroad by any outward affection, is the state of a spiritual man." B. ii. c. 6.

QUESTION.—What is to walk with God?

ANSWER.—It is to be occupied internally with God; and this occupation requires three things.

1. The first is a continual attention to the Presence of the Lord, on Whom one thinks incessantly, and Whom one cannot forget, because one loves Him entirely, and labours for Him Alone. When a soul has firmly resolved to serve Him, and when she has during the day different exercises which bring her back to Him, should she wander ever so little, she has no difficulty in returning to His Presence, because the holy resolution she has taken, never to remain far from Him, having become a habit, she cannot lose the sweet remembrance of her Beloved.

2. The second thing necessary in order to walk with God, is to do everything upon principle and through Grace, following the light of the Holy Spirit, and in entire dependance on assistance from on high. This

mode of acting distinguishes interior persons from those who are not so; for the latter decide on all they do, from merely human motives, consulting only their own natural reason, guided only by their own self-will, and loving only what they themselves choose, and at most avoiding only what is manifestly sinful.

Devout minds adopt a very different rule. They converse with God within, and all their works are above nature, being the fruits of prayer; they labour to subdue their appetites, and to mortify their self-will; they undertake nothing without commending the issue thereof to God, and whatever they do, they seek always to please Him. In this manner every thing succeeds with them, for Heaven never fails to second their designs. Others act from whim, or by chance, or with the view to some human interest; these regard God Alone, and wish only what they know to be agreeable to Him. Their intentions are always upright; it is Grace which ever leads them to act; Grace, which regulates all their actions; they bind themselves to her, never willingly quit her; in a word, they strive, as far as it is possible, to reach a state where they may possess God, be united to Him in spirit, and have no other guide nor Master than Him.

Those who have not experienced what we describe, will fancy that nothing could be more sad and irksome; but those who have tried it are persuaded of the contrary: they find nothing but happiness in it; for besides the extreme joy which the presence of their Lord occasions them, they have also this advantage, that He is always ready to give them salutary advice; as our author says, "If you would retire within yourself to converse with God, you would hear the answers He would make you:" and again, "Blessed is the soul which heareth the Lord speaking within her, and receiveth from His mouth the word of consolation." B. iii. c. 1.

This, perhaps, cannot be attained all at once; but by the continual exercise of the presence of God, a devout soul, whose intentions are always pure, becomes worthy at last that He should discover to her the designs which He has for her.

3. The third thing which the soul must do, in order never to lose the presence of her Beloved Spouse, is to become familiar with certain practices of piety, which may help her to rise continually towards Him, without ever relaxing or falling back into coldness; accustoming herself to internal exercises, by which she may learn to enjoy God and gently to enter into familiar intercourse with Him.

Now these exercises are, to meditate often on the Passion of Jesus Christ, to labour zealously either in acquiring some virtue which one has not, and in perfecting one's self in it, or in subjugating some vice to which one is liable; and other similar efforts, which recall a man within himself, lest he should give himself up entirely to outward employments, inconsiderately and without profit.

Many satisfy themselves with the performance of duties to which they are strictly obliged, and from which they cannot reasonably be exempted. They join in prayer with tolerable attention, they go to the Choir at stated hours; and watch sufficiently over themselves to guard against committing gross sins; but beyond this they pass their lives softly, forming no lofty schemes for improvement, and making no extraordinary exertions to attain to perfection. It is not thus with those who may be termed interior and spiritual.

They are always occupied within themselves, always on the watch to correct some defect, to purify themselves more and more, to grow in holiness, to walk in the presence of God, and to cherish familiarity with the Saints. "Blessed," says our author, "are they who enter far into things internal, and who endeavour to prepare themselves more and more, by daily exercises, for the receiving Heavenly secrets." B. iii. c. 1.

QUESTION.—What is not to be kept abroad by any outward affection?

ANSWER.—It is to take no interest in all that is without: it is to be insensible, and as it were dead, to all that is external, however fascinating it may be, except as far as it may tend to the glory and service of God.

The world is filled with persons lamentably remote from this degree of perfection. Objects of sense have charms which win them; if the work which they are about pleases them, they cannot leave it. They must not then be called interior men, for this disordered affection makes them love to go out of themselves. That it rules in their heart is evident, for on occasion of a mere nothing it raises a great tumult within them and the strongest stirrings of the soul. A glass broken by chance throws them into a passion; one man burns with a longing wish to go to the theatre, or to be present at some show; another to see a prince with his retinue. What is there which will not stir up a restless and dissipated mind?

How often, even amongst those who profess higher things, do we see those who find pleasure in seeing fine houses, splendid palaces, even turning out of their road to satisfy their curiosity! Such things, they say, are not without their use in conversation; one should be able to speak on all subjects. They are never at a loss for specious reasons to cover their self-indulgence; but secretly it is the things themselves to which they are attached. How many religious await with impatience an order from their superior to leave a house of which they are weary, to go into another which they hope will suit them better! How many others long passionately to see certain persons, and to hold intercourse with them, not in order to advance in virtue, but simply for their own gratification! A man truly spiritual is dead to all that flatters his senses.

But you will say, Must not a man be perfectly stupid, not to be affected by anything? Oh happy he who is insensible to that degree, that nothing touches him but the interests of God Alone! Assuredly a soul which has once devoted herself to God, should be ashamed of loving and desiring anything but His glory! Our author might complain with reason that in these times "there are very few contemplative persons." B. i. c. 31. He does not mean there are very few hermits; by "contemplative," he means those whose heart and mind are perpetually fixed on God. He does not mean either, that one is obliged for this purpose to renounce all external occupation, since many of the saints have been able so happily to unite contemplation with action, that, without relinquishing their meditations on God, they have been employed day and night for the salvation of souls.

All that he requires is, that we should be so entirely detached from all that is external, as never to take a single step in order to see anything, however new or delightful, to which we are not induced by the consideration of some service to God. Even then we should carefully examine our motive, lest it should be a pretext to colour our self-love. We must go direct to God, and so fix our eyes upon His glory, as never to follow a certain natural excitement whereby most men are guided.

CHAPTER II.

(On these words)—" If thou attain to the full contempt of thyself, know that thou shalt then enjoy abundance of peace." B. iii. c. 25.

QUESTION.—How can one obtain perfect contempt for oneself?

ANSWER.—There are three steps, as it were, to arrive at this.

1. The first is, to have no regard for our own interests, to be insensible to all that regards ourselves, to have little esteem for ourselves, so that, if we are attacked, slandered, or insulted, as long as our own honour and reputation only are at stake, we should not complain of it, should not be in the least moved by it, and if some slight resentment is excited, should suppress it instantly. This it is to despise oneself; for he who thinks well of himself, and wishes to be somebody, thinks it strange if he is attacked without regard for his rank or merit. It is true, if we may believe him, it is not the affront that he resents, still, things so false are ascribed to him, that he cannot but require an explanation! Besides, it is necessary for the edification of others, that he should justify himself and the truth be known.

Such is the language of a vain man who seeks some cloak for his pride. For he who has a real and perfect contempt for himself, leaves all to God, is always tranquil, and gives himself no trouble about what is said against him. If any murmuring thought, any suspicious or bitter feeling surprises him, he stifles it instantly, for although he might flatter himself with feeling, "I do not yield to my vexation; I let the world talk, I care as little for its contempt as for its applause," still, however little he may dwell upon all this, he is unavoidably more or less disturbed. The shortest and surest way is to put away at once all such thoughts, to offer up one's resentment to Christ Crucified, and to seek true repose in the Cross. By such means one ensures that internal peace after which the whole world strives in vain; safe sheltered, we can no longer have anything against any one, are free from all anxiety for one's own interests, willingly renounce the right (so reasonable in the eyes of certain so-called philosophers, but bad Christians,) to defend one's honour and repel calumny even to the extent of demanding full satisfaction, contrary to the injunction of our Saviour, *Of him that taketh away thy goods, ask them not again.* Luke vi. 30.

The true friends, perfect imitators, and faithful disciples of Jesus, that Divine model of gentleness and humility, never repine about their rights, because they are persuaded that if He had not renounced many of His, there would be no salvation for them.

This mode of acting, equally humble and noble, is always acceptable to Him; for He wishes us to love but Him, to prize only His friendship, to seek only His glory, and after the example of St. Paul, to count all the rest *but as dung.* Phil. iii. 8. In this manner we obtain the peace of the heart, sweet and abundant peace, and this is the first step towards perfect contempt for oneself.

2. The second consists not only in never resenting the insults which are offered us, and in never complaining of those who humble us; but in welcoming humiliation, in yielding willingly to others, in taking everywhere the lowest place, in preferring contumely to respect, in regarding ourselves as worms of the earth in the eyes of God, and, in the sight of the world, as

the lowest of men, in loving the shame of the Cross, in finding our delight in it, and placing our treasure in it. These sentiments are nourished by a consideration of our sins and demerits, and by a fervent desire of imitating our Lord, Who sought and loved humiliation. "Abase yourselves," says our author, "that the whole world may trample you underfoot as the mud of the street." He who thus retires into his own nothingness, enjoys a peace which cannot be expressed: for when God sees a soul humbled in His Presence, He loves to visit her, He communicates with her; and the soul, having no earthly clog to prevent its union with God, forgets herself wholly, and thinks only of pleasing Him.

On the other hand, the ambitious man, who seeks only for opportunities of display and aggrandizement in the world, is always uneasy, always dissatisfied; and God hath pleasure in mortifying him, because he is not satisfied with God, and his whole passionate longing is to see himself honoured by man.

Those lowly hearts who seek God Alone, find Him everywhere; and as soon as He has revealed Himself to them, He communicates to them His peace, He makes them sharers of His joy. For, exalted as He is, He hath no greater pleasure than in descending to those who make themselves little before him. It was this that made the Blessed Virgin say, *He hath regarded the low estate of His handmaiden.* Luke i. 48. *Though the Lord be high*, says David, *yet hath He respect unto the lowly, but the proud He knoweth afar off*. Ps. cxxxviii. 6. There is then no more certain mode of pleasing God, and deserving His favour, than to humble oneself.

With this view many great princes have embraced the religious life, as being mean and contemptible in the eyes of the world.

But what doth the religious, who, full of the spirit

of the world, and weary of living under obedience, thinks of promotion! He dreams of the highest dignities of the Church; his head is full of the episcopate. If he has friends, he hopes to attain it through their assistance; and sometimes his hopes are not deceived. Very different they who are more mortified and more wise; they flee honours, imitating St. Ambrose, St. Martin, and many others; they shrink from them, like hidden shoals; at least, they wait till God calls them; even when they are obliged to accept them, there is nothing they would not do to escape from them.

We are told in Ecclesiastical History, that a German monk, about two hundred years ago, being torn from his cloister, was made a Bishop and then a cardinal. This holy man was so humble, that he declared when dying, that the thing which had caused him most grief was, having been obliged to leave his monastery, and that it would have been far more profitable for him to have taken his turn in the kitchen there, than to be raised to dignity in the world. Admirable lesson for those who aspire to honourable posts, and who cannot endure poverty and humiliation! After all, if their intrigues succeed, and they find means of gratifying their ambition, we do not see that their minds are calmer, nor do they appear more contented than they were in solitude and in communion with God. For nothing can make a man's happiness during his life, but that which will form his consolation and joy at his death.

3. The last step by which we reach real contempt of ourselves, is that which St. Ignatius, the Founder of the Company of Jesus, recommends so earnestly to his children, when he exhorts them not only to remain in an abject condition, but even to desire and take pleasure in it; and to welcome calumny and slander with no less joy than people of the world feel in honours and dignities. Indeed, they are special gifts

from Heaven, since chiefly through the shame of the Cross do we grow like our Saviour.

In this frame of mind we seek only how to abase ourselves and truly learn self-contempt. The love we have for the Saviour, makes us happiest then, and to feel that there is no greater happiness than when plunged, by some unforeseen circumstance, into a degrading situation, in which we are pointed at as a nothing, an object of indignation or compassion. He who finds, upon calmly submitting to this, that he has no other view than content to resemble the Suffering Jesus, has, it seems, reached the highest stage of self-renunciation. St. Ignatius accordingly regards this as the most exalted degree of humility, and he holds it out to his fraternity as a source of many graces. In truth, all who can attain this, derive from it an ample store of blessings. "Abundance of peace" is their recompense, B. iii. c. 25., for Heaven showers continually upon them torrents of joy and rapture.

Some suppose that the Saint intended to give us merely an idea of heroic humility, but that he was well aware that it was far easier to wish for it than to obtain it. They acknowledge that it is the height of perfection, but feel that without extraordinary grace it is useless to aspire to it. I grant that the state of a mind which glories in shame and makes it a subject of joy, is indeed a very elevated one, but it is not beyond our power to desire it earnestly, to make it an object of our prayers, to ask it of God, and to make it the principal subject of self-examination. We may all purchase this *pearl of great price*, of which the Gospel speaks; and to obtain it, we have only to meditate seriously on Jesus Christ nailed to the Cross; to endeavour to form ourselves after this Divine model, and to unite ourselves to Him in closest love.

Led by this spirit, we reach by degrees the height

of perfection of which we have spoken, till at last we prize nothing but contempt—we are dead to the world and to ourselves—we have burst all human bonds, and are buried with Christ in God. Thus we possess, if we may so speak, the key of the treasury of heaven; its precious gifts are within our reach; its holy joys are abundantly poured on us; and light from on high is never wanting in our time of need. This is the fountain of internal peace—especially when we are conscious of a resemblance to Jesus, and when we can calmly delight in inward communion with God. There is, in fact, no path leading so surely to gain the friendship of one's Lord, as contempt for oneself.

We meet, however, with abettors of self-love, partizans of our corrupt nature, who, on the principles of a philosophy altogether Pagan, urge that man is to take great care of his honor, as of a natural good, and a precious treasure which he should preserve at the expense even of his life. It is true that it is every man's duty to avoid all occasions of scandal; and it is thus we should interpret the words in Ecclesiasticus, xli. 12, "Have regard to thy name." But the saints condemn overstrained anxiety on this matter, all agreeing with one voice that it is praiseworthy to leave one's good name wholly in God's hands, and to be ready to sacrifice it for His glory.

Hence it has happened, that many of them, inspired by Heaven, have not chosen to clear themselves from atrocious crimes of which they have been accused; and this accords with the doctrine of St. Ignatius, who teaches in his constitutions, that a religious should be glad and even desirous that the world should despise him; and that provided he does no wrong, and that his life is irreproachable in the sight of God, he ought to rejoice in opprobrium as much as worldly men rejoice in honour. Our author, as we have already remarked, holds the same opinion; he teaches that the perfect imitators of Christ ought so to abase themselves, and make themselves so little, that they may be trodden underfoot.

But how then can any venture to maintain that it is an error of the mystics to believe that we are allowed to wish to be accounted fools, and to despise so great an advantage as a good reputation! The most ardent wish, generally, of those who love God with their whole heart, is, that it may please Him to suffer them to be contemptible in the eyes of the world, when this may be without His own glory being diminished by it. St. Ignatius, when advising us to love shame and confusion, teaches us, that to obtain it, we must seek the most complete self-contempt and self-renunciation! Indeed, how is this possible, if we are to believe those philosophers, that we are obliged to guard our reputation with extreme care?

The same Saint, in his exercises, when describing the third gradation of humility, goes further still ; for he says, that if a really spiritual man had his choice between two conditions, one obscure and the other brilliant, in both of which he should be equally capable of glorifying God, the one desire of imitating Christ Crucified should determine him to prefer humiliation to grandeur, ignominy to glory.

What can those preachers of comfortable morality say to this, who require an express command from God, to yield in the slightest instance in a point of honor? Whoso truly loveth contempt is never satisfied with disgraces ; the worst treatment is his dearest delight; and as humiliation is the path which leads to humility, he desires it, seeks it, embraces it with ardour, when he is not checked by a yet higher consideration, such as the greater glory of God ever is. In a word, if we regard contempt in connexion with

God, and not as connected with the world, we shall see that there is nothing more ardently to be sought, since it is a source of infinite blessings, being a sure means of dying strictly to self to please the Lord, and to be united entirely with Him.

They say that God has no delight in seeing His servants in shame and suffering—that there is nothing desirable in contempt, since it is an evil in itself, as well as pain, and that God cannot like what is evil. I answer, that considered in themselves, shame and sorrow are not attractive, but that still God sends them to us because He knows them to be necessary for our salvation, and for our perfection. Even the heathen philosophers were not ignorant of this, for Seneca says, that to see a good man struggling with misfortune, was a sight worthy of God Himself.

We must not then be surprised to find that God loves to see His servants in a condition in which their own nothingness is forced upon them—in which they annihilate themselves before Him, and have innumerable opportunities of growing in virtue. Great souls have always ardently felt this: witness Saint Theresa, who cried out so often, "suffer or die;" which we must not understand of martyrdom only, but of all sorts of crosses and mortifications, which have this in common, that they purify man of his vices, elevate him above himself and all created things, not in themselves, as we have already remarked, but by Divine grace. The sight only of Jesus Dying, inspired the saints with a love of suffering, and they were persuaded, with St. Bernard, that it is a shame to see delicate members of a Head pierced with thorns.

CHAPTER III.

(On these words) — "All things are comprised in these few words: Forsake all, and thou shalt find all." B. iii. c. 32.

QUESTION.—How can we forsake all?

ANSWER.—In three ways principally;

1. First, by depriving ourselves thoroughly of all temporal goods, in order to follow literally the counsel of the Son of God: *Go thy way, sell whatever thou hast, &c.* Mark x. 21. This is done by all who enter the cloister; they abandon their father and mother, quit their property, and put it out of their power ever to acquire or possess anything of their own.

The Apostles once said to the Saviour, *Behold, we have forsaken all, what shall we have therefore?* Matt. xix. 27. He replied that He would give *everlasting life* to them, and to all who should follow their example in ages to come. Whoever then renounces all, obtains all, for God Himself is his recompense. Thus, Saint Francis, having made himself poor, could say with truth, God is my portion, *He is in Himself every thing to me.* And, in fact, a man who strips himself of all external things, delivers himself from so many obstacles to his perfection; he deprives the evil one of the means of tempting him, and of drawing him into his nets; he empties his soul of creatures, and fills it with God.

It is not that if a Christian had all the riches of Abraham, he might not, like him, be devoted to God, and possess God; but it is difficult, and the Saviour did not without cause exhort His disciples to quit all things, that they might go freely to God. Most of the saints have followed this course; and even those who have been constrained to return to the possession and control of those worldly goods which they had quitted, have done so only to dispense them in the service of God. Thus, so many holy prelates, taken almost by force from monasteries, and from poverty made rich against their own will, have disposed of their revenues, rather as stewards than as proprietors and masters. It is observable, too, that as soon as the Spirit of God makes a strong impression on the soul, and inspires her with a great aim at perfection, she deprives herself of all, that our Lord, ever a Lover of poverty, may come to her, and that she may have grace to possess Him.

Saint Francis Borgia, Duke of Candia, having quitted the great riches and the great honours which he enjoyed in the world, was so filled with God, that he said that if he had possessed all created goods, and had them for ever, he should not have tasted among them all so much sweetness as he felt in one Communion. And this happiness was not only that he believed with certainty in the Presence of his God, but because he truly enjoyed It within him. In this manner we may say boldly, " Forsake all, and you shall have all." It is not then a little thing truly to renounce all the goods of this world, to restore them into the hands of the Lord, and to yield to Him all claim on them. Those who give up their present goods for the love of God, receive as a recompense the inestimable wealth of the faith, as the Apostle St. James says, *Hath not God chosen the poor of this world, rich in faith?* James ii. 5., rich in solid and eternal goods, in goods which they not only hope to possess one day, but enjoy now, and which make their happiness in this life, being spiritual goods, more capable of fully satisfying them than all the goods of the earth.

Saint Paul says, that the faithful are so full of *the grace of God, which is given them by Jesus Christ, that they come behind in no gift.* 1 Cor. i. 4. 7. This is, however, only a foretaste of the perfect possession of God; for in this world we do not see Him openly, though we feel His Presence, and being united to Him by love, " we truly enjoy Him, and find rest in Him," as our author says. He is far, however, from discovering and communicating Himself to the soul at the first step as afterwards, but however little He discovers Himself, it always feels the truth of this promise of the Saviour: *There is no man that hath left house, or brethren, or sisters, or father, or mother, or wife, or children, or lands, for My sake and the Gospel's, but he shall receive an hundred fold, now in this time.* Mark x. 29, 30.

2. There is a second way of forsaking all, when we not only abandon all that we have, and deprive ourselves of it, but when we feel no attachment to any thing, and can say without deceiving ourselves, that we love God Alone, and wish only to see His will done. A man, for example, who has this disposition, though he likes his place of abode, may say with boldness and sincerity, that he is ready to go wherever he is sent, as soon as he knows God's will respecting it; he may say, also, that whatever pleasure he finds in the conversation of those with whom he has long lived and been acquainted, he has no difficulty in renouncing it.

For if he still feels a strong unwillingness to quit them, though resolved to do so, he may believe that he has a desire to do well; but this natural inclination to live with our friends, and this difficulty in leaving them, are a sign that he has not yet acquired the true spirit of interior destitution, and that his heart is not detached from all; for if this were the case, he would be equally satisfied with every place, and with all sorts of persons: he would avoid all engagements and reject every thing which might diminish his freedom. For, to be wholly free, we must love no good, no employment, nor even any man soever, except with a view to the greater service of God. "What thing more quiet than the single eye?" says our author, "and what more free than he that desireth nothing on earth?" B. iii. c. 31. Can one who has not attained this perfect liberty, think himself in a state to enjoy the Presence of God, while the least mote is capable of troubling the eye, and hindering it from beholding its Object? Here is matter to occupy a man who aspires to eternal happiness. Let him often examine himself, that if he discovers any too human affection, any attachment, however slight, binding him to creatures, he may quickly rid himself of it, for otherwise his work will never be ended.

3. The third and last manner of forsaking all, is to forsake oneself; and this is a more perfect way than the others. Our author sets before us a man who seems to have abandoned all, and asks if he can do more. He replies, that "there is much wanting;" for he adds, "having left all, he must forsake himself." B. ii. c. 11. You think, perhaps, that there was nothing to add to the second degree of renunciation; but you are mistaken; self-love must be overcome in the tenderest point, and that is, self-seeking even in spiritual things.

The mean of mortifying it is to put in practice this precept of our author: "Wherever you find yourself, quit yourself:" that is to say, the moment you feel any secret attachment to your own will, your own opinion or taste, renounce it instantly. Represent to yourself our Lord addressing you in these words: "Forsake thyself, and thou shalt find Me." B. iii. c. 37. God is ever ready to enter a disinterested soul: He delights in enriching her with His gifts; He makes her pass through trials which serve to purify and detach her from the world; so that thinking of God only, she desires and enjoys God Alone, and finds her whole happiness in Him; she so conjoins herself with God, as to find no pleasure but in doing what He requires.

It is this which prepares for her a Paradise, even here, from which she never departs, because she sees that all things are done as Providence ordains, and is infinitely better pleased than in doing her own will. She regards only the glory of God, seeks only to please Him, reposes sweetly on Him with a pure and disinterested love, possesses and embraces Him lovingly in her inmost heart, and in order to be more closely united with Him, detaches herself from all that might separate her from Him, so as to forget self, to despise health, life, and reputation, and to think of nothing temporal and passing, in order to devote herself wholly to that which concerns the honour, the service, and the will of God, the " God of mercy and love."

Then is accomplished what the Saviour, speaking of His beloved disciples, said to His Father: *I in them, and Thou in Me, that they may be made perfect in one.* John xvii. 23. One in themselves, and with us. The Father loves them in like manner as He loves His Son; He bears them in His Bosom, He gives Himself to them, they enjoy Him; and this is the effect of the promise of the Saviour Himself, Who said, *I will come again, and receive you unto Myself, that where I am, there ye may be also* (John xiv. 3.); that is, in the Bosom, in the very Heart of My Father, and that ye may dwell there for ever. A holy soul, though enclosed in a mortal body, shares these advantages, which are the fruits of the Divine love that the Holy Spirit kindles in the hearts of the righteous. But the Heavenly Spouse does not communicate Himself, and fill her with His favours till we have made great efforts to render ourselves pleasing in His eyes by stripping ourselves of every thing in the way above mentioned; for we cannot gain His Love without doing ourselves great violence; and though He gives to whomsoever pleaseth Him, it is certain that by overcoming ourselves nobly, we obtain great favours from Him. *If a man love Me,* said He, *he will keep My words, and My Father will love him, and we will come unto him, and make our abode with him.* John xiv. 23.

CHAPTER IV.

(On these words) — "The more thou withdrawest thyself from all solace of creatures, the more will I heap upon thee spiritual joys." B. iii. c. 12.

QUESTION.—How must we despise those consolations which come from creatures, to obtain those which proceed from the Creator?

ANSWER.—By renouncing all satisfaction and support that might be hoped from creatures, to lean upon and rejoice in God Alone.

The spiritual and supernatural life consists in so detaching ourselves from created things, as to have God only for the object and aim of all our designs. Thence comes an abundance of Divine consolations, which are augmented in proportion as we reject those which come from creatures. These are of three sorts. The first are completely carnal; the second less material; the third still a little less gross, and more spiritual.

In order to belong to God only, and to repose in

Him Alone, it is necessary to reject them all. This seems hard; but it is the way to arrive at perfect repose, according to the maxim of our author, who assures us in a hundred places, that the more we despise the delights of the earth, the more we render ourselves worthy of those of Heaven.

1. The first sort of consolations and pleasures that the world offers us, is entirely carnal, and consists of all that flatters the senses. A lady, for example, who is absorbed in the world, seeks for satisfaction in the pleasures of life, such as cards, balls, banquets, promenades, parties where they jest and laugh; in these she tries to get rid of her ill humour, and to relieve her low spirits, persuaded that she could not exist without them. In consequence, the things of God, and the exercises of devotion, are a weariness to her. If she had resolution to withdraw from these vain amusements, and to moderate her passion for pleasure, she would find solid happiness in God. At first the remembrance of her past joys might trouble her, and be a temptation; but if by a noble effort she broke all the ties which bind her to the world, if she devoted herself to good works, if she associated with pious persons, if she loved to hear the word of God, and often went to worship the Lord where He is present in the church, she would soon feel wonderful peace and tranquillity. Whenever she felt dejected, she would only have to shut herself up in her oratory to unburden her heart to God; she would often come out cheered. And if she hates solitude, a single conversation with devout and spiritual persons, would be a greater relief to her than all the diversions in the world.

To assure herself of the truth of what I say, she may ask persons of her own station, who make a profession of piety, and learn from them if they are happy, and if their minds are at rest. There is none who will not answer, that amidst the greatest austerities her heart is more full of joy than it was among the delights of this world, which, being false, ever leave the heart full of remorse and vexation. Worldly people, when they suffer any pain, either of body or spirit, generally seek to divert themselves with things without, to see and hear curious things; they give themselves hotly and eagerly to such pursuits, and have their minds so full of them, as to be always talking of them.

This separates them much from God, though the objects which attract them are often not altogether evil in themselves. One who seeks God, who desires in good earnest to love Him, does otherwise. She withdraws within herself, has recourse to our Lord, takes comfort in Him. As for external things, she takes what are necessary, without becoming attached to them: and then God gives her such overflowing joy, communicates to her so much strength, that continually despising the things of the world more and more, her heart is filled with perfect satisfaction.

2. The second and less gross sort of consolation drawn from creatures, is that which is sought in outward things by many men, otherwise virtuous and opposed to the false maxims of the world, who forget that by these external joys, they deprive themselves of much heavenly consolation.

They seek it, indeed, in indifferent things; but they sin in this, that they rest on them, as on a solid foundation. For example, in a religious community a handmaid of God, otherwise well-intentioned, has a confidante to whom she unfolds her troubles, without whom she thinks she could not live; and when she has related all that weighs on her heart, she feels herself relieved of a burthen. Yet we often deceive ourselves. We think to have relieved ourselves, and are more oppressed than before, because in thus opening our hearts, our view was to satisfy ourselves, rather than to please God, and enable ourselves to serve Him better; which leaves a weight that depresses the spirit instead of relieving it, though we are not conscious of it. "If there lurk in thee," says our author, "any self-seeking, behold, this it is that hindereth thee, and weigheth thee down." B. iii. c. 11.

People think they gain much when they tell all their sufferings to a friend in private. But they murmur, they complain, they mourn over their sorrows, they give way to self-love; and as they lean on the creature, and not on God, they find themselves left in a narrowness of heart, which is the effect or the punishment of too much self-seeking. A noble and generous spirit will easily deprive himself of all human consolation; and if in affliction, will be contented to speak of it to God, when conversing with Him, and when God communicates Himself in prayer; or if he needs counsel, will turn to some spiritual person, who will encourage him to bear his cross courageously.

There are indeed interior sufferings, which proceed not so much from the weakness of the soul, as from the temptations of the Evil One: in these we must often have recourse to a prudent director, not only to ask counsel, but also to seek courage and fortitude. And this sort of self-seeking is not a sin, it is reasonable and necessary, and I condemn those only in which much time is lost in useless conversation. We undoubtedly do ourselves great wrong, when, for want of confidence in God, we seek in creatures a relief and a cure which are to be found in Him Alone.

To know how to converse with Jesus in our heart, is the first and most useful of all knowledge. When we can make it our custom, we receive from it the fruits of perpetual consolation, solid peace, and an abundance of all sorts of spiritual wealth. B. ii. c. 2. We should accustom ourselves to it early, instead of seeking in created objects a relief for pains which we suffer only because we do not labour to mortify our passions and to rid ourselves of our vices. None but spiritual persons who always seek the presence of our Lord can attain to this familiar intercourse. Those who love the society of the great, who delight in hearing news, in jesting, and telling amusing tales, cannot inwardly rejoice in Him.

Of all things in the world it is most desirable to be able to withdraw within ourselves, and the only way to learn this thoroughly, is to avoid company, and to converse with Jesus only. *The Master is come, and calleth for thee.* John xi. 28. If you are wise, arise quickly, and come unto Him. Imitate Magdalen, who, knowing that Jesus was come, hastily left the Jews who were with her in the house to comfort her, so impatient was she to speak to Him and to hear His words.

3. The third sort of consolation which is received from creatures, is specious, and appears very innocent. It appears wholly good, and tending to God's honour. Yet we must be content to part with it; it is God's will; that we may say, the Lord is all my Good, and all my consolation. It is His pleasure, for example, that we should not be too eager to hear a certain preacher, to visit a certain church, to converse with a certain devout person, to perform certain other practices which we think very holy, but in which self-love has often a great part.

It is not that we absolutely condemn them, or forbid their use, when they are necessary or profitable to the soul which desires to be wholly devoted to God; but we must be ready to leave them, when there is danger of our secret attachment to them turning us from a greater good; and God is not pleased that we should complain of His Providence, when He deprives us of the opportunity and means of making use of them; for then we cannot do better than attach ourselves to Him, and trust in His infinite goodness.

What I say may also be applied to the voluntary penances, and other pious exercises in which some put their whole confidence. Whatever pleasure and profit we find in them, God often permits us to be compelled to interrupt, or abandon them entirely, or to retrench them much more than we would. It is incredible how much we profit by this in simple love, because we make it our happiness to do what God pleases, to enjoy God Himself, and not the means which He gives us to attain to Him. We learn this by experience, when He deprives us of certain spiritual pleasures which supported our devotion. If we complain of it, and lament, it is a sign of undue attachment, and of want of resignation to the will of Him, Who, infinite as He is, cannot fully satisfy our desires.

In such cases we cannot enjoy the sweet comfort which our Lord is wont to give to mortified persons, who feel only disquiet and contempt for all that is not God. These persons being attached to Him, He gives them a full and abundant share of His joy, which penetrates them wholly, and fills them with inexpressible happiness. This is the fruit of an entire abnegation of self, when, having put all our interests, temporal and spiritual, in the hands of the Lord, we desire only to obtain from Him what it is His will that we should ask. Thus a good man is fully satisfied when God is pleased; His whole pleasure is to see God's will done, according to these words of our author: "Frame thy desires wholly according to My good pleasure; be not a lover of thyself, but an earnest follower of My will." B. iii. c. 11.

There are truly other consolations which are the resources of self-love in aridity and sorrow; but that which alone supports and rejoices a soul that truly loves our Lord, is the accomplishment of God's designs in us, and this is acquired by purity of intention, which leads us in all times and in all things to regard only the Divine Will; "Say thou this in every thing, Lord, if this be pleasing unto Thee, so let it be." B. iii. c. 15.

The more a man strives to purify himself, the sweeter and more spiritual are the consolations which he receives from Heaven. Now he purifies himself by the care that he takes to purify his intention, which is the more holy, the less he regards his own desires, and the more he seeks those of God. And what is God's great desire? Undoubtedly that His Will be done, for His Heart and His Will are the same.

We may even say, that all the perfections of God are, as it were, contained in His Will; for He wills what His Wisdom prescribes, what His Justice ordains, and what His Goodness demands; and in consequence we cannot unite ourselves more closely to Him, than by abandoning ourselves entirely to His guidance. The shortest way of arriving at perfect resignation, is to mortify our desires; for the more dead we are to ourselves, the more capable are we of the gifts of God. "Since few strive to die entirely to themselves, most men remain so enslaved to their passions, that the Spirit never gains the mastery over the flesh." Therefore our author concludes thus: "All lieth in our dying," B. ii. c. 12, renouncing ourselves entirely.

To this the Saints exhorted their disciples. St. Ignatius recommends nothing to his followers so much as entire abnegation, and continual mortification in all things. St. Ambrose, and after him all founders of religious orders, made it a first precept to their children, to overcome themselves, and to raise themselves above all earthly things. St. Francis took great care to instruct and accustom his to despise the praise of man, and not to put their trust in creatures. All, in a word, have done the same. St. Paul said to the first believers: *Ye are dead, and your life is hid with Christ in God. They that are Christ's, have crucified the flesh with the affections and lusts.* Col. iii. 3. Gal. v. 24. The Book of the Imitation of Christ is full of this doctrine.

CHAPTER V.

(On these words)—" Rejoice to be thought guilty, that you may be innocent in the sight of God."

QUESTION.—Who is he that is willing to be thought guilty, that he may be innocent in the sight of God?

ANSWER.—This may be said of three sorts of persons.

1. First, of those who, when blamed, do not excuse themselves. Innocence is very often calumniated, but one who looks simply to God, and considers that the only important thing in this world is to please Him, that He Alone sees the ground of his heart, and that we are holy only in proportion as we are united with Him; one, I say, who has these views, cares little for the contempt of man; whatever is done to decry him, he remains always contented, provided that God's honour is not concerned; and that he may judge well of this, he never consults or hearkens to self-love.

When, therefore, care for the honor of God does not oblige him to justify himself, he has no difficulty in allowing himself to be thought guilty; he can even make most profitable use of this opportunity, to grow in the knowledge of himself, and enter more deeply into familiar intercourse with our Lord. For, being repulsed by the world, he takes refuge with

Him Who knows the sincerity of his intentions, and the merit of his works; he reposes sweetly in Him, and becomes more strongly attached to Him, when he figures to himself the only Son of God, the Holy of Holies, accused and counted by the Jews as an impostor, and an enemy of the law. In these circumstances his silence causes him to be thought guilty, but serves at the same time to make his innocence brighter in the sight of the Sovereign Judge, because an injury joyfully received, when we could defend ourselves, is an inestimable merit in the sight of God.

Corrupt nature is always ready to exculpate itself, to dissemble and colour its faults. Adam and Eve excused themselves, when they heard the voice of the Lord reproving their disobedience. Most of their children imitate them, for they have always a thousand specious reasons to avoid a reproof; and though they cannot be unaware that they have erred, they lay all the blame on others who are innocent, and even on God Himself, like the first man, when he said, *The woman whom Thou gavest to be with me, she gave me of the tree, and I did eat.* Gen. iii. 12. They thus sometimes reproach the Creator, saying that they should not have said or done the thing for which they are reproved, if they had not been naturally passionate and of a fastidious temper. Thus they condemn Providence, instead of imputing the evil to their own irresolution and want of mortification, and their neglect of grace given.

The more we try to justify the dealings of God by attributing our own faults to ourselves, the more pleasing are we to Him, which verifies this saying: "Love to appear guilty before man, and in the sight of God you shall be innocent." We are so full of pride, that we have great difficulty in owning what we are in truth. The humble and sincere soul will acknowledge honestly that it is he who has failed, will own it, and share with none his deserved confusion.

It is said, and commonly, I own that I am far from being as perfect as I wish, and ought to be, but I cannot be so without special grace, such as God has been pleased to give to the Saints. People say this; but they do not see, that if the Saints received great assistance from Heaven, as they assuredly did, it was always their principal care to co-operate with it; that they laboured much, did themselves much violence, that they spent ten or twenty years in conquering themselves and mortifying their passions; in a word, that the perfection that they acquired cost them much, and that it is with extreme labour that they arrived at it.

What have these people to say to this, who seem to require God to do all, and who are, on every occasion, asking for extraordinary graces? Grace helps us, but we most often are wanting to grace. We are so weak, that at the least effort to be made, the least shame to be endured, we draw back and lose courage. If we have only not to eat something pleasing to the taste, or not to let our eyes rest on an object which awakens curiosity, we cannot do it.

It is incredible how much the Saints mortified themselves, how faithfully they responded to the inspirations of Heaven. One of a true spirit hides not his defects; attributes his small progress in virtue to his own weakness only, and remissness; accuses himself before God, humbly entreats pardon of Him, and prostrate on the earth, with tearful eyes, and confusion of face, implores His mercy.

Those, on the other hand, who think that they have done a great deal for God, and that He owes them much, review all the good that they think they have done, recount the years they have spent in His service, and close their eyes to the multitude of their offences. True wisdom acknowledges its faults, and owns itself guilty; for, by humbling ourselves we become just in the sight of God, Who knows the inveterate evil of the human heart, and Who always hath wherewith to confound the proud. *In Thy sight,* said the Prophet, *shall no man living be justified.* Psalm cxliii. 2. What is there more shameful than to see a man, who is but dust, swelling with pride, as if he could of himself do great things?

Vain spirits, full of yourselves, hear the great Apostle telling you, that *if a man think himself to be something when he is nothing, he deceiveth himself.* Gal. vi. 3. None has nearer access to God, than he who, pierced with the consciousness and sorrow for his faults, confesses that without the Divine help he must remain for ever in corruption and filth. So feel the Saints, who, lost in their own nothingness, always think themselves the last of men. So felt St. Paul, who thought himself *the chief of sinners.* 1 Tim. i. 15. "Set thyself always then in the lowest place, and the highest shall be given thee." B. ii. c. 10. Be persuaded that you are the most guilty, and your place shall be with the holiest.

Yet there are false critics, who dare to condemn those whose wisdom and holiness are universally revered. Their narrow minds are accustomed to argue by formal rules, and dispute on all subjects. They treat the most essential maxims of the Gospel as errors, and visionary. "A Saint beloved of God, and of consummate virtue," say they, "cannot be the chief of sinners. For what is more opposed to vice and sin than eminent virtue? They are mistaken then, in calling themselves most guilty of all." Such is their reasoning, founded on knowledge which does not go beyond the light of nature.

The Saints, through faith, perceive things in a way to which human reason cannot attain. What they say is true in a sense which the Holy Spirit teaches them, and which they alone comprehend. It is enough to know that St. Paul and St. Francis were enlightened from above, and that they said nothing of which they were not fully convinced, nothing which they were not able to assert without exaggeration or deception. If others do not understand it, how can they dare condemn it?

2. The second sort of persons whom God loves because they consider themselves great sinners, are those who, in public calamities, suffer not for their own sins, but for those of others; for, by the Providence of God, the innocent are generally afflicted with the guilty. These general chastisements, in which both the good and evil are involved, must be most just, for they are the effects of Divine Justice, which though many may be unable to understand, all ought to receive with submission. God often punishes whole nations by terrible scourges, from which the good are not exempt. Then the truly humble, far from complaining, accept the punishment, however severe it be, thinking themselves always sufficiently guilty to deserve it.

In this spirit, the ancient Prophets and the Priests of God said, *We have sinned, and have committed iniquity, and have done wickedly.* Dan. ix. 5. Ps. cv. 5. Saint Dominic, before entering any town or village, knelt and prayed that his sins might not bring the curse of God on those whom he was about to instruct. Saint Catherine [a] always feared that the evils which in her days afflicted the whole Church, were the punishment of her unfaithfulnesses. The lives of the Saints are far above ours, and our feeble reasonings cannot approach them.

This way of regarding ourselves as guilty, however innocent and unblameable we be, is very pleasing to

[a] Of Sienna.

God, and gives no truce to the pride which blinds us; so that the time when we have most reason to mourn is when we are most satisfied with ourselves. Generally speaking, confidence in the Divine Mercy is very good, but that which is founded on a vain presumption of our innocence is very dangerous. *All our righteousnesses are as filthy rags.* Is. lxiv. 6. Thus, the way to appear righteous before God, is to consider ourselves sinners. Oh, how incapable of discerning this great truth are they who reject, as imaginary, the most laudable and spiritual sentiments of the Saints! When we judge of them by the false light of reason, they appear so untenable, that instead of humbly revering, we combat and condemn them.

Lastly, the third sort of persons who do not dream of excuses and apologies, are those who, being unjustly accused and blackened to the world, say nothing in their own defence. Of this number were Saint Theodora, Saint Peter Martyr, and some others, who chose rather to live long in disgrace, and to endure rigorous penances, than to clear themselves of the enormous crimes with which they were charged. They rejoiced to be treated as great criminals, and suffered this humiliation in silence for the love of our Lord, Who at last took their cause in hand, and made their innocence known. The truth being then acknowledged, their past shame served greatly to increase the renown of their sanctity.

Our author, by the words which I have quoted, encourages those who find themselves in any similar circumstances, to profit by them, gladly to receive this portion of Christ's Cup as the most precious treasure in the world. The way to do this is to consider contempt and dishonour as a very great advantage. And hereby the maxims of those worldly philosophers, of whom I have spoken, are manifestly condemned. For they maintain that we are not permitted to neglect our reputation, and that we must defend our honor at the expence of worldly goods and life, if only it can be done without offending God. What offence would Saint Peter Martyr have committed, if, when he was accused of having introduced females into his cell, he had confessed that they were sainted women, who came from Heaven to visit him? Does it not appear that God would have been thereby more honored, since he would have prevented the scandal caused among his brethren by his silence? Yet he did not defend himself; he resolutely concealed the truth, being desirous to imitate our Lord, Who, during His whole Passion, spoke no word to justify Himself from the great crimes of which He was accused. We find that God approved of his conduct, and bounteously recompensed his rare and heroic humility. But these great examples are far beyond the reach of our human wisdom, which teaches us only to love honor, to avoid contempt, and to seek our own interest in all things, instead of following Christ, Who saved us by the foolishness of the Cross.

CHAPTER VI.

(On these words) — "Set thyself always in the lowest place, and the highest shall be given thee." B. ii. c. 10.

QUESTION.—Wherein can a humble man seek the lowest place?

ANSWER.—He can do so particularly in three things; first, in the station of life which he embraces; secondly, in his employment; thirdly, in his spiritual conduct.

1. Those truly abase themselves in the station of life which they choose, who, being great, rich, and

powerful in the world, make themselves little and poor in a religious life. We have illustrious examples of this in many kings, princes, and other persons of distinction, who having left all, and entered the Monastic life for the love of Jesus Christ, have employed themselves in serving their brethren, as if they had been the lowest of all. By this means they arrived at a high degree of perfection; and we may venture to say that they obtained with God a rank as far raised above the mass of men, as their former station surpassed in grandeur and dignity the lowly state which they chose in order to annihilate themselves before God.

Amongst these last we must reckon those who, in the religious life itself, having it in their power to rule, and being worthy of the highest offices, have solicited earnestly to be employed in the most abject ministrations; or, who having all the merit and capacity necessary to become Priests, have refused that dignity, that they might be of less consideration among their brethren. This was done by Saint Francis, and by the blessed brother Jacobon, who desired to be cook in the monastery, though he was learned, and capable of the most important employments. This is done in all religious communities, both of men and women, by an infinite number of devout persons, whose sole ambition is to be employed in the lowest offices.

To these may be added those who, already holding a high rank, take pleasure in employing themselves in whatever is most humiliating. St. Francis of Borgia, and Father Vincent Caraffa, both generals of the company of Jesus, both of illustrious birth, were not ashamed to perform, even in public, the meanest functions of the house. And in most well-regulated communities, it is seen daily that those who occupy the highest places have no greater joy than to humble themselves, and to show that the most obscure station is that which they love, and most gladly embrace.

2. The second sort of voluntary abasement is practised in employments even of a spiritual nature, when we carry them out in a simple modest manner, free from all appearance of pomp; and when, far from seeking for display, we love obscurity, and avoid all that makes a noise in the world, that causes admiration, or shows much capacity and talent. Yet public professors must not, through excessive modesty, affect to teach only the less elevated part of the sciences, whether divine or human; on the contrary, they must give proof of their capacity. A theologian, for example, must study to fill the minds of his hearers with sound doctrine; he must explain the most sublime mysteries with as much subtlety as plainness, when that serves to make them more clearly and deeply understood.

I say the same of all other sciences. But as in general *knowledge puffeth up*, it is necessary to avoid with extreme care all that savours of vanity and ostentation. A preacher who ascends the pulpit only to instruct the people, to excite them to penitence, to teach them to live a godly life, must not seek either for too much acuteness in thought, too much force in reasoning, too much art in composition, or even too much elegance in language. He must speak the common language, and choose those reasons which are most adapted to convert sinners, and to lead them to the love of God. He who with simple faith and true zeal, seeks in the Gospel for the truth alone, without losing time in subtle and obscure reasonings, which serve rather to dazzle the ignorant than to edify the faithful, this man possesses the true talent of preaching. He accordingly is animated by the Spirit of God, Which softens the most ferocious, overcomes the most rebellious, and gives repentance to the most hardened sinners.

The Holy Spirit communicates Himself more readily to those who never wander from orthodox doctrine, and who join simple and natural manners to ardent zeal, than to those who seem as if they would fain rise above the sky, and distinguish themselves from common men by the sublimity of their style and of their thoughts. We have seen preachers, remarked for no extraordinary qualities, who simply and plainly explained the truths of the Gospel with a modest and serious air in ordinary language, and produced more fruit than others far more polished and eloquent. God takes pleasure in raising by His Grace those who do not misuse their natural talent, and who humble themselves to the comprehension of the most rude and ignorant.

Lastly, we must beware, even in the spiritual course, not to seek to soar too high. For there are spiritual persons, who, knowing that God leads some by extraordinary paths, do their utmost to enter them without being called. If they speak of the things of God, it is in lofty terms, hard to understand. If they teach practices of piety, they will have none that are not sublime and new, instead of recommending and practising those which the saints have given us. If they write on some mystery of religion, they always subtilize and refine very dryly, without unction and without devotion.

This is because they seek to rise too high. These words should often be repeated to them: " Humble yourselves, and ye shall be exalted." What can be imagined more divine than the sentiments of St. Theresa, of St. Catherine of Sienna, and of some other holy persons? But how did they attain to them? Was it by soaring at first, and rising to the most sublime contemplation? No; it was rather by humbling themselves at the feet of Jesus their Beloved Spouse, Whose love and endearments they obtained by the mortification of the flesh, by exercises of penitence, by noble deeds of charity and humility.

There are some who imagine, that the higher they rise in thought, the more they will enjoy heavenly things. But strive as they will, they can gain no more than if they sought to obtain water from a dry sponge. For it is not there that the dew of true piety is found. The graces of Heaven are poured abundantly on those alone who love their own abasement, and who prefer Christian simplicity and modesty to the vain grandeurs of the world.

St. Theresa yielded to none in elevation of spirit, and yet there was nothing more simple and natural than her words and expressions. Her behaviour was so unstudied and so unworldly, that according to the testimony of her confessor, she esteemed herself a fool, that is, she sat at the feet of our Lord, as one who needed instruction in the smallest things. She had no pleasure in displaying her knowledge, though our Lord had filled her with a wisdom which, together with the power and quickness of her mind, caused her to be considered one of the most gifted women of her time. She never used extraordinary terms except when obliged to treat of mystic theology, which she understood admirably.

Many esteem and praise natural talent: and it must not be despised, for it may be very usefully employed; but we must always set a far higher value upon the gifts of grace, which contribute incomparably more to the execution of those great things which are done in God's service. When people see a man of talent, who thinks well, and expresses himself nobly, they form a high opinion of him, and there is nothing of which he does not seem capable. But they should first enquire if he is humble, if he does not take credit to himself, and trust too much in his own talents and insight, for by this we should judge for what he is fitted, and what he may accomplish, since the success of the greatest designs is generally a fruit of humility.

It is sometimes said in a community, Here is a daughter, of quick talent, ready answer, who understands the affairs of life; with a little virtue, she will make an excellent nun. On the contrary, one is despised who acts simply, and by a very holy conduct hides, for a time at least, the excellent qualities with which God has endowed her. I would say to those who judge so ill, Learn the true sentiments wherewith devotion, ever drawn towards humiliation, inspires the Saints; humble yourselves; beware of following the inclinations of nature, which loves honour and show; and God, who exalts the humble, will communicate His Spirit to you, and will fulfil you with His grace. Say not then that she really possesses less talent than the other, because she displays less in civilities and courtesies merely secular. Perhaps she could succeed in this better than any, but she neglects such trifles, and avoids applying herself to them, because one who acts on holy principles will ever value worldly talent far less than that wisdom which cometh of grace.

CHAPTER VII.

(On these words)—" I cause all devout persons to pass through severe trials [a]."

QUESTION.—Who are the truly devout?
ANSWER.—Those who are resolved to live well, and

[a] Probably, B. i. c. 13. "All the Saints passed through many tribulations and temptations, and profited thereby;" or, iii. 49. "The faithful servant of the Lord is wont to be tried."

think only of increasing in virtue, and becoming ever more closely united with God.

There are some who make a profession of serving God, who appear good sort of people, and are so in fact, but who yet are not all which would entitle us to be called devout. The perfectly devout are those who, not only in idea, but in practice, prefer nothing to the honour of God, and the accomplishment of His Holy will, above all, in what concerns their own perfection. But even among those who have some concern for their salvation, and some fear of God, there are too many who are yet unable to comprehend this doctrine. What then we must well consider, and what our Author particularly remarks, is, that God disciplines severely the truly devout, that He sends them very heavy trials, and that it is thus that He deals with those who devote themselves for ever to His service. These trials are of three sorts.

1. Of the first are contradictions and hindrances from man. How many Christians do we see living in great tranquillity, and apparently prospering in all things! They are esteemed, praised, and preferred above others; they are well satisfied with themselves, and when they reflect on the state of their affairs, they perceive nothing but prosperity and peace. But if they thoroughly examine their own hearts, they must acknowledge that they have not yet firmly resolved to give themselves up wholly to our Lord, and to place their whole joy and happiness in Him. Our Lord, on His part, does not reckon them among those whom it is His pleasure to try, to perfect, to conform to His own Image, as the Apostle says, *All that will live godly in Christ Jesus shall suffer persecution.* 2 Tim. iii. 12.

A doctor, much enlightened in spiritual things, has said boldly and well, that God would rather suffer Heaven and earth to perish, than His own to be untried. Saint Theresa asserts, that from the moment that a person conceives the design of devoting himself wholly to God, a thousand tempests arise against him. Hence it appears, that too great a calm is not a good sign. And this because our nature, always passionately desirous of pleasure, cannot die to itself, or reach any high degree of holiness, except through suffering.

For years, and even to the hour of death, it is the will of God that some, for the good of their souls, be considered by their whole community as criminals. When the causes are investigated, it is at length discovered, that either none exist, or they are very slight. Yet before the truth is ascertained, the subject is much canvassed, murmurs and complaints abound, all is suspected, all misunderstood.

In fact, it appears manifestly that God is pleased to exercise further the virtue of those who are resolved to live a holy life: *Because you are pleasing to God*, said the Angel to Tobias, *you must needs be tried by temptation.* Tobit xii. 13. Vulg. The religious King David suffered most bitterly. Abraham, Joseph, and innumerable other Saints, trode the same path; and he who is not always ready to endure calumnies, persecutions, outrages, can hardly attain to a moderate degree of virtue.

It is certain, then, that the true spirit of God's children has ever been to seek no rest in this world, but to wear themselves out in labours for the love of our Lord. It is by the narrow way that Providence leads them. Alas! how grievously self-deceived are they who, seeing themselves welcome everywhere, esteemed and sought by all, imagine themselves much beloved by God, and worthy of blessings from above! One says in his heart, "I live in peace in the monastery; I have no enemies; my superiors think highly of me." "I am liked abroad," says another, "and everybody esteems me." This comforts and rejoices them. But if they sought for the cause of this sweet repose, this general approbation, they might undoubtedly attribute it to their lukewarmness, and to their want of zeal for spiritual improvement. This is the real cause why they are so tranquil, and why, while others are tempest-tossed, they abide yet in calm.

I know that some of the righteous enjoy great tranquillity; but if they are not persecuted, they have inward crosses, which, though concealed, are for them true martyrdoms. Our Saviour began to suffer from men from the time that He began to teach them, and did suffer from them till His death. Everywhere St. Paul met with enemies who sought only to destroy him. St. Benedict encountered almost insurmountable difficulties in the institution of his order; St. Ignatius was hardly ever at rest, and his life was a series of persecutions. The societies in which God is best served, are those most cruelly warred against by the world. How much did the order of St. Francis suffer in its beginnings! and what difficulty had St. Theresa in establishing her reform! Were not all nations, all the powers of the earth, opposed to the establishment of the Church?

Know then, that if you once resolve to serve God, you must endure severe attacks from the world, which hates holiness. This is because the evil one, whenever he has power, stirs up his partizans against those who strive to do well, and God permits it to accomplish the designs of His providence on the elect.

2. The second sort of trial for the Righteous consists in inward sufferings. For as soon as a man is resolved to walk in the narrow way, God, who takes great delight in contributing to the execution of so noble a design, sends him crosses of this nature; and it is thus that He commonly deals with those whom He sees prepared to make great progress in spirituality. We must

pass through frightful deserts, and endure long nights; that is, we must remain long in barrenness and darkness, said a holy man, if we desire to be detached, not only from external things, but from ourselves, and thus to conquer the self-love which is so natural to us. Now this is done by the privation of spiritual joys, and by struggles with temptation. For these compel the soul to make the greatest efforts to overcome itself, and to resolve again and again that it will live for God alone. It is thus by these that it acquires great habits of virtue.

God established this law from the time that our first parents sinned, and it has ever been His custom to give His friends something to exercise their patience from within or from without, often from both. St. Ignatius being asked, whereby he thought a man might most profit in the spiritual life, replied, by sufferings. When there are none from without, God causes them to arise from within; and when He has some great design for a soul, He treats it as He treated Job formerly, He afflicts it in every way; and the afflictions which He sends it are not slight, they are very severe, and apparently beyond human endurance.

In this He follows the order which He has established in nature. The labourers have sowed, then comes winter, during which the corn takes root, and all plants gather strength, to put forth their flowers in spring, and bear their fruits in summer. Thus after the reception of grace, the chill of aridity comes instantly, that the Divine seed may germinate, and in due time produce excellent fruits of all good works.

3. The third trial of the virtue of great Saints consists also in inward sufferings, but of so strange a nature, that we need not fear to compare them to those of another world. Undoubtedly, these exercises of heroic patience, when well used, draw down upon persons perfectly resigned to the Divine will extra-

ordinary graces; but these occasions are rare, and there are few capable of enduring such excessive sufferings. Yet God, who is pleased to try His own severely, sends them from time to time to those in whom He especially delights, and it is a sure proof that He desires their perfection; for by these violent shocks devotion is more deeply rooted in the soul, which thus strengthened produces far more excellent and more frequent acts of virtue. Besides, as we hereby make much satisfaction to Divine Justice, we ordinarily come forth more clean and more enlightened. Thus the light as well as the comfort received are more pure and more abundant.

There are many, however, who make a jest of all this, and say boldly, that grace has no part in these sufferings, and that they are only the effects of a gloomy melancholy. But the experience of so many innocent persons, whom God has thus severely tried, shows that there is here a secret, hidden to human philosophy. St. Gertrude writes of herself, that she endured very great sufferings. The blessed Angela suffered terribly. Those who have written best on the mystical life, as the blessed Jean-de-la-Croix, Blosius, Jean-de-Jesus-Maria, and many others, have composed books on purpose to explain sufferings of this kind. Of those whom I have known to be most attached to our Lord, a large proportion have suffered strange internal combats.

Many, knowing nothing of this thorny path, counsel those whom they see walking in it, to distract and divert themselves. But this is useless; for their torment continues, and none but God can deliver them from it. He will not do it so quickly, because by permitting them still to suffer, He deals with them as a gardener does with his garden, when he carefully prunes the trees, and roots up the weeds. As for those who fear these sharp trials, and dare not resign themselves into the hands of our Lord, they will assuredly ever remain imperfect, though they often flatter themselves that all is well, and though they appear quite contented with their state.

CHAPTER VIII.

(On these words)—"It is matter of great skill to know how to hold converse with Jesus; and to know how to keep Jesus, a point of great wisdom." B. ii. c. 8.

QUESTION.—What is "to know how to hold converse with Jesus?"

ANSWER.—It is to know how to commune with Him in our inmost hearts in this mortal life; and this consists in three things, the first of which is to abide in His presence, and to seek never to depart from it.

Few give their principal attention to this exercise, which is, however, the source of all spiritual good. We may practise it by thinking that God is really within us, that His only Son, Jesus Christ, also dwelleth there through His grace, and through the power of the Sacrament of the Eucharist; considering also that the Divine Word, having vouchsafed to become man for love of us, has imprinted His own Image both on our souls and bodies; and lastly, that being united with Him, as we are by His grace, we possess Him, so to speak, and He dwells in each of us as in a temple.

Thus each may conceive to himself Jesus Christ within him, and commune inwardly with Him, because, in an inexplicable manner, He in such wise renders Himself present to the soul as to make her hear His voice; He gently enters into all its faculties, and penetrates it entirely, so that, full of delight, it exclaims with the Apostle, *I live; yet not I, but Christ liveth in me.* Gal. ii. 20. St. Catharine of Sienna told her confessor that she effectually felt the presence of Jesus

Christ. We must, then, accustom ourselves by degrees to feel Jesus Christ within us. The whole secret of this is, to represent Him well to ourselves by frequent acts of simple faith; to unite ourselves closely to Him by the continual exercise of tender love, to which the special gift of His grace, exciting the faithful to converse familiarly with Him, greatly contributes. Our Author speaks of this gift in the eighth chapter of the second book.

The best preparation that we can make for this is, to meditate continually on the Saviour, never to forget His precepts, to have His Life and His Death ever before our eyes. By this means we form insensibly a very lively and very sweet image of Him, which opens a great entrance to familiar communion with Him; and this image is impressed on the soul, not by great efforts, but as it were naturally, and without exertion, by the frequent remembrance of the Holy Humanity.

2. The second means of conversing profitably with Jesus is, faithfully to observe and follow His Divine Inspirations. To feel thoroughly the attraction of Grace, we must first take great care to conduct ourselves in all things according to the light of reason and faith; for this attractive influence gains by degrees upon a well-disposed soul, and makes it follow without resistance, never turning aside through fickleness, weakness, or a feeble yielding to nature, which would gladly be free, and exempt from all constraint. The more faithful we are to God in this matter, the more we grow in grace; which is the cause that spiritual persons find so much ease in conversing with their Saviour in prayer.

All do not enjoy this practice; but the undoubted reason why they give so much liberty to nature, and afterwards find themselves in darkness is, that they fail to reply to the inspirations of Heaven. Blessed is he who knows how to avoid separation from our Lord, how to embrace Him inwardly, and to rest sweetly in Him! As all are permitted to give themselves to this exercise, all should love it, and all are invited to it by the Saviour Himself, Who says, Come unto Me, all ye, &c. Matt. xi. 28. Now this is to be done, not 'by the way,' that is, not while seeking to divert and distract ourselves, but it is to be done by applying ourselves to hear the voice of the Lord, and to follow the motions of His Grace. "Blessed are the ears that gladly receive the pulses of the Divine whisper." B. iii. c. 1. Our Author takes great pains to show us the importance of this attention, and to excite us to it. His book is in the hands of all, is read by all, and yet there are few who take pleasure in an occupation wholly spiritual, wholly inward, because outward things, which strike the senses, enter more readily into the mind, and make more lively impressions.

It is true that at the beginning we find great difficulties, and that we cannot learn to love contemplation without great efforts; but the treasure of spiritual wealth which we afterwards discover, causes forgetfulness of all past sorrows. If I am asked then, what is the inward life of a perfect Christian? I can only reply, that it is a continual attention to respond to the Grace of our Lord, without ever following the false lights of a reason enchanted by external objects, and corrupted by the motives of the deceitful wisdom of the world. One who is unfaithful in this respect is incapable of the occupations of the inward life.

Some imagine that this sort of communion and intimate union with God are fitting only for solitaries, and for persons greatly devoted to contemplation. But I ask them, what they think was the design of our Author, who, throughout his second book, treats of this alone? Do they imagine that he wrote only for contemplatives and solitaries? Assuredly those Apostolic men who consecrate themselves to the service of mankind, and in general all whose great aim it is to please God, should make use of this practice. For without this, what assurance can they have of preserving the life of grace, among so many outward occupations and labours? How could they seek God in all things, and free themselves from all love of creatures, if they did not maintain a perpetual inward communion with God, who animates them, supports, and assists them to perform very difficult things, and far surpassing their natural powers?

St. Francis Xavier formed within his heart a kind of solitude, where our Lord was always present, and where he enjoyed a sweet repose in the midst of his labours. "Blessed are the eyes which are shut to outward things, but intent on things eternal. Blessed are they that enter far into things eternal." B. iii. c. 1.

The Book of the Imitation of Christ recommends nothing more than the love of meditation, than self-renunciation, and inward mortification. St. Ignatius knew it so well, and used it so familiarly, that every day he read two chapters, that at which the book happened to open, and the next following. Those who read it attentively cannot fail to perceive the necessity of devoting themselves to the inward life, and of replying to the inspirations of Heaven.

3. The third thing necessary to converse rightly with Jesus, is humility. For as it is the principal study of courtiers to pay their court well to their Prince, so is it the great endeavour of our Lord's true servants to approach Him inwardly in the most humble and reverential manner possible. Therefore said our Author, "Teach me to live worthily and humbly in Thy sight." B. iii. c. 3.

One who disregards the inspirations of Heaven, or speaks unworthily of the presence of God, lacks this humility. We must in all times and in all places show profound reverence for the Divine Majesty. And this is not a weariness to souls which are wholly devoted to the Lord; for He is in such manner their King, that He is also their Spouse[a]. He loves them, He does not willingly afflict them. He requires them only to abide ever faithful to Him, and He recompenses their fidelity at last with fulness of joy and heavenly pleasures.

QUESTION.—How can we follow Jesus, and dwell ever with Him?

ANSWER.—A soul which has once known the blessings of this close communion with her Saviour, if she is wise, strives to the uttermost to maintain it, and fears nothing so much as its loss. But the foolish, instead of carefully preserving the grace which she has received, neglects it: and this precious perfume, for want of being secured, speedily evaporates. The wanderings of the heart, and dissipation of the senses, cause great failure here. For those who love glory or pleasure dwell entirely in outward things, they seek only for diversion or for the acquirement of reputation in the world. Thus do they drive our Lord from them, Who, having forsaken them, leaves them to follow their appetites, and indulge their passions, but to their own ruin.

Those who are possessed of Heavenly Wisdom never suffer their lamps to go out; they have ever oil enough to support the flame of devotion. They cherish it by pious meditations, by continual reflections on the Life and Death of Christ, and by other similar considerations, which are never wanting to them. They do not employ themselves in vain and curious enquiries; even the thoughts of study and of

[a] Ho. Q. 18, 19.

business, though innocent, do not occupy them overmuch; they give them no more time than is necessary, not suffering them to engross their affections; their delight is in God alone; they think of Him only, like a faithful servant, always employed in his master's service, following him everywhere, and rarely losing sight of him. Thus it is their only and passionate desire to possess Christ, and that He may so fill their heart as to leave no space for worldly things, that the things of sense may be entirely excluded. At the same time, they labour continually, and undertake all things for the service of God. However, in this there is nothing painful to them; or if at first they find some things difficult, the difficulties are soon levelled, and afterwards they find therein only pleasure. They take also the greatest care to preserve the love of God. Their intention is very pure, and they ever strive to overcome themselves, without which it is impossible to do any thing considerable for God's glory. No man is master of his calling without much labour, and certainly it were wrong to complain of the trouble which is spent in acquiring the high degree of perfection of which we speak.

CHAPTER IX.

(On these words)—" A certain person by loving Me entirely, learned divine things, and spake that which was admirable.
" He profited more by forsaking all things, than in studying subtleties." B. iii. c. 43.

QUESTION.—How is it that we profit more by forsaking all, than by studying all the subtleties of the schools?
ANSWER.—Because by forsaking the riches and

profits of the world, we render ourselves capable of receiving the Light from above, which teaches many things unattainable by reading or by speculation. To comprehend this rightly, it must be understood, that there are two very different ways of acquiring knowledge. The one is to study deeply, to read much, to listen to teachers, to devote the whole mind to the search for truth: the other is to cast aside every affection and every tie that binds us to created things, to watch unto prayer, and to draw near to God. By this second way, the soul is insensibly and almost unawares taught from above, and raised to a sublime acquaintance with the Divine Perfections, and with the mysteries of our religion. Much more, it often acquires a great degree of knowledge with regard to natural things, and discovers secrets at which the world wonders, which are known to few, but in which the saints find powerful motives for right conduct, for kindness towards their fellow-creatures, and to honour and praise their Creator.

It is seldom, however, that God bestows this kind of natural knowledge upon simple and ignorant people, though He enlightens their minds with regard to supernatural things. We see, in fact, unlearned people, and even women, who through prayer are wonderfully instructed in the Faith. But this abundant light is commonly given only to those whose minds are in some degree prepared, and who have begun to take delight in the things of God. However this be, there are some who, by the exercise of prayer, and by abnegation of self, become so enlightened, that there is nothing in the order of grace, or even of nature, that they cannot penetrate.

This has been seen even in the holy Doctors, as in St. Buonaventura, St. Thomas, and according to some authors, Albert the Great. For great as their penetration might be, we may venture to say that it was at the foot of the Cross[a], and by the aid of light from Heaven, not by reading an endless number of books, that they obtained their wisdom. They gave indeed much time to study; but their knowledge was owing more to Grace than to the power and acuteness of their own mind. In fact, nothing more raises the mind, and prepares it better for Divine illumination, than perfect purity of heart, with a complete renunciation of all created things, and an absolute resignation of self into the hands of Providence.

Those who bury themselves in their studies, and are satisfied with the light of nature, will never rightly understand the things of God. They will speak of them as men in general speak; they may even discourse of them from their pulpits with great applause; but their notions will always be very different from those of the holy Doctors, and they will not find that enjoyment which the Saints found in them; they will misunderstand the maxims of Christian morality, and will reject, as low, the loftiest teaching of the Gospel: what they cannot understand, they will call error, and the commonest truths, which present no difficulty to a spiritual man, cannot enter their minds. It was of this that Gerson spoke, when he said, that some doctors laugh at the devout as ignorant persons who know not what they say. For if they have no perception of the easiest things, it is no wonder that in those which are most startling to human reason, as some feelings of the Saints, they are altogether blind.

When they are told, for instance, that St. Paul and St. Francis believed themselves the chief of sinners, that St. Ignatius considered himself the most imperfect of all his company, although inferior to none in merit and in holiness, these are paradoxes and

---

[a] Au pied du crucifix.

riddles beyond their comprehension. How, say they, could these holy men, knowing the grace that God had given them, truly declare that they knew none more imperfect or more wicked than themselves? These are, they add, some of those pious, yet visionary thoughts, which often come into the heads of spiritual persons blinded by humility. Thus speak those who examine all things by other rules than those of the Gospel, who philosophize upon all things, and believe nothing unproved by formal argument. We do not blame philosophy, or those who teach it; it is of great use; but those who are determined to reason on certain sentiments wherewith the Holy Spirit inspires exalted minds, deceive themselves.

There can be no doubt that those Saints who forsake all, and who receive great illumination from above, understand very well what they say; at least, the eternal Wisdom which enlightens them, leaves not the slightest doubt on their minds. It so persuades them of all that it teaches them, that they are thoroughly convinced of it, and convince the most learned. Thus St. Francis de Paula gave admirable answers to those who asked him for explanations of the most difficult passages of Scripture. This is because their souls, detached from creatures, free from all earthly affections, have nothing to hinder them from receiving supernatural light, and because one ray of this Divine Light discovers to them more than they could learn by long and painful study. "I am He," says the Uncreated Wisdom, "Who, in one instant, do raise the humble mind to understand more of eternal Truth, than if one had studied ten years in the schools." B. iii. c. 43.

END OF THE FIRST BOOK.

BOOK II.

CHAPTER I.

(On these words)—" Learn to despise outward things, and to give thyself to things inward, and thou shalt perceive the Kingdom of God to come in thee." B. ii. c. 1.

QUESTION.—What is to despise outward things?

ANSWER.—It is to have in the depth of our souls so complete an indifference for all external things, and for all which does not tend to render us more pleasing to God, as to take no interest in them, and above all, never to set our affections on them.

1. The first thing required then is, to beware of cherishing esteem or affection for any outward object, or of permitting it to make an impression on the senses, unless it can be made use of in some manner to the greater service of God. But in the latter case it is no longer a question of outward things, since God and that which concerns God are deeply interior, there being nothing, either in ourselves or in any other creature, that can be more closely present with us than the Creator, whom St. Gregory of Nazianzum therefore calls the centre of all things.

From this it appears that the spiritual man is one whose heart and mind are continually attached to God. For though created things present themselves before him with all their charms, he does not linger with them, but passes onward; and if his glance fall on them for ever so short a space, he immediately lifts up his thoughts to Heaven, and despises their natural beauty, considering only that part which may lead him to love and enjoy God more. One who dislikes contemplation, on the other hand, has no greater pleasure than to dwell on objects of this kind; he admires them, praises them, is eager to possess them; his desires become so impassioned, that he thinks no more of God, but so forgets Him, as even to prefer his own satisfaction to the obedience due to Him. Our Author exhorts all who aspire to perfection to depart as far as possible from sensible objects, that they may draw near to God, Who is the basis and foundation of all things, and Who is present in all His works.

Thus the truly spiritual, whithersoever they turn their eyes, see God alone; in all they behold the image of God, and all speaks to them of God; and as the human mind, with its limited capacities, cannot dwell on created objects without losing much of its intentness on things Divine, they try to separate themselves completely from the creature; they despise all that is below God, all that has no relation to God; they desire only to please Him, and to gain His love by striving to purify their hearts, by seeking to fulfil His Divine Will, and by approaching as closely as possible to Him; by practising charity and justice towards their fellow-creatures, and by exercising themselves generally in all that concerns the spiritual life.

But after all, what is it truly to despise outward things? It consists, first, in not suffering those things which dazzle the senses by vain outward show, to seduce the imagination and deceive the mind. For when those who delight in outward things see the worldly grandeur, the rich attire, the superb palaces, the magnificent trains of the kings and princes of the earth, they are filled with admiration, they envy those to whom all these things belong, and cannot refrain from calling them happy. But the spiritual man judges otherwise. He sees in all this nothing but illusion, error, and vanity; all is little in his eyes, because he is convinced that nothing in the world is greater than God.

2. Secondly, to attain to a due contempt for earthly goods, it is necessary to guard ourselves against the dangerous impressions which they are apt to make on the mind and heart. We must repress the too great desire, felt so commonly, of seeing fine houses, splendid furniture, pictures, and other exquisite productions of art; or, if there be some reason why we cannot avoid seeing them, we must always beware that it be not through a spirit of curiosity; for many people delight in taking long journeys, in traversing provinces and kingdoms, with no design except that of observing all that is rare and beautiful in great cities. This strong passion shows plainly that they are led solely by the desire of gratifying their senses. One who loves God and desires Him alone, will not purchase such a vain pleasure by so many fatigues, and at the expense of repose.

3. Thirdly, a perfect contempt of outward things is always accompanied by great moderation; which leads us, when we have to speak of them, to express ourselves coldly, at least without hyperbole, to avoid extravagant praises, and whatever savours of exaggeration. Thus, also, is obviated a degree of excitement, never free from much dissipation and trouble of mind, which is seen in some people, when it is necessary, for instance, to adorn the house upon some public occasion, to make preparations for some extraordinary festival, or to receive some great personage. There are many whose minds are so occupied by such cares, that they can think of nothing else, but are quite absorbed in them; they even accuse those who are less excited than themselves, of indolence, laziness, and insensi-

bility. The spiritually-minded man is not disquieted by all these things; he cares more for peace of heart, and an intimate union with God, than for all the outward things in the world.

When therefore some unforeseen misfortune happens, such as the fall or death of an important personage, curious people speak much of it, they reflect and reason on these occurrences, and imagine a thousand consequences, mostly erroneous; but those who are interior, withdraw into themselves; and as for those things which depend on themselves, they are contented with providing for them as prudence dictates, without neglecting anything.

QUESTION.—What is it to give ourselves wholly to things inward?

ANSWER.—In the first place, it is to have God present with us. For the presence of God calms the mind, and prevents the wanderings of the heart.

In the second place, it is so to regulate our interior, that all may be in order, and that we do not resemble those whose heads are ever full of vague and changing thoughts, who form an endless number of useless desires and projects, and who thereby bring on themselves a great confusion of thought; after which, finding their minds a chaos of disorder and confusion, they throw themselves more and more on outward things, and there, according to our Author, they set up their rest. Those who wish to abide in peace, and to be ever united with God, must begin then by bringing all the powers of their soul into subjection, and well-ordering its functions.

In short, to apply ourselves to the internal life, is to examine carefully all that passes within ourselves, to reflect profoundly on it, and never to indulge in the least irregularity or a shade of carelessness. Those who know nothing of the inward life do not trouble themselves about the state of their conscience; they totally neglect it, particularly when anything happens which draws their thoughts outward. But the others dwell at home, watch unceasingly over themselves, and are always most careful, 1st, to walk always as in the sight of God; 2nd, to do nothing which may be displeasing to Him; 3rd, to say nothing unbecoming; 4th, in all things to follow the motions of grace, and to respond faithfully to the inspirations of Heaven. This is not unknown to those who have tried it, and is most important in their eyes, though the world in general thinks little of it.

QUESTION.—What is meant by the kingdom of God abiding in us?

ANSWER.—It is the happiest state that it is possible to desire in this life; for one who has attained to it, feels that God guides him inwardly, that He is the Lord of his heart, that He rules him in all things, and that even in outward things He gives him sensible tokens of His love, which is the true happiness of this present life.

Further, what is here called the kingdom of God is the peaceful possession of those good things which God pours out abundantly on the soul. These good things may well and truly be compared to a kingdom; for kings are raised above their people in dignity, they possess great riches, they live in pleasure, and all things contribute to their enjoyment. In like manner, the souls in which God reigns are infinitely honoured by their close communion with their supreme Lord. They share both the kingdom and sufferings of Christ[a], and to use the words of the Apostle St. Peter, *the spirit of glory and of God resteth on them.* 1 Pet. iv. 14.

---

[a] Rev. vii. 14. 2 Tim. ii. 12. "If we suffer, we shall also reign with Him."

They are, moreover, filled with spiritual riches; *having nothing, and yet possessing all things.* 2 Cor. vi. 10. Their understanding, ever united with the Fountain of light, receives Its fulness, and possesses all the treasures of Divine Wisdom and Knowledge. In short, the holy joy with which these souls are filled surpasses expression. We have spoken of this elsewhere, as our Author also does in many places, as when he says of the interior man, that "God visiteth him often, and hath with him sweet discourses, pleasant solace, much peace, familiarity exceeding wonderful." B. ii. c. 1.

All these advantages are common to those who flee from things outward to retire within themselves, and to enjoy peacefully their hidden wealth. *The kingdom of God*, said our Saviour, *is within you.* Luke xvii. 21. Renounce all creatures then; remember what is here said, and practise it resolutely. You will thereby undoubtedly arrive at the kingdom of God, that is to say, at an intimate union with God, in which you will find both true holiness and perfect happiness.

CHAPTER II.

(On these words)—"He that judgeth of all things as they are, and not as they are said, or esteemed to be, is truly wise, and taught rather of God than men." B. ii. c. 1.

QUESTION.—What is that wisdom which we need to make a good use of the things of this life?

ANSWER.—That which leads us to consider them as they are, not as men esteem them.

To comprehend this rightly, it must be understood that all things have two faces, and may be viewed from two different sides; 1st, as they are in themselves, and in the sight of God; 2nd, according to the common opinions of men, and the misrepresentations

of self-love. It is then true wisdom to regard them
only with relation to God's judgment, and to the end
for which they were created. For, in moral conduct,
it is extreme folly to follow the opinions of men,
whose minds are too frequently occupied by some
criminal inclination.

What is it to be a bishop, for instance? It is to be
a shepherd of souls, to be appointed by God to lead
the faithful in the way of salvation, as the Apostles did
by our Lord's command. This charge must, then, in-
dispensably bind those who are invested with it to
consecrate themselves to the service of their flock, and
to labour to the utmost of their power for the sanctification of the numerous souls of which they must
render an account to Him Who ransomed them with
the price of His own Blood. Such is the episcopate
in the sight of God. In the eyes of the world it is
quite otherwise. It is a station of grandeur, power,
and authority, become an object of ambition and
avarice to many who desire only the honours and
great wealth which they see to be attached to it. The
Saints, who were not guided by the opinions of men,
but by the standard of Truth, regarded bishoprics
with different eyes. Far from seeking, they avoided
them, and it was with difficulty that they were induced
to accept them.

What is it to be a King? It is to be God's Vice-
gerent on earth; for men, made for society, require
a Head to govern them, to maintain peace and justice,
and preserve true religion among them; and this
Head must render an account to the Lord of the
whole earth. Such is royalty according to the decrees
of God and the judgment of the wise. But the mass
of men represent it to themselves as a lofty station,
whose occupiers are independent of all, give laws to
nations, and are enabled to do whatever pleases them.
A monarch who, in his seat of power, desires and seeks

only to do God's will, conducts himself prudently and modestly, as the Saints have done; but one who desires only to reign, to enjoy the pleasures and other advantages of his dignity, according to his sinful nature, and the common error of the world, such an one walks in the way of perdition, following an infinite number who have perished in those great honours.

The same may be said of all important offices. What is it to be president of a supreme court? It is to be the deputy of God, and of the Sovereign; to administer justice to the people, and to confirm them in the obedience they owe to both. But what is the general opinion of it? It is thought a means of acquiring wealth and of living honourably; of gaining friends, and of sharing many of those privileges which are enjoyed by the magnates of a republic. It is acting wisely and in accordance with God's will, to undertake these offices with a determination to exercise them worthily; above all, to satisfy their most essential obligation, that of rightly administering justice, and keeping good order: but, on the contrary, how common is the folly of seeking these sort of employments for mere worldly considerations, for rank or wealth!

Thus, as I have asserted, all things have two appearances. On the one hand, faith places them before our eyes, as they exist in truth, and as God would have us see them. By faith we perceive that the Three Persons of the All-Holy Trinity created this visible world for man, and man for Themselves; gifted his spiritual nature with all needful faculties to know, love, and serve Them, appointed the high to govern the low with prudence and kindness, and formed living creatures, and all the fruits of the earth, to supply the wants of men; designing that the rich should impart of their wealth to the poor; that thus all the children of God, provided with the things necessary for this life, may dwell in peace, may bless their Heavenly Father, and serve Him with all their heart, with all their mind, and with all their strength.

On the other hand, a worldly spirit leads a man to make use of creatures in a way that the Creator has not ordained, to gratify his own avarice and ambition; his mind being thus darkened, and accustomed to follow its natural tendency to evil, he neglects the duty of charity, thinks only of enriching himself, refuses the guidance of reason, abandons himself to vice and sin, speaks of perishing things according to the false ideas which he forms, and to the deceitful colouring of the passion which blinds him; a strange but common folly, which has been fatal to very many. None then are truly wise, but those who judge soundly, following the rule which we have laid down; and these are in truth taught by a light from above, which, showing them the straight path of perfect holiness, makes them *walk in truth*[a], as the Apostle St. John speaks; and this is the meaning of our Author's words. Assuredly our faults are almost all occasioned by the perverseness of our judgments, and by our failing to consider all created things with regard to their original, as the children of God should do. Thence arise all the errors and illusions into which men fall, when they consider things with an unpurged eye. There are three means by which a spiritual-minded man may guard himself against them.

1. The first is, that in all his occupations and all his affairs, he regards things in their origin, which is God, not resting in outside and appearances, but going to the centre, and examining what is their principal object, according to the rule of Faith. If he is a married man, and God has given him children, he

[a] 2 John iv.

considers God's design in instituting matrimony, which is, that the man should live in peace with his wife, ever joined with her in the bands of true charity, and that he should so bring up his children as to make them true Christians, without being too anxious to establish them in the world, and to leave them great wealth. If he is an ecclesiastic, he fixes it firmly in his mind, that he did not become a priest to be more at liberty, or to be indolent, or to make a kind of traffic in holy things, but to serve God with greater purity and fervour, and to labour with all his strength for the salvation of souls. He regulates his life accordingly, never failing to consider the nature of things and the design of God, and always on his guard lest he should be carried away by the torrent of the false opinions and evil customs of this world.

2. The second means of which the righteous make use, to keep themselves in the way of salvation, is, that they often withdraw into themselves, and thereby become capable of Divine Illumination, God being averse to tumult, and communicating Himself only in silence and solitude. This withdrawal should be practised two or three times a day; for otherwise the soul becomes accustomed to dwell in darkness, and to set little value on that inward light which the Holy Ghost sheds abundantly on the purified spirit.

3. The third means is, often to ask of our Lord the grace to judge of things as He truly judges of them Himself, and not by appearances which can but deceive. The wise man says, that *the bewitching of naughtiness doth obscure things that are honest, and the wandering of concupiscence doth undermine the simple mind.* Wisd. iv. 12. In fact, the world and the devil so bewitch most men, and so fill their mind with false ideas, that the wisest find it difficult to free themselves from common errors. People seek a benefice as a means of living comfortably,

without thinking of the obligations inseparable from it. They aspire to an office as a thing necessary to distinguish themselves or to support their family, without a thought of the debt incurred to God, to the sovereign, and to the public. Let each individual, then, beseech the Lord to enlighten his mind, and to strengthen his will. Let him hearken to the whisper of the Holy Spirit in the depth of his heart, without regarding the voice of the world. This especially regards preachers, prelates, superiors, and all others whose employment is to serve their fellow-creatures. For they must often seek from God the gift of discernment and knowledge, that they may know the true value of created things, and be saved from those delusions to which such as regulate their conduct only by opinion or example are subject. And, in fact, one who is not enlightened from above does infallibly fall into the snares of the devil, the father of lies, who employs all manner of stratagems to turn him from his duty, to lead him into evil, and to induce him to prefer his own will to that of God.

CHAPTER III.

(On these words)—"The more holy violence thou usest against thyself, the greater shall be thy spiritual profiting." B. i. c. 25.

QUESTION.—What is the surest means of attaining perfection?

ANSWER.—Using violence against ourselves in the practice of virtue, and hardening ourselves against all difficulties which are to be found therein. But for this we must have powerful aid from God. Yet, as our spiritual progress depends on our own co-operation with Grace, we can advance in the paths of God only in proportion as we overcome ourselves.

This is, because perfection is altogether a divine and spiritual state, and far above our nature, which is in itself low, gross, and earthly. It is God's will that man, being endowed with reason and capable of merit, should do all that lies in his power to acquire that degree of perfection for which he is intended. Man must, therefore, strive to follow the leading of Grace, because he cannot follow it without surmounting great obstacles, and the efforts which he makes for this, shall obtain for him a reward proportionate to his labour and to the infinite liberality of God. It is this which leads our Author to say, that the more violence we use against ourselves in obeying the inspirations of God, the more merit we shall acquire, and the greater shall be our spiritual profiting.

QUESTION.—What are the things in which particularly we should use violence against ourselves?

ANSWER.—There are three principally, of which the first regards the recollected and attentive thought which we should give to the things of God. There is much more to be done here than we imagine; for the natural man is carried away by outward things; sensible objects attract and charm him; he dwells in them, he delights in them, in them he finds satisfaction and repose. But the virtuous man loves to retire into himself, and to hold familiar converse with God. He is not like those unsettled spirits of whom the Prophet complains, when he says, that *no man layeth to heart* (Jer. xii. 11) those things which alone deserve his whole attention. He abides in the Presence of the Lord, and avoids all objects which might call him forth from it, having no curiosity to see or to hear what passes in the world. But because man naturally hates retirement, and seeks only for diversion, he must put force upon himself, like children who are made to study against their will. Without this voluntary constraint, he will never know the things which concern his peace, and will be too feeble in spirit to fulfil those things for which Providence designed him.

It is a general maxim, that one who desires to profit in the spiritual life, can never succeed unless he excites himself by all manner of considerations to overcome himself, to oppose his own inclinations in a thousand ways. Above all, he must repress the too great desire of knowing useless things, or those which concern him not. For these things being once impressed on his mind, arouse the passions, which now, freed from restraint, cause him to commit grievous faults, and to depart entirely from God. But if he has courage enough to moderate himself, to resist his constant inclination to be always moving, always speaking; if he keeps silence, and devotes himself to prayer, he will make great progress, and will begin to enjoy those exercises which he once found unendurable. This also will be an excellent means of gaining the love of God, and of attaining to perfection.

But to come to particulars; on what occasions should we try to overcome ourselves? When, for instance, we perceive that we are going to hear some piece of news that bears no relation to piety or to religion, for then we must try to turn our minds away, and to retire into the depths of our own souls. When, again, our friends invite us to go and see a prince make his entry, or to join a company of people accustomed to feasting and jesting; if we refuse, we have gained rather a victory over ourselves. This is the way to practise our rule, and the more frequently we strive to practise it, above all, in those things against which nature most revolts, the more easily shall we obtain the spirit of prayer, and draw down on ourselves the consolations of heaven.

THE MEANS OF ATTAINING PERFECTION. 65

2. The second thing, in regard of which we have need to overcome ourselves much, is freedom of heart; for as nothing helps us more to attain holiness and perfection than an entire detachment from created things, so we must spare no pains to acquire it. Suppose the case then of a person who is bound by attachment or interest to some other individual. What must he do? His first care must be to break his bonds, to renounce every too earthly affection, and to arrive at as great an indifference for the beloved object as for one unknown. And this must not be long delayed, for the smallest delay is always a hindrance to perfect union with God.

You may, perhaps, have received a present which is very pleasing to you; you feel that your heart clings to it, and that it would give you much pain to part with it, if it were only on account of the person who gave it, and whose remembrance you wish to preserve. Renounce it instantly, if you are wise, and if you have any remains of zeal for your spiritual progress. *If thine eye offend thee, pluck it out*[a], said the Saviour. This is for you a cause of offence; banish from your heart all that may hinder its liberty.

Saint Francis once felt some slight satisfaction in composing a little work; the idea of it returned upon his mind during his prayers; he rose immediately and burned it. Those who desire true freedom of heart should imitate this example; and the more diligent they are in casting off all natural feelings, the greater progress they will make towards perfection. This gives the poor a singular advantage in uniting themselves to God. There is nothing in which we should labour harder than in breaking these sort of attachments; for God cannot permit that a heart which desires to be His, should divide its affec-

[a] Mark ix. 47.

tions between Him and His creatures. An imperfection proceeding from weakness alone, a sudden movement of impatience or self-love, does not separate us from Him in such a degree as a voluntary attachment to any created thing whatever.

3. The third thing in which we must strive to overcome ourselves and to show our courage, is in correcting the too great liberty of the senses, and repressing the impetuous motions of rebellious appetite. The man who seeks to be truly spiritual, not only must not yield to the violence of his passions, but he must seek to combat and subdue them, so that he may be always master of those sudden movements which lead him to say all that is in his mind; and the more he restrains himself, the greater will be his merit. Let him then wage a continual war against himself; and God, seeing how he labours to overcome his evil inclinations, will bless him abundantly. It is, moreover, natural, that an opposite should yield to its opposite. It is most certain, that our spiritual progress can only be proportioned to our endeavours at self-mortification.

Many aspire to perfection, but few make use of this path to arrive at it. They enjoy the things of God, they consider them, meditate on them, converse gladly with devout persons, apply themselves to reading, love spiritual books, willingly read that of the Imitation of Christ, and approve of its maxims; but when they are required to overcome their appetites, to yield their own opinions, to believe themselves undeserving of all good, to be silent when attacked, to abstain from all sorts of jesting, to avoid sports and spectacles, to mortify their taste, to refuse themselves the satisfaction of reading and studying curious and diverting things, to chastise the body, and finally, to persevere in things of this kind, there are few generous enough to resolve on it, and to determine to be virtuous at this price; and therefore, very small is the number of those who are truly zealous for perfection. There are many who, under an imposing air of wisdom and probity, conceal strong and unmortified passions; their indocile spirits do only such things as please them, and refuse to be restrained; yet they pass for good people, either on account of the outward appearance of goodness, or of the sanctity and perfection of their state.

CHAPTER IV.

(On these words)—" Presume not upon thyself." B. i. c. 7.

QUESTION.—How can we presume upon ourselves?

ANSWER.—In three manners principally. The first is very gross, the second somewhat less so, the third is more subtle and more spiritual.

The first, then, is that of those who seek only their own interests, who love themselves alone, who in all their affairs reckon only on their own industry, their own carefulness; who think and labour for nothing but their own pleasure and glory, and in nothing else show activity, resolution, and ardour. These people show great weakness when what they love is taken from them, when they are shown how little ground they have for confidence in themselves, and are deprived of that vain satisfaction which they derive from the temporary possession of those good things in which the world delights: then are they most sad and dejected.

A learned and eloquent man glories in his knowledge and his talents; a Cavalier in his valour, his great exploits, his family, his handsome appearance, his magnificent train, and other such things. Deprive them of that which renders them so vain, and which feeds their pride, you will see them weak, annoyed, confused. A richly dressed woman, who thinks herself handsome, and who is considered witty, is always proud and disdainful; but deprive her of these sources of vanity, she will instantly be so changed that you cannot recognize her: a sure symptom that she presumes upon herself, and that her trust in these natural advantages is the cause that she desires to rule everywhere, and that in all conversations she speaks first, and with the tone of one who will make herself heard. In fact, without this she would care neither for balls, nor for the society in which she is desirous to appear, to shine, and to attract admiration.

The interior man cares not for all these things: his only support is virtue, and the testimony of a good consience: his designs, his affections, his discourses turn upon this; and as one who desires to lift a heavy weight rests his lever on something solid, thus, in all his undertakings, he rests on God, and not on himself; on truth, and not on vanity: far different from the wise men of this world, who expect all from their own skill, their industry, their cleverness, and who thus feed their pride and self-love. One who desires to give himself wholly to God, is completely detached from self, and values a good conscience and a firm resolve to please the Lord, incomparably more than all the advantages either of nature or of fortune.

2. There is a second manner of presuming upon oneself, which is not gross, like that of worldly people, but more spiritual, and is found in those who addict themselves to good works. These are not discouraged when some temptation of the evil one comes upon them: their resource is the recollection of the good

that they have done; and they rest on this, instead of going directly to its principle, which is God. As for the worldly, when they are in sorrow, they recal to their mind the grounds of comfort which they can find in themselves, and thus support themselves with ideas chimerical enough of many things flattering to their self-love.

Those of whom we speak have a more subtle kind of self-trust for desiring comfort; they say to themselves, "I have long employed myself in good works; I hate the amusements and vanities of the world; I do penance, and communicate often." Thus they try to recover themselves from the dejection into which they fall at times. Truly, a good conscience is a joy to those who have no cause for self-reproach; but a pure and really virtuous soul makes no such reflections. Persuaded that those works which we think holy are but *as filthy rags,* (Is. lxiv. 6,) to eyes enlightened from above, she goes to God, and is lost in Him; totally forgetful of self, thinking neither of the good nor even of the evil that she has done.

We must then beware of these two different methods of proceeding; the one gross, and seen in the imperfect, who are filled with esteem for their own good qualities, and make them their comfort and their rejoicing; the other more subtle, and observed in people who are not without virtue, but who having, as yet, too little, reckon much on their good works. In the most holy communities people are to be found, who, thinking that they have acquired much virtue, say in their hearts, I am not like many who do nothing, for I alone fill many offices; the superiors are well pleased with me, and I am at peace with all. They form and cherish in their imagination vain ideas of their merit, and instead of obliterating them to remember God only, they recal them constantly, principally in seasons of dejection, when they desire comfort. This is a sure sign of being still very far from perfection. We should bury these things in eternal oblivion, and meditate attentively on this saying of the Saviour, *When ye shall have done all those things which are commanded you, say, We are unprofitable servants.* Luke xvii. 10.

It is indeed dangerous to set our own virtues before us, as is often done without much reflection, instead of quickly turning away our eyes from them. If we closely examined those whose secret pride triumphs in their own good works, and displayed to them their hidden imperfections, they would be much astonished: for on meeting with the smallest mortification, or feeling themselves despised, they show extreme vexation, because they are accustomed to believe themselves exempt from failings. A sovereign remedy for their presumption is to do what our Author elsewhere recommends; so completely to renounce ourselves, that " retaining nothing[a]," attributing nothing to ourselves, we may entirely forget all that may tend to our honour. It is truly giving ourselves to God to quit ourselves in this manner.

Lastly, those who presume not at all on themselves are those holy and perfect persons who find nothing solid but the love of God, who give a place in their heart to no creature, in order that Jesus may fill it all, that He may be their only support, and His Cross their sole dependence. You must put no trust, said Saint Vincent Ferrier, in yourself, nor in all the actions of your life, nor in all your possessions, but must rest on Christ Alone, Who made Himself most poor and most abject, and endured the extremest shame and death itself for you. This is truly resting, not on self, but on Christ. God commonly takes from the soul which zealously seeks

[a] B. ii. c. 11.

perfection all matter for vain-glory: and instead of those good things of which she thinks herself possessed, which can only be an occasion of pride, He communicates to her His Sacred Love, to the end that she may live and act by love, full of fervour, resolved to serve her God, to honour Him, to please Him, to fulfil His Divine Will, which supplies to her the place of all.

When the soul finds nothing else whereon to build, or whereto to cling, when she is in such a state that neither the favour of man, nor honours, nor health, nor the delights of the senses, nor even spiritual joys, can satisfy her, then is she compelled to have recourse to Him Who is her only refuge, she throws herself into the arms of her Lord; Whose good pleasure is more dear to her than her own life, and she completely fulfils this precept, " Presume not upon thyself." Thus stripped of all, she is hid with Jesus Christ in the Bosom of the Father, there to dwell peacefully with Him, according as He said to His Apostles the evening before His Passion, *I will come again, and receive you unto Myself; that where I am, there ye may be also* [a] for ever.

CHAPTER V.

(On these words)—" False freedom of mind, and great confidence in ourselves, are very contrary to heavenly visitations." B. ii. c. 10.

QUESTION.—What are these heavenly visitations?

ANSWER.—They are an effect of grace fortifying and elevating the soul, and producing in her a supernatural feeling, without which she is incapable of

[a] John xiv. 3.

making the smallest progress in the spiritual life: for the Spirit of God must be present, to enlighten her, to give her strength and courage, to make her enjoy the exercises of virtue, above all, to prevent her from falling back into her original weakness. Therefore Job said, *Thy visitation hath preserved my spirit*[a], and prevented it from perishing. Righteous souls are most careful to seek these visitations, knowing how precious are their uses. Worldlings, on the contrary, neither esteem them as they ought, nor strive to render themselves worthy of them. For that they receive them so rarely is a punishment of their sins, and, above all, of those which our Author mentions, I mean, too great freedom, and extreme confidence in themselves.

The former of these two defects makes them neglectful of certain feelings of remorse produced in them by the grace of the Holy Spirit, Who desires the perfection of men, and suggests to them those things which He sees to be profitable towards their attaining it. And because these inspirations are a bridle to nature, which ever passionately desireth liberty, those who wish to be free obstinately reject them, notwithstanding the reproofs of the Spirit of God, Who, being infinitely pure, can endure nothing unholy.

Further, this Divine Spirit, opposed to all violence, does not compel the soul to obedience; He suffers her to follow her own will, but when she resists Him, He makes her feel deeply His just indignation. After having essayed to gain her by gentleness, if she persists in refusing to yield subjection to grace, He gives her up, speaks to her no more, abandons her at last to her own will. This was the cause of the grief of the Son of God, when weeping over

---

[a] Job x. 12.

Jerusalem, He said that that unhappy city *knew not the time of her visitation*, Luke xix. 44, and that as the punishment of her wilful ignorance, she should be sacked and destroyed to the ground. The same thing befalls the soul which refuses our Lord's visitations too often; for she thus deprives herself of the assistance, without which she is unable to resist the attacks of her besieging enemies, who, after a feeble resistance, make themselves her masters, and bring her to utter desolation and ruin.

2. The second thing which hinders the frequent visitations of God, is confidence in ourselves; a greater and more dangerous sin than is generally imagined. There are some who may be called virtuous, but whose virtue is very ordinary and imperfect, who are almost always in a state of dryness, and devoid of sensible comfort. They think that God leaves them in this manner solely to try them, and console themselves with this idea; but when all things are considered, the cause of this inward desertion is, too commonly, the liberty which they allow themselves to say and do whatever they please, without regard to the illumination and motions of Grace. These are not spiritual men, nor have they a spirit of mortification, for they know not what it is to overcome themselves, and they permit themselves very many and considerable faults. This very criminal licence is caused by their valuing their own discernment and reasonings too highly, despising the prudent warnings of pious people, and rejecting as ill-grounded scruples those things which they should regard as real duties, and true signs of faithfulness to God.

Now, of those who thus trust in themselves there are two sorts. The first are far separated from God, the others less so. Among the former are freethinkers, who imagine they know every thing, and who decide on all subjects, not excepting matters of faith, and the incontestable dogmas of theology. Young people are subject to the same fault; they cut, they prune, they judge the things of religion, they criticise the lives of the Saints, and scarcely do holy Scripture and the teaching of the Church escape their censure. These people are all so far from Grace, and so unworthy of the visitations of the Holy Spirit, that there is nothing more pitiable, nothing more to be compassionated, than their state. They can enjoy nothing which does not flatter their sensuality or their pride, and therefore God abandons them; and it is not surprising, for they so completely abandon God, that the most Christian sentiments appear to them mere weakness of mind. We may say that obstinacy is their only strength, as the whole strength of rocks consists in their hardness.

Some years ago a courtier died at Paris. His confessor exhorting him to prepare for death, presented to him a crucifix, by which he appeared very little moved. Another seeing this, and wishing to show that he was one of those free-thinkers of whom we speak, told the confessor that men of sense were not moved by objects which were good only for the lower classes; that he ought to know how to distinguish them from ordinary people, and not to tell them common things. I suppose he imagined that Seneca was to be quoted to him, and that the sight of the crucifix was only for devout women, while such a great genius required profound reasonings; as if Saint Bonaventure had not a sufficiently lofty mind, of whom it is said that he had worn out his crucifix by frequent kisses: as if we were to reckon among narrow minds Saint Augustine and Saint Thomas, who, in divine things, were simple and humble as children. Saint Augustine says, that God communicates Himself to the great, but not to those who are great in themselves, that is, in their own esteem, such as courtiers, idolaters of worldly honour.

2. The second sort of persons who show this false confidence are those who have much probity and uprightness, who are engaged, by their profession itself, to a good life, but who trust too much in their learning and reasonings; for which reason they have little enjoyment of God, and rarely receive His visits. These think themselves very enlightened, and imagine that to reason philosophically enables them to judge well of divine things. Therefore they always find something to blame in the conduct of the masters of the inward life, and of those who devote themselves to it; even going so far as to believe that loving devotedness to God renders them credulous and easily deceived. They sometimes even imagine that the tenderness of devotion enfeebles the mind, and takes away much of its firmness.

As they find no pleasure in pious exercises, they consider this dryness as the character of a masculine and solid virtue. They say that they are not like women, who weep for nothing, and that God does not treat them like novices; that when they were children, little things affected them, but now being men, they see plainly what they have to do. Thus their learning, used as they use it, serves often but to strengthen them in their evil customs. They pretend that the spiritual Fathers cannot reason as they can; they despise the sensible joys and comforts with which God favours the simple spirit, and think little of the ardour with which He inspires them for penance. Yet we know that St. Francis wept continually, and that St. Ignatius, holding fast to God in heart and spirit, nearly lost his sight from shedding tears.

What is the reason, then, that they have no share in these visitations of Heaven? It is that they do not value them sufficiently. Some of them complain of their own hardness of heart; and as they are ignorant of its cause, they blame their occupation, which, by obliging them, as they say, to be constantly treating of dry and speculative subjects, gradually dries up in them the springs of devotion. But they deceive themselves; for application to study is not the true cause of their insensibility to the things of God. St. Thomas, St. Bonaventure, and many other holy Doctors studied constantly, and were still filled with spiritual pleasures. Their indevotion, then, springs only from their too great self-confidence; and it is this which leads them to speak contemptuously of the truly devout; to set a high value on certain talents and actions which are entirely natural and human; to turn into ridicule many terms of which the Mystics make use in their writings; daringly to condemn Denis, the Carthusian, and many other authors equally renowned for sanctity and learning, because they have not always defined things according to the rules of Aristotle, though their whole teaching shows profound wisdom.

Thus they are supreme judges of all, and would have their words regarded as so many oracles. This is the cause why the visitations of Heaven are not for them, and why, for want of this assistance, they fall into thick darkness, and are even overcome by disgraceful passions. Some of them make a mock of the secret operations of the Spirit of God in the soul; and if the Saints endeavour to express in lofty and mysterious terms what passes in these Divine operations, they alter their terms, and explain them in a low sense, to make jests of them. It is presuming strangely on oneself thus to attack those Doctors and Saints for whom the excellent of all ages have felt the greatest veneration. Those who follow the teaching of the Holy Spirit, and not human reasonings, do quite otherwise; for the communion of the soul with God inspires no less humility than confidence.

CHAPTER VI.

(On these words)—" In whatever instance a person seeketh himself, then he falleth from love." B. iii. c. 5.

QUESTION.—How may we lose the love of God?

ANSWER.—By loving and seeking ourselves. Fully to understand this truth, it must first be remarked, that one who desires to make much progress in the way of perfection, cannot do better than to direct his whole intention towards God, and, in all things, to seek Him simply. This is the principal effect of divine love, and he who aspires to perfect holiness, must needs follow this path to arrive at it; he must propose to himself as his only aim, to please our Lord; and thither must all his thoughts and all his desires tend. For if he dwells on himself, instead of lifting up his mind to God, after the manner of those who faithfully seek Him, he falls, and becomes earthly and carnal, full of self-love, and the slave of his passions, from whence proceed three great evils.

1. The first is, that he loses that light, without which it is impossible to walk safely, and then becomes blind, because he cannot receive illumination from above. But one who looks ever to God, and who approaches Him with true humility, receives light, *God being Light,* (1 John i. 5;) and the instant that he turns away, this Divine brightness disappears. That which separates him from God, is attachment to his own interests; for one who thinks only of himself, who loves himself alone, is always in darkness, and

cannot, in this state, perceive the truth, because he sees all things in the false colours with which self-love depicts them to his imagination, as when we look through a blackened glass, all that we see appears dark.

2. The second evil is, that we are soon discouraged when things do not succeed as we desire. This is the reason that if, after making some efforts to break our bonds, and to lift up ourselves to God with an upright intention, we begin once more to mingle a little self-love in our good works, we feel an internal weight and suffering, of which we can hardly guess the cause. How often has it happened to us, in the ordinary course of our lives, to find ourselves weary, tired, and dissatisfied! This was caused, and is almost invariably caused, by a secret self-seeking. We think we have the best intention possible; we could swear that in the undertaking we have in hand, we regard God Alone; and yet we are sad, and feel a certain distaste which troubles our peace of mind. This is to be attributed only to this unregulated self-love. On the one hand, we have strength and courage, through the motive of the honour of God; on the other, we are weak, feeble, languishing, when we consider our own interest. "If there lurk in thee any self-seeking, behold, this it is that hindereth and weigheth thee down." B. iii. c. 11.

Often, after having performed some good work, you are delighted to be praised and thanked for it. This vain joy is caused only by the part that you have had in the affair. But if, having met with bad success, you are reproached and ridiculed, this is sufficient to fill your heart with bitterness for many days. Whence proceeds this vexation which you try to conceal, but which gnaws you inwardly? It is that things have not succeeded as you hoped. You would fain take a lofty flight; but hardly have you power to drag yourself along and crawl on the earth. Perform all your actions for God, propose to yourself nothing but His glory, you will be entirely free, and without self-reproach.

Few enjoy entire freedom of heart, because there are few who so love God as to desire nothing beside Him; and the greater number, thinking only of themselves, and of what others may say or think of them, make themselves voluntarily slaves of the world. "Separate yourself from yourself," said St. Augustin, "for there is nothing which troubles you more than yourself." That which gives you uneasiness is, not the affair which you have to conduct, nor the employment with which you are charged, it is the attachment to your own interest, and the fear of something vexatious happening to you. Think no more of that; be wholly devoted to God: beware lest you be like those who, not endeavouring "perfectly to die unto themselves, therefore remain entangled in themselves, and cannot be lifted up in spirit above themselves." B. iii. c. 53.

How can a bird fly when its wings are glued, or a weight is attached to its feet? Too great desire of being at ease, and of succeeding in every thing, hinders us from going to God. When the interest is great and pressing, when our whole property is endangered, when an attempt is made to ruin our reputation, what efforts do we not make to prevent and turn away this misfortune! Why is it that we then take so much trouble, and leave all our other occupations? Why are we incapable of doing many things which before we did very easily? It is that all the powers of the soul are, as it were, bound to one single object; it is, that we have not entrusted the conduct of this affair, or the care of refuting this calumny, to the hands of Providence. The soul thus retaining but very little strength to perform her duties, we need not wonder that they are done very feebly and imperfectly.

3. The third evil which befalls those who seek themselves is, that they commit innumerable faults. For being deprived of the light from heaven, weakened by the passions which have acquired dominion over them, and completely occupied in seeking their own comfort, they cannot do otherwise than fail in many particulars of their duty. They suffer many disorders which they are bound to prevent, thus betraying the cause of God by a base compliance with scandalous sinners; they bend and yield when they should display firmness; they flatter when they should reprove; they fly on occasions when they ought to face the enemy; they sleep while the house of God is in flames. This is extremely displeasing to the Lord, whose service ought to be preferred to all human interests. Thus they walk amidst the shadows of a dark night; they wander, fall, and are wounded, for want of seeing the path they ought to follow.

The cause of all these irregularities, is the want of an upright intention, of love for God, and of faithfulness and zeal for His Glory. God's true servants care nothing for their own concerns, but despise themselves; and this makes them more ready and more free to employ all their powers in that which regards their Master's honour. For this reason, also, it is, that the Saints constantly preach to us this one thing, that the surest way of serving God is to forget ourselves, and to sacrifice all to the glory of the Lord. To lose our credit, to be deserted by those whose esteem we deserved, is very hard for the unmortified; for one who is not entirely dead to himself, can hardly turn his eyes away from the things that flatter his passion: thus he deprives himself of many graces, and falls into innumerable sins.

Self-love is the root of all the passions. When it has excited them, they are like impetuous winds, causing violent agitations, which are commonly followed by lamentable shipwrecks. When once we have renounced our own interests, we are sheltered from those storms which destroy so many lovers of themselves and devotees of pleasure. "If thou hadst but once perfectly entered into the secrets of the Lord Jesus," says our Author, "and tasted a little of His ardent love; then wouldst thou not regard thine own convenience or inconvenience." B. ii. c. 1. Would to God that we did taste the sweetness of that love, which, binding our hearts to the Heart of Christ, makes us share His feelings, and embrace His teaching! We should care very little what the world might say or think, and the uprightness of our intentions would be preserved uninjured.

QUESTION.—What then must we do to avoid this self-seeking, and to renounce our own interests?

ANSWER.—First, whatever is our age, whatever our situation, we must resolve to refuse nothing to God, and to desire nothing but God. We must believe that in no other way can we destroy our self-love. We never rise above flesh and blood, said St. Augustin formerly: we are always employed in seeking honour and pleasure; nothing moves us much which does not regard our own credit or repose. We do not entirely forget the things of God, but we are very negligent and weak in them; we look at them afar off; and if we sometimes apply ourselves to them, it is only on extraordinary occasions; in general we think only of the success of our own little designs.

2. The second thing for which we must labour, is to die continually to ourselves; to overcome ourselves, not only on great occasions, but even on little ones.

"For it is no small benefit for a man to forsake himself even in the smallest things." B. iii. c. 39. St. Ignatius commands the members of his company particularly to study self-abnegation, and an entire and continual mortification. The man who makes this his principal study, will infallibly drive from his heart the enemy of divine love, which is the love of self.

3. The third thing to be done is so to devote the mind and heart to the right direction of our intention, that with a simple and sincere eye we may see God in all things, do all for His glory, and be careful never to turn aside our look, either for want of reflection, or through natural impetuosity. Thus shall we be free to fly to God, and to unite ourselves very closely with Him, according to the law of perfect love.

CHAPTER VII.

(On these words)—"Simplicity doth tend towards God; Purity doth apprehend and, as it were, taste Him." B. ii. c. 4.

QUESTION.—What are the motions of the soul which desires to be united with God?

ANSWER.—Those three noted by the bride in Solomon's Song. *I sought Him whom my soul loveth.* She says, *I found Him, I held Him, and would not let Him go.* Can. iii. 1. 4. The soul strongly attached to her Beloved, who is her Divine Spouse, begins then by seeking Him, by seeking finds, and having at length found Him, holds Him fast, and so clings to Him, that nothing can separate them more. She seeks Him by simplicity, and finds and possesses Him by purity.

WHAT IT IS TO SEEK GOD.

QUESTION.—What is it then to seek God?

ANSWER.—It is to try in all things to lift up our heart to heaven, and to fulfil the Divine Will, which consists in three things.

1. The first is, to walk as in the presence of God, without ever losing sight of Him, as the Holy Spirit says by the mouth of His prophets: *Seek ye the Lord while He may be found : seek His face evermore.* Isa. lv. 6. Ps. cv. 4. That man seeks the Lord who remembers Him in all his actions, forgetful of himself, and of all creatures. Cowardly souls love not the remembrance of God; they dread His inspirations and enlightening, because they fear lest they should be obliged to alter their life. Those, on the contrary, who desire to be faithful to grace, have God always present to their mind ; they constantly implore His government, His support, His assistance in the practice of virtue; and directly this help fails them, directly they begin to lose their joy in God, they are in constant disquietude till they have regained it; their whole care, their utmost efforts, are directed to recal to their memory the sweet idea of Him, Who alone was their happiness, and Who alone can lead them to perfection. They are unlike the lukewarm and imperfect, who calmly suffer the privation of the Divine Light, without feeling their misfortune. They cry, they groan, they cease not to call on the Lord, till at length they find Him once more. Such is the fruit of a holy simplicity, which looks to God Alone.

2. The second means of seeking God, is to have a simple and direct intention, to strive to the uttermost to find Him, to do in all circumstances what pleases Him best, to crush in our hearts all which inspires human respect and vain-glory ; in a word, it is to think of nothing but honouring and serving God. Whosoever does otherwise, seeks himself, and not

Christ Jesus[a]. Simplicity acts thus, because it has but one object, and turns away its eyes from all things beside. There is in fact but one path for the simple soul, while there are a thousand for the deceitful and wayward. The straight road is the only one, and they who follow it have nothing in view, but to do what God requires of them. Those who have but little love for God, and little zeal for His service, become attached to all things that please the senses; but those who truly love Him, desire only what pleases Him, and this is rightly called seeking God; this is what our Lord recommends, when He desires us to seek *first the kingdom of God.* Matt. vi. 33. Ps. xiv. 2. But God justly complains in many places of Scripture, that *there is none that seeketh Him,* Ps. liii. 3. and that goeth to Him with a simple and efficacious intention of pleasing Him.

3. The third means of seeking Him, is to do the utmost in our power to return to the good path directly we discover that we have quitted it. If you perceive then that you have discovered too freely your hidden life, have been too wandering, too much carried away by the diversions and the conversation of the world; if you feel your soul weighed down by the pursuit of perishing things, or relaxed by indolence and lukewarmness, retire immediately within yourself; fortify yourself by prayer; regulate your interior carefully; for those who place their supreme happiness in sensual delights and worldly pleasures, at length find in them their extreme misery. As for pure and faithful souls, nothing can be more painful to them than the coldness into which they think they have fallen. They are impatient to rekindle the first fire of their devotion, to unite themselves more strongly than ever to our Lord, to renew their

[a] Phil. ii. 21.

vigilance and fervour, both in their prayers and in their works. Thus they seek God, and continue till at length they find Him.

QUESTION.—When may we say that we have found God?

ANSWER.—When the soul which has sought Him faithfully, at length arrives at a state in which God unites Himself to her, and she unites herself to Him so closely, that she feels Him in her heart, from which she has banished sin, and in which she enjoys a serenity, a peace, an inward joy, which the presence of God alone can bring. Serenity is the effect of the great illuminings which chase away all darkness from her: peace springs from the removal of all that might trouble her: joy from the Grace with which she is wholly imbued, and which fills all her powers. Then may we say truly that she has found what she sought, and gathered the fruit of her long perseverance.

God hides Himself from some, either to punish their unfaithfulness or to try their virtue; the good feel this trial bitterly, because, when God withdraws Himself, life becomes to them more insupportable than death. They say weeping, *I sought Him whom my soul loveth, but I found Him not.* Can. iii. 1. But if after an absence of many days, sometimes of many years, He shows Himself to them once more, if by their prayers and sighs, their penances and voluntary mortifications, they at length constrain Him to return, their joy is beyond conception, and they are well assured that they have found Him, because they feel an inward calm, a strength, a happiness which can proceed from Him alone.

Holy Scripture and the masters of the inward life exhort all people in general never to weary of seeking God; and it was in this sense that Christ said, *Ask, and it shall be given you; knock, and it shall be opened unto you.* Luke xi. 9. The proper means to recover Him when He is lost, are prayer and patience. *Seek,* said our Lord, *and ye shall find.* Ibid. We seek by prayer, by humiliation, by self-mortification, and then God reveals Himself to the soul, of which we have a figure in the woman in the Gospel, who found her piece of silver[a]. The diligence with which we should seek the Lord is simply expressed by the eager carefulness of this woman. She sweeps her own house, lights her candle, moves every thing, searches everywhere; and the extreme joy which she shows when the piece of silver is found, represents the state of the soul on recovering the Grace which she had lost.

QUESTION.—What is it to hold God fast, and retain Him within ourselves?

ANSWER.—It is to possess Him, to enjoy Him, not to suffer any thing whatsoever to separate us from Him. This takes place when, after much seeking, having found our supreme good, and enjoying that inward peace in which we taste and see how gracious the Lord is[b], we attach ourselves to Him, and obtain by our fidelity, that He shall leave us no more. Thus to possess God is the privilege of the pure in heart[c], for when once they have succeeded in casting away their vices, and washing themselves from their sins, when they have uprooted their evil habits, the Holy Spirit, who desires nothing so much as to find abodes worthy of receiving Him, communicates Himself and unites Himself to them.

Purity, then, is the virtue which has the advantage not only of knowing the Supreme Good, but of feeling and tasting His sweetness, and binding itself for ever to Him. As its ardent love for God makes it seek in all things what is most pleasing to Him, it causes

[a] Luke xv. 8.   [b] Ps. xxxiv. 8.   [c] Matt. v. 8.

it also to feel a horror of all that may displease Him; thus the soul, purged from her sins, and with her natural inclination to evil diminished, the soul, I say, has then reason to hope that the Heavenly Spouse will come to dwell within her. Two things in consequence must be her whole occupation.

The first is, to attach herself inseparably to that Supreme Goodness Which alone can give her the succour both of light and strength which she needs rightly to perform her duties. The other is, to live in a state of great fervour, and to be always faithful to Grace. For as the good of the soul is to possess Christ, so the good thing which Christ requires of the soul is, that she be always most faithful to Him, and that by extreme vigilance she avoid even the smallest faults, and the slightest imperfections, and labour for nothing but to satisfy and please Him. This is the only way to render oneself worthy of possessing Him.

When one who loves his own interest has acquired some perishable good, he says in himself, as Pharaoh said when he was pressed to suffer the people of God to go out of Egypt, I will not let it go, (Ex. v. 2,) it shall not escape me, I will keep it to the last. One who is attached to God by the bonds of pure love, also protests that he will never leave Him, but abide eternally united with Him; that he will rather lose life than His love, will be always faithful, and will thereby constrain Him to fulfil him continually with His favours.

The conclusion of the whole matter is this, that the happiness of the enjoyment of God is the recompence of purity; that constant fidelity retains and preserves it; and that finally, by means of these two virtues, we abide in that Divine Union which makes all the sweetness of this present life, and is the reward of past labours.

CHAPTER VIII.

(On these words) — "He that can best tell how to suffer, will best keep himself in peace." B. ii. c. 7.

QUESTION.—By what road can we arrive at true peace in this world?

ANSWER.—By patience. This path is difficult, and almost unknown to those who think that peace consists in abundant worldly goods, and in sensual pleasures, being unable to believe that it can be found elsewhere. It is true that it is found only in satisfaction of some kind, but not in that which they love and seek so passionately. For there are two sorts of satisfaction, one low, the other lofty. The first, which serves only to delight the senses, is the most loved, and is preferred to the second, which is pure, and wholly spiritual. Yet peace is contained in this last, and we can never possess it, except we repose on truly good things; that is, on those spiritual treasures that God has promised and reserved for His servants. Those who imagine it to be found in fleshly enjoyments are grossly deceived. In truth, it cannot be obtained but by the way of suffering; for it is impossible in this life to content both flesh and spirit, and to satisfy the spirit, we must mortify the flesh.

Moses says, in speaking of the flood, that *the waters increased, and bare up the ark, and it was lift up above the earth.* Gen. vii. 17. In like manner we may say, that afflictions, signified by these waters, assist the soul in raising itself and approaching to Heaven. When a sudden inundation covers the lower story of a house, we mount to the second floor; and if the waters continue to increase, we climb even to the roof. Thus the good man who is afflicted in his flesh and in his senses, that is, the lower part of his soul, takes refuge as we may say in the upper part, where he finds peace, and the God of peace Himself: but he does not leave this lower part, unless tribulations attack him there; and as long as he abides there, he is a sensual man, constantly exposed to the temptations of the evil one, and in danger of perishing.

A man should consider that it is natural to him to love those things which gratify his sensuality; but that there are a thousand obstacles to hinder him from satisfying this violent passion, and thus he never enjoys solid peace. All is serene in the upper regions of the air; it is in the lower that thunderstorms and tempests are found. The true spring of peace is freedom of heart. Is it possible to conceive a greater blindness than that of the world, which makes it a rule to flee from all that causes pain? People desire to be well treated, well lodged, honoured and applauded in all things. Those who set up their rest in good things of this kind cannot be fully satisfied, because their joys are mixed with innumerable sorrows. Those, on the other hand, who despise them, and who love sufferings, have their minds calm even in the midst of affliction, by virtue of that grace which strengthens them. But it is to be observed, that in the enjoyment of this peace, which is the effect of a long habit of suffering, there are, as it were, three degrees of perfection; so that from the first we ascend to the second, and from the second to the third.

1. The first degree consists in receiving placidly all vexations here below; and this is called patience. The patient man, who is desirous only of imitating the Saviour, most willingly accepts poverty, sickness, the inconveniences of cold or of heat, persecutions,

and in general all things that are most hard and unendurable in life, for the love of the Cross alone, through a generous desire to crush in himself all self-love, whose ordinary nourishment is the delight of the senses.

In this the soul feels a pleasure which sweetens all bitterness, calms all uneasiness, and removes her natural repugnance to endure insults without excusing herself or accusing others. Thus she becomes hardened to sufferings, and is at last in such a state as no longer to apprehend present evils; being fully persuaded that they are sent her by God, and that He is pleased to try her patience, as He has done that of the Saints, without sparing even His own Son. She therefore resigns herself to the Divine Will, feels no impatience, abstains from all complaint, and thereby acquires a placid calmness, wherein consist true peace of mind. As for those who resist Grace, and rest on created things, they enjoy indeed some slight pleasure, but not perfect satisfaction, such as that of the lovers of the Cross, who, by accepting sufferings, raise themselves above sensible objects, in which the others think to find their blessedness on earth.

2. The second sort of peace obtained by those who learn to suffer, is no less sweet, but it is more firm and more constant than the former. It is a disposition of mind which abandons itself, and even takes pleasure in adversities, in humiliations, in sufferings, with humble submission to the Divine Will, and with the design of seeking conformity to Jesus' Suffering. When a man thus resolves upon patience, and can overcome the weakness of nature always averse to crosses, he feels within him a calm, a firmness of courage, a strength and a power able to resist persecutions, and the severest pains. He appears immoveable as a rock amidst the waves, and is never more firm than when he seems overcome, so that he may

say with the Apostle, *When I am weak, then am I strong.* 2 Cor. xii. 10.

This extraordinary strength proceeds from Grace, which endures all things, and which renders him so courageous, so eager for sufferings, that he says boldly to God, " Give me crosses, Lord, give me crosses; more, yet more; augment my toils, multiply my sorrows." His fervour arrives at such a pitch, that he cannot endure to live without suffering, and that when he does not suffer, he languishes like a man pressed and tormented by hunger; but directly God begins anew to afflict him, his strength and courage return, and he is vigorous as after repose. As soldiers, accustomed to a hard life, despise delicacies and comforts, so a generous spirit asks not for consolations, but rather for hard trials, and painful labours for the glory of Christ.

Those who desire to strengthen children, and to accustom them to fatigue, nourish them with plain food, occupy them in laborious exercises, and give them a horror of every thing approaching to effeminacy. So does God deal with those whom He destines to be instruments of His glory. He sends them afflictions, that suffering may become to them a custom and a pleasure; and when they are fully convinced of the great advantages of the Cross, He gives them such a taste of its fruits, that they cannot do otherwise than desire them, that they seek them eagerly, that they can never have enough of them, and find them wonderfully sweet and delicious. In this peace there is then not only sweetness but strength; and the man who obtains it becomes so fervent, that, like the Apostles, and many other Saints, he ardently desires to be ill-treated, outraged, persecuted even to death. Divine love is like a lamp, and the oil which maintains it is labour and suffering. The knowledge of the excellent fruits produced by the Cross, gives to lofty souls an insatiable desire for suffering, and a constancy in afflictions far greater than is shown by others amidst the pleasures of life. They must either "die or suffer," said St. Theresa.

The third sort of peace is a sublime and tranquil disposition of the soul which loses itself in God, and which finds in that Fountain of true pleasures satisfaction, a rest, which St. Paul calls *the peace of God, which passeth all understanding*, Phil. iv. 7, and which is found, neither in the good things of this world, nor in good things above this world, which are not the supreme Good ; a peace, in short, whose sole foundation is the joy of beholding the satisfaction of God ; a happiness incomparably greater than all sensible joys.

In this state man is most closely united with his Creator, and begins to live a heavenly and more than human life. From thence it often arises, that those who, in the extremest anguish, abandon themselves to the will of God without once swerving, however desolate they be, speak of the things of God in so lively, so animated, so touching a manner, that they give marvellous comfort to the most afflicted. That which gives so much energy to their words is, that their peace is in the higher part of their spirit, and depends not on the operations of their senses, either external or interior. It even happens sometimes, that though some of them, overwhelmed by the deepest melancholy, think themselves cast-aways, they do not cease to convert sinners, and to lead them efficaciously to love Him by Whom they think themselves abandoned. This comes not, and cannot come, from any sensible pleasure, for in the lower part of their soul there is nothing but gloom and sorrow. It can then proceed only from that peace which is above the reach of disquiet and of trouble.

But what is the cause of this perfect tranquillity ?

It is suffering; and we may venture to say, that the more the soul is afflicted to her inmost depths, the more her peace enlargeth, there being nothing which contributes more to establish it than privation of spiritual joys, inward desertion, and many other sufferings, which are the favours that God bestows upon His chosen friends. He is pleased truly to treat them as strangers and enemies, but it is only to teach them to trust all things to Him, and that dying to themselves, they may rest peacefully within His Heart, that lofty Heart[a], inaccessible to all sorrows, according to the words of the Prophet, *There shall no evil happen unto thee, neither shall any plague come nigh thy dwelling.* Ps. xci. 10. He offers them, then, His Heart as a place of refuge. There they dwell with Him, forgetting themselves, regarding Him alone, loving and desiring none but Him. There also is shed over all the powers of their soul a secret virtue, which so fortifies them, that no evil accident has power to shake them. "Lord," say they, "Thy will be done," and not ours; fearing nothing in this world but the anger of God. God alone acts on their will, and on their reason, He only has the key of their heart, and this is the cause that in the superior part of the soul they enjoy a peace which all created things together can never trouble.

CHAPTER IX.

(On these words)—" What is not savoury unto him, to whom Thou art pleasing ?" B. iii. c. 34.

QUESTION.—What is the way perfectly to enjoy God ?

[a] Ps. lxiv. 6. lxiii. 7. Vulg. Accedet homo ad cor altum.

ANSWER.—It is to have no pleasure in created things.

QUESTION.—How can we have a holy enjoyment of created things?

ANSWER.—By perfectly enjoying God. Rightly to comprehend this mystery, it must be understood that there are two sorts of pleasure to be found in creatures. The one low and imperfect, which serves only to satisfy nature; the other, excellent and elevated.

2. The first, quite opposed to the second, prevents a man from raising his heart to heaven. Therefore must he rid himself of it as an obstacle to true happiness, which consists in the enjoyment of the Supreme Good. One who has learnt to enjoy God, enjoys all things in God, as in their principle; so that the simple view and the pure love of that Uncreated and Infinite Good make him equally satisfied with all things, both bitter and sweet, that he sees, and that befall him in this life. This is what our Author expresses in these words, "He to whom all things are one, he who reduceth all things to one, and seeth all things in one, may enjoy a quiet mind, and remain peaceable in God." B. i. c. 3. What he says of sight may be applied also to enjoyment. It being thus impossible perfectly to enjoy God, without at the same time enjoying all things in God, we cannot be dissatisfied; for the general pleasure that is found in God raises the spirit, and detaches it from those particular objects which might cause vexation.

Those who offend in this matter, are those who desire certain employments only, who like some sorts of good works, and cannot endure others; who willingly undertake what is in accordance with their choice, and refuse all the rest. For if they have to do something contrary to their inclination, they cannot help showing annoyance. For instance, a Religious likes to dwell alone in his chamber; he studies there in peace, he has his regular hours, to which he has long been accustomed; he goes, at the sound of the bell, to take his repasts, which are neither highly flavoured nor rich, but which are sufficient for a man accustomed as he is to live frugally. It would be difficult to imagine that self-love could mingle here; and none assuredly can deny that the Religious would be far more to blame if he frequently left his monastery in order to be more at liberty. But after all, he may be attached to the life that he is leading; for if it is proposed to him to go and pass some time in the country among secular persons, on some occasion when he might render considerable service to God, or to a fellow-creature, for the love of God, he will feel repugnance to do so; he will say that there is nothing like living in community with his brethren; that amongst worldly people there is no order, and that, with his utmost endeavours, it will be impossible to have his regular hours and occupations. But if God is truly pleasing to him, he will not be hindered by this difficulty, especially if his vocation leads him to labour for the salvation of souls; for his whole pleasure will be to do what God demands of him.

St. Francis Xavier passed his life sometimes on sea, sometimes on land, most frequently among savages. What repose would he have had, what trouble would he not have endured, if he had suffered himself to be carried away by this false delicacy? But as he sought nothing but God, he found Him everywhere. Those who seek only their own will, and care for themselves alone, are incapable of that universal enjoyment which finds pleasure in all things. It also happens very often, that for want of knowing ourselves well, and examining our intentions, we feel a repugnance to certain things prescribed to us by obedience, without knowing, or to speak more correctly, choosing to know the cause, so much concealment and disguise do we use with ourselves. We find reasons to excuse ourselves, which are nothing but pretences; the true cause is self-love.

A man is sent to a place where it is thought that he may advance the glory of God. He cannot make up his mind to it, and excuses himself by saying that it would be an offence if he were seen among persons who do not make a regular profession, as he does.

Search the bottom of his heart, and you will see that what hinders him is, that he fears to find no comfort, and not to be honoured there, and that it is his interest only which attaches him elsewhere. A man is satisfied everywhere, and seeks himself in nothing, fears nothing, and desires nothing, when he takes pleasure in God.

QUESTION.—What are the means to obtain this universal enjoyment which leads us to find good in all things, and to be disheartened by nothing?

ANSWER.—There are three, of which the first is,

1. To free ourselves from all attachments to created things, to give our whole heart to God, not to dwell too much on the attractions of various things, but to turn away our eyes from them, as from things which strike us and deceive us at first sight. It is natural for a man when some employment is proposed to him, to look directly on its advantages, and to accept it with this view alone, that it is pleasing or honourable. These considerations are often in our mind, but there is nothing more contrary to perfection. We should desire nothing but to fulfil the will of the Lord; this is the only thing we ought to value, and we should but despise all besides.

2. The second means is, that when we have undertaken any affair, or engaged ourselves in some employment, and are happy enough to succeed, and

meet with applause, we must beware of giving way to a low and natural joy, which seems only to nourish pride. For we are apt to take a certain pleasure in it, which destroys that feeling of sweetness which we should find in general in all that proceeds from God. Our affections then must be given only to the service of our Lord; and in difficult cases we must do ourselves violence, and banish from our minds all thoughts besides.

3. Lastly, the third means is, that if we meet with bad success, and sadness seeks to take possession of our heart, we must try to prevent its entrance; so that for no temporal loss whatsoever we may ever sink into dejection, but may lift up our spirit to heaven: by faith we must enjoy God, and thus free ourselves from those sorrows which are commonly occasioned by misfortunes and losses; and after all, we must even be as well pleased as if we had lost nothing, either in reputation or in wealth. Those troubles, though slight, which bring with them dejection and uneasiness, are a great injury to the soul, for they render her incapable of rising from the earth, and drawing nigh to God; and therefore acting no longer with the design of pleasing God, she remains enslaved by creatures; ever disquieted, ever the captive of innumerable objects which share her love, and can but trouble her peace.

BOOK III.

CHAPTER I.

(On these words)—" Wheresoever thou findest thyself, renounce thyself [a]."

QUESTION.—When is it that a man finds himself?

ANSWER.—1. It is when he feels a secret inclination to seek himself, away from God. When some harsh or contemptuous word has been addressed to us, we feel in our hearts a movement of indignation excited by pride against the person who we think has offended us. Thence arise sentiments of aversion and bitterness, quite contrary to peace of mind, and then we find ourselves. For it is most evident that we are very sensitive to all that concerns ourselves, and that self-love is our ruling passion. A man truly dead to himself, on such an occasion, humbles himself, and abandons himself to the hands of the Lord; even considering the loss of his property and the diminution of his honour as great advantages.

2. There is also another way of finding ourselves, and that is, when we appear to be forgotten, and those from whom we expect some marks of kindness, neglect us, abandon us, and reserve their favours for others. Then regret at seeing ourselves forgotten

---

[a] The exact words have not been found, it is the substance of B. iii. c. 37. iv. 2.

The following passages are like it :—

" Learn in all things to overcome thyself." B. iii. c. 42.

" What do I require of thee more, than that thou study to resign thyself entirely to me?" B. iv. c. 8.

and despised, while others are objects of consideration, and overwhelmed with benefits; regret, I say, torments and distresses us. We feel bitterly the wrong that is done us, and cannot avoid mourning and lamenting over it. This is properly what is meant by finding ourselves, for it is regarding ourselves as something, and forgetting that in truth we are nothing. The things which present themselves to our eyes, in general move and attract us, when we hope to profit by them; but in this very thing it is evident that we find ourselves, since our inclination and attachment to these things is but one effect of the unregulated self-love which is natural to us.

3. There is a third and last manner of loving ourselves, quite different from the other two, and having nothing vicious; it is when we see ourselves menaced by some evil which we may reasonably avoid; as when we find a thing to be injurious to our health. In which case we do well to abstain from it, unless some important reason calls on us to risk all. But this is not seeking ourselves in the sense of our Author. We seek ourselves, and to our own loss find ourselves, when thinking ourselves unjustly attacked on some point which concerns our honour, or even our life; we resent it, and try to do ourselves justice, which can proceed only from an excess of self-love.

QUESTION.—When do we quit ourselves?

ANSWER.—When in the circumstances that we have mentioned, we always seek what is right, without any concern for ourselves, or regard for our own interests; and in order to do this three things are necessary.

1. The first is, to sacrifice to our Lord those resentments which arise sometimes from anger, sometimes from shame at seeing ourselves either despised or too

little esteemed. We sacrifice them, either for the love of God, or by the consideration of the shame of Jesus crucified. It is by such thoughts that we try to make appetite yield to reason, and nature to grace, whether by repressing those unregulated movements, which trouble our peace of mind, or by turning our thought elsewhere, or by suppressing it with a thought of greater power. Thus, when I am deserted and despised, I represent to myself the extreme contempt and desertion of the Saviour during His life and in His Passion; and this is like throwing water on the fire, or a great quantity of earth on a dead body, that this fatal and frightful object may be seen no more.

2. The second thing necessary to be done is, to commit all our interests and designs into the hands of our Lord. For innumerable things happen here below which we cannot foresee, and which give us pain, in which we commonly feel and show how far human weakness can go. A sovereign remedy against this evil, is to yield ourselves to the guidance of God, to trust in His infinite mercy, and to renounce all cares but that of obeying and pleasing Him. A wife, for instance, hears no news of her absent husband, and this disturbs her: let her resign herself entirely to the Divine Will, and her spirit will be at rest. To be free from all trouble, we must, in like manner, commit to the disposal of Providence, our honour, our health, and our life.

3. The third thing is, to apply ourselves to some exercise contrary to the inward inclination which, at the present time, torments the mind. If my inclination then leads me to pleasure and indulgence, if I am excessively careful of my body and of my health, I must perform some penance, in order to prove that I am resolved to overcome my flesh, to hold it in subjection, and never weakly to yield to it. If I feel some movement of pride and anger at being

neglected, I must seek for an opportunity of practising gentleness and humility, by doing some good office to the person who seems to despise me. Thus we may quit and renounce ourselves, not only by not following the movement of nature, too sensitive to the smallest mortifications, but by resolutely opposing it, and doing the very contrary. Thus we break all attachment to self, we get rid of self-love, that irreconcileable enemy of divine love, and whenever we feel too earnest a desire for our own interests, we resist it with all our might, neglecting nothing.

CHAPTER II.

(On these words)—"It is, therefore, no small matter for a man to forsake himself even in the smallest things." B. iii. c. 39.

QUESTION.—What are small things?

ANSWER.—They are of two kinds: the one small in appearance and great in effect; the other, small both in effect and in appearance. To these we might add those which appear great, but are, in truth, small. These last ordinarily cause great trouble to those timid and scrupulous minds which torment themselves about nothing.

But what are those which we call small both in appearance and effect? They are slight faults, whose principle is not very bad, or which, at least, cannot have very evil consequences.

There are others little in themselves, but considerable in their cause and in their effects. A thoughtless look does not appear a great evil, and yet it sometimes causes death and the everlasting destruction of the soul. A patch on the face of a young lady is nothing in itself, and yet it shows great vanity, and is sometimes a sign of great disorder.

To abstain from a curious look, to refuse ourselves some delicate morsel at a repast, appears very little, yet it is great when it is done with the design of mortifying ourselves after our Lord's example. It even shows a real desire for perfection; and we see, by experience, that those who, for the love of God, deprive themselves of many small things, have generally much virtue. This induced our Author to say, that "it is not little to renounce ourselves even on the smallest occasions."

Great holiness is required to be exact and constant in thus overcoming ourselves in the smallest things. One man gathers a flower and smells it innocently; another will not touch it; he prefers sacrificing to God the slight pleasure he would find in its odour. Blosius says, that the action of the one is as far removed from that of the other, as heaven from earth. We see, too, that the Saints who desire to live for God alone, refuse themselves all pleasures and conveniences which they believe unnecessary; and then the retrenchment of the smallest thing is very meritorious. In the life of Father Lessius, the Jesuit, we are surprised to find that when he writes to Father Olivier Manar, whom St. Ignatius had received and trained himself in the company, he asks him for instruction on very easy and well-known subjects connected with the spiritual life. If we judged of this simplicity according to the spirit of the world, we should ridicule it; but I consider that nothing can more plainly show the deep humility of this man, no less celebrated for his virtue than for his learning.

QUESTION.—Why do the Saints regard small things so much?

ANSWER.—This proceeds from the Spirit of God, by whom they act, and Who cannot permit in them any thing which does not originate in a virtuous

principle; and although, when He possesses the soul
which yields herself wholly to His guidance, He so
occupies all her powers, that He suffers not her attention to be divided amongst minute details; yet when
she has to labour for the acquirement of some particular virtue, He requires her to reflect on the smallest things; He makes her know that nothing must
be neglected, because all that depends on the human
will should be guided and sanctified by Grace. As
there is not a wheel in a watch which has not its own
use, and the want of a few teeth is enough to stop or
derange it; thus, in man, when all should conduce
to the glory of the Creator, it is necessary that the
smallest actions should be regulated; and none can
be neglected without the soul, which must give
account of all, suffering notable injury.

The consequence of this is, that when we care
little for things which appear inconsiderable, we are
in danger of greatly displeasing God, and even of
being great losers, as the wise man says: *He that despiseth little things, by little things shall he fall.* Eccles.
xix. 1. One of the first things necessary in order to
arrive at perfection, is to die entirely to self; and
therefore, all who truly aspire to it, gladly suffer
mortifications, and wage a constant war against self-love, fully persuaded, that to attach importance to
these small things, is not the sign of a weak mind,
but of a character of solid virtue. Thus do those
souls that are taught and guided by the Holy Spirit,
break through even their smallest attachments to
created things. " Forsake thyself perfectly, as well
in small things as in great. I except nothing, but
do desire that thou be found naked, and void of all
things." B. iii. c. 37.

CHAPTER III.

(On these words)—" That I may not feel myself." B. iii. c. 21.

QUESTION.—What is it to feel ourselves?
ANSWER.—It is to find satisfaction and pleasure in things which concern ourselves, and have no relation to God. There are three degrees of this fault.

1. The first is, that of those who take pleasure in considering and admiring themselves, who make the remembrance of their own good qualities their principal occupation, comfort, and support; who, when alone, can converse agreeably with themselves, never wanting a subject, since their own perfections, and the other good things of which they think themselves possessed, furnish them with enough. People of this character often reach such an excess of self-love, that not content with amusing themselves with this chimerical fancy, they are vain enough to make their own portraits, or, to speak more correctly, their eulogium; to paint themselves in bright colours, to note not only their virtues, but even the very features of their face, their figure, their complexion, and, in general, all things in themselves which they think deserving of praise, hoping thus to immortalize their memory. But what they succeed in showing more is, an extraordinary blindness, of which the very heathen would be ashamed; for, whereas, there is nothing more important or more glorious for them than to forget themselves entirely, and to think only of God, they make of themselves an idol which they carry everywhere, and show to their friends, thinking to attract adoration, where their pride generally does attract nothing but ridicule.

This method of proceeding shows three very considerable disorders. The first is, an indolence of mind, which, depriving them of all serious occupation, leaves them leisure enough to reflect on vain and ridiculous things, which reason alone ought to efface from their mind. The second, great presumption, with so high an idea of themselves, that infatuated with their own merits, they imagine that the whole world must be thinking of them, and acquainted with all their affairs. The third, a foolish itching desire to talk of themselves, and to make great boasting of things which people of common sense cannot hear without indignation and disgust. This exact consideration of our past life is never good, but when we desire to make a general confession; for then the penitent is obliged attentively to consider what may render him deserving of punishment in the sight of the Supreme Judge, and contemptible in his own. But to employ much time in searching out what is good in ourselves, is to be intoxicated with self-love, and to act in direct opposition to the teaching of the Saviour, Who said to His disciples, *If any man will come after Me, let him deny himself.* Matt. xvi. 24. It is precisely contrary to what our Author desired of God in these words, " Grant, Lord, that I may not feel myself;" as if he would say: " I desire, O my God, to be so occupied and filled with Thee, that I may feel no more what I am, but may live on the earth as if already in heaven."

St. Vincent Ferrier found in himself so little cause for vanity, that he looked on himself with horror, and was unendurable to himself. St. Ignatius wished after his death to be refused Christian burial. St. Catherine of Genoa said, that she would rather see a demon, however hideous, than herself in the state she was in. The Saints, by thus despising and annihilating themselves, obtained the enjoyment of God, while those who do otherwise, separate themselves from Him by their vanity, according to these words which our Author makes Him speak: "The more thou canst go out of thyself, so much the more wilt thou be able to enter into Me." B. iii. c. 56. To go out of ourselves, is to think not at all of ourselves, nor to speak of ourselves, except when we are obliged to do so, or when we are about to confess.

2. The second degree of the vice of which we speak, is somewhat less gross than the former; it is that of such people as approve of nothing which is not in accordance with their own ideas; like none but persons whose dispositions sympathize with their own, and avoid all others, unless they will accommodate themselves and yield to their ways. This is indeed being sensitive to what concerns themselves; it is also departing far from that perfection towards which he tends, who, our Author says, asks of God that he may cease to feel himself.

Some men love solitude, not because God calls them to it, but because they have an unsocial temper. A conversation which wearies them ever so little, is torture to them; the love of liberty overpowers all other feelings; they must live in their own way, and for an empire they would not constrain themselves. But, after all, their greatest torment is their capricious and wayward temper, which causes them to meet with endless vexations. Undoubtedly, they are a heavy burden to themselves, and must be conscious of it. A spiritual man does not delight in these self-willed methods of proceeding; he is satisfied with all, he accommodates himself to all, he has no attachment to his own ideas; but exactly follows the counsel that we gave in the 4th chapter of the 2nd Book, in explaining the words, "Presume not upon thyself."

The third degree of this vice is found in many persons who have acquired real virtue, but have not yet been able to overcome their natural feelings, and who suffer but too often from the injurious mixture of these human feelings with those wherewith God inspires them; in which they are far less happy than those devout souls that are entirely dead to themselves, and insensible to all their own concerns. God suffers this, and permits the weight of nature to drag them aside against their will for some time, that being not yet cleansed from the remains of their sins, they may acknowledge their own weakness, and mourn to see themselves so inclined to evil. They feel themselves, then, as a heavy burthen, under which they fear every instant to sink, whilst those who are full of God, feel Him alone, and think of nothing else. What is good in them is, that this mixture of feelings, high and low, natural and supernatural, is no longer to them, as in former days, a reason for relaxing, and a cause for self-love, but an exercise of patience and humility, which, far from turning them from God, leads them to sigh after Him, and to desire to enjoy nothing beside Him.

CHAPTER IV.

(On these words)—"If thou wouldst perfectly empty thyself from all creatures, Jesus would willingly dwell with thee." B. ii. c. 7.

QUESTION.—What is it that hinders the Saviour from dwelling in the soul?

ANSWER.—It is, that He does not find it perfectly emptied from all creatures. The greater number of those who profess to serve God, do not wholly renounce created things, and therefore Jesus cannot dwell with them.

QUESTION.—How does Christ dwell in the soul?

ANSWER.—Not only by habitual and sanctifying Grace, but also by a joy and a delightful feeling caused by His Divine Presence, which is greater or less, according to His different way of giving and applying Himself, so to speak, to the soul in which He takes up His abode. Sometimes He communicates Himself to her in such a manner as entirely to fill her, and then she is overflowing with joy, like a man who sees his coffers full of money, or one who comes forth well satisfied from a magnificent feast, or one who by some sudden good fortune has gained a large sum of money. If such a man thinks himself happy in the possession of good things which pass away, if he is fully content, shall not the soul which possesses Christ in the manner of which our Author speaks, and to which Christ unites Himself very closely, whether by the Holy Eucharist or by prayer, feel a like satisfaction? When I say a like satisfaction, I mean only one resembling it; for in truth there is no comparison between them.

This joy, this perfect satisfaction, produced by the immediate presence of our Lord, is not a favour common to all the just, nor, perhaps, even to all who have renounced the world, although they do not repent of having quitted it, and consecrated themselves for ever to God in the religious life. This gift is only for those who, by complete self-abnegation, and a general renunciation of all that is not God, and that does not tend to God, have perfectly emptied themselves of all creatures. It is to them that our Lord communicates Himself, He honours them with His familiar converse; with them He discourses confidentially and openly. He is their guide, their companion, their support, their counsel, their All; He fills them, satisfies them, rejoices all the powers of their soul, so that they possess and enjoy Him, not by seeing Him clearly, but in such a way as to feel Him within themselves, by a lively faith and ardent love.

QUESTION.—How must we renounce all creatures?
ANSWER.—Entirely, and in such manner, as to rest only on God and on what is in God, and to die to all beside. Few reach this high degree of perfection; and therefore there are but few who are free from all affection and attachment to created things. Let us take, for example, an Ecclesiastic, a Religious, in a great town, the capital of a great kingdom, where innumerable pleasing objects are presented to his eyes without need of his going far to seek them, where he exercises his functions with reputation, and where the first people follow him, hear, admire, and applaud him; he feels, in this, a true joy, which creeps into his soul without his perceiving that there is any thing wrong; for, after all, he is entirely occupied in ministrations which regard the glory of God, and the good of souls. But the heart enjoys this pleasure far more human than divine, and finds in it a nameless sweetness. It is easy to say that all is directed to God's glory; this is not said till after the man has contented himself, and given to nature the satisfaction it desires. Then, but too late, he lifts up his mind to God, and protests that he desires to serve Him, and to seek His Glory; as if that consisted in performing actions, good in themselves, with earthly views, and, as if the principal point were not to purify the heart from all love for worldly things, and to fill it wholly with God.

His most certain means of judging rightly whether

he is truly full of God, is to examine what would be his feelings if he were obliged to quit this pleasant abode and go into a village to catechize the peasants. Would he leave it willingly? And supposing that he could resolve to do so, would not the desire of returning and seeing once more those things which it pained him to quit, cause him fresh grief? If so, this is an evident sign that he has not yet perfectly renounced all. Some man may say perhaps, "I do not make this my great object." Granted; but you make it your satisfaction and your rest, and this must be carefully avoided.

See if you feel no repugnance to live in a poor and obscure place, where you will find none but God. But if you have virtue enough to prefer villages to the largest towns, think not that all is done. Perhaps in the most solitary place, if you do not love the inward life, you may find means of satisfying your self-love. Nothing more is needed to divert you than some curious study; the things that you have read will return to you continually, and your heart and mind will be full of them. A soul emptied of all creatures thinks only of the things of God; this is her whole pleasure; she thinks and acts only with the intention of pleasing the Lord.

After all, we would not condemn those outward employments which are suited to the vocation and the disposition of each individual. What we blame, is that natural satisfaction that is sought in them without any consideration of the Divine Will. Thus perfectly to empty ourselves of all things is difficult; but it is the cross of the true children of God, who, after many victories gained over themselves, and a long practice of mortification, at length obtain that God comes to dwell in them, occupies their whole soul, and fills them with such great joy, that they can neither rejoice nor repose but in Him.

CHAPTER V.

(On these words)—"Where shall one be found who is willing to serve God for nought?" B. ii. c. 2.

QUESTION.—Wherein consists this free and disinterested service that should be done to God?

ANSWER.—In a fixed intention to do those things which God requires of us, solely through the desire of pleasing Him, without any consideration of our own interests. Our Author speaks of this disinterestedness as very rare; for, although many people profess to serve God, they may be divided into three classes. Those who belong to the first do all with a view to their own good, their salvation, and their everlasting happiness. The second are gained by the loveliness of virtue, and by reason, which teaches them that the creature ought to obey the Creator. The third and last are actuated solely by the desire of pleasing God, of Whom they have so lofty a conception, that nothing but the consideration of His infinite greatness can move them. This consideration so animates, inflames, and strengthens them, that they need no other incitement to well doing than to know that there is a God infinitely good and infinitely gracious, and that His kindnesses to men proceed from unmixed love.

Saint Catherine of Genoa says, that the most perfect love is that which acts for God, without any thought of self: like that of God, Who loves us without expecting any thing from us. Thus a soul which has a pure love for God, like that of the blessed in heaven, has no thought of what she is to receive for serving Him; she does all that lies in her power, thinking of the great reward promised ; and in this there are, as it were, three degrees.

1. The first is, when a man has no attachment to health, life, honour, or repose, and leaves all to the disposal of Providence, without caring what may happen, or even seeking or desiring any thing but the honour of God. In this sense Saint Francis Xavier explained the Saviour's words : *He that loseth his life for My sake, shall find it.* Matt. x. 39. He considered that we should expose ourselves to all sorts of dangers, to shipwreck, torture, death itself, without once reflecting that we hazard all.

2. The second degree is, when he appears to neglect even the gifts of grace and the merit of his good works ; that is, when he throws himself entirely on the goodness of God, and thinks not at all of them ; not through contempt, but because being resolved to think henceforth of God Alone, and to forget himself, his mind does not dwell on the rewards of God's service, nor does he make this either a subject of rejoicing or a ground of obedience. It is not, however, to be imagined that these spiritual advantages are really neglected : on the contrary, he is careful of them, and omits nothing to preserve and increase them ; but not for his private interest ; he has no other object than to please the Lord ; and the soul which regards him as her spouse, loves Him with a love at once so tender and so noble, that all the desires and emotions of her heart are only directed to please Him ; and she finds this the most powerful motive to all her good works.

3. The highest degree is when he leaves in the hands of God even his everlasting salvation ; troubled about nothing ; neither seeking nor desiring to know any thing more than God is pleased to reveal ; because he loves Him Alone, and disinterestedly. This is not a blameworthy and presumptuous sentiment, failing

in conformity with those of the greatest saints who dreaded the judgments of God, or opposed to the saying of the Saviour: *I will forewarn you Whom ye shall fear.* Luke xii. 5. All that it seeks is to fulfil the first and great commandment, *Thou shalt love the Lord thy God with all thy heart, and with all thy soul, and with all thy mind.* Luke x. 27. *Perfect love*, says Saint John, *casteth out fear.* For he who fears thinks of himself, and of the evils which menace him. Such thoughts are not useless; they are good, and must be made use of in time of need; because man, being frail by nature, must make use of all that can aid in guarding him from sin. But when the soul is perfectly free, she desires God Alone; and the love with which she burns inspires her with so much confidence, that nothing is capable of causing her fear.

This has led many Saints to say surprising things. St. Theresa declared that she had no fear of death, because she knew that in dying she should fall into the hands of Him Whom she loved the best. Another Saint, carrying in one hand a torch, and in the other a pitcher of water, said that she desired with the one to burn Heaven, and with the other to extinguish the flames of hell, that she might think no more but of love, and that henceforth she might serve God for His goodness only. St. Ignatius, the founder of the company of Jesus, once said, that if he saw heaven opened, and it depended only on himself to enter, and God proposed to him to remain still on earth to render some considerable service to His Divine Majesty, at the risk of perishing himself, he would not hesitate an instant to take this latter portion, and to hazard all, rather than to lose so good an opportunity of giving glory to God.

For myself, I am fully persuaded that one who loved our Lord perfectly would willingly renounce all the glories of paradise, for a time at least, for the smallest interest of Him to Whom he owes all. Those who burn with the pure and ardent fire of divine love, leave to God the decision of their everlasting happiness or misery; they leave their lot to Him; and so repose on Him, that they take thought for nothing but how to do His most Holy Will. But where shall we find these men dead to themselves, attached only to Heaven, and having continually in view "the greater service of God," as St. Ignatius says? We may venture to say that they are rare; for there are few sufficiently mortified to prefer the glory of God in all things to their own honour, their own life, and all perishing things.

The true way to reach this lofty state is to forget ourselves, and at the same time to forget all that concerns our comfort, our reputation, and our repose; that, whatever happens, we may sanctify all things by referring them to God through simple love. This cannot be done but by a long habit of renouncing self, by protesting to God frequently that we desire nothing besides Him, and never suffering ourselves to be carried away by delight, for all the praises of man, nor for all the prosperity and wealth of the earth.

Some who pass for spiritual persons, and who make a profession of being so, both think and speak like perfect men; but their intentions are not pure, and human nature mingles largely in them. If they are going, for instance, to some place to labour for the salvation of souls, they begin directly to think that they are known there; that they have made friends; that they are esteemed, and apparently will meet with success there. This thought rejoices and encourages them; whereas they should love only the Cross, humiliation, and contempt, attach themselves solely to God, rejoice only in seeing Him glorified; and if praise is offered to them, they should return it to Him without taking any share, without desiring to enjoy the gratification found in it, which so delights the proud spirit.

CHAPTER VI.

(On these words)—" If thou seekest thyself, thou shalt also find thyself." B. ii. c. 7.

QUESTION.—What is it to seek ourselves?

ANSWER.—Nothing else, as I have said many times, than to seek our own interests, low and earthly interests, which have no connexion with those of God. Thus the greater number of those fickle souls that are still possessed by a worldly spirit, and know not what it is to aim at perfection, find no pleasure but in such things as flatter the senses. The excessive love of enjoyment makes them employ themselves in seeking the vain pleasures of this world, and renders them incapable of finding satisfaction in any thing else.

QUESTION.—What is it to find ourselves?

ANSWER.—It is to feel our poverty and wretchedness, as is the case with those who, passionately loving pleasure, and finding no true comfort away from God, meet with deserved punishment for their endeavours to find some satisfaction in creatures; for, after much useless trouble, they find nothing of what they desire, any more than those who seek for water to refresh themselves in a dry and sandy place. Men, born with a desire for true happiness, and thinking to find it without going out of themselves, discover their self-deception at last; and nothing remains to them but the vexation of seeing that, instead of a real good which they sought, they have found a false good, a feeble empty creature, incapable of satisfying them. What do they find then in themselves, if they seek not to find God there? Three things fitted to make them unhappy, —hardness, bitterness, and indigence. Hardness deprives them of repose; bitterness, of pleasure; indigence, of the means to fill and satisfy themselves.

It is natural for men to love peace, pleasure, and abundance; and those who are full of God possess all these things in Him as in the source and fulness of all good; but as for those who are so blinded and governed by passion, that, instead of seeking God in themselves, they seek themselves in all things, they gain only some apparent good, and suffer immediately from the three evils of which we have spoken, the first of which is hardness.

A man who likes to live in peace, delights in a place where nothing interrupts or troubles his repose. He is like a traveller oppressed with weariness and slumber, who requires a good bed to sleep softly. All is uneasy to one who seeks rest in himself, and not in God. Thus thought St. Augustine, who said, "Lord, there is no rest but in Thee, and all beside Thee is hard." When we have extracted all the juice of a plant, there remains only the pith, which is hard and dry. In like manner, when God is no longer in a soul, we may say that she has lost all goodness, she becomes dry, and almost wholly useless; there remains to her only her own nothingness, into which she falls once more, as soon as she leaves Him Who sustained her.

Thence arise a thousand troubles; above all when the things which she loved passionately, and in which she had set up her rest, are taken away from her. For then, seeing herself deprived of all support and of all sensible joy, she mourns and weeps inconsolably.

In this state she finds the truth of St. Augustine's saying, that away from God all is thorny, and it is impossible to move without being wounded. When a man who trusts in the favour and protection of a prince falls into disgrace, it is very hard for him to have nothing to rest on but himself, being deprived of all succour and support. For what can he find in himself, who has nothing, and can have nothing but by the assistance of the creatures that surround him, or by the mercy of God, Who will be pleased to dwell in him if he offers himself to receive Him? If both God and creatures fail him, he has no resource, and is like a man in an unfurnished house, with no other bed than the earth.

2. But after all, what does he who seeks himself find in himself? No sweetness, and much bitterness. Aristotle says, that meat should have a pleasant taste, and experience shows plainly that none like bitter food. Now bitterness is the portion of those who, instead of seeking God, seek themselves. A lady, for instance, is in company with people of high rank. If it is for some good work, she will go away contented; but if it is to show herself, to acquire esteem, she will carry away nothing but shame; for God will permit some contemptuous word to be addressed to her, or will suffer her to say something unseasonable, which will amuse the company. Thus she will return home covered with confusion. What can be more mortifying to one whose ruling passion is vain-glory? But whence comes her vexation? From self-seeking, and from the pride which possesses her, and which is a source of bitterness; for this word spoken imprudently by herself, or that addressed her with a disdainful air, or in a mocking tone, returns continually to her mind; it is a sting in her heart, which wounds her to the quick, and often brings tears into her eyes.

This weakness is common to all who are full of

self-love. A man who has to speak in public, or who loves to be applauded, is always in danger of drawing down vexation on himself; for if he does not succeed, or another succeeds better than he, it causes him much sorrow; whereas, if he looked only to the glory of our Lord, his spirit would be at rest. It is certain then that they who seek themselves find themselves at length, but to their own harm; and nothing torments them more than their own vanity. How unhappy are the ambitious, the avaricious, the voluptuous! They have always some wound in the soul, some bitterness in the heart; for if they succeed once, they fail a hundred times. And this is all that is gained by those who seek and find themselves, for in themselves they find nothing but vices and sins whose root is equally bitter with their fruits. Some are always sad, always in ill-humour, always sunk in deep melancholy. This is only to be attributed to self-seeking. The great advantage of perfect virtue is, that it quits itself, and is lost in God.

3. There is yet a third trouble which befals the unmortified, and that is indigence. The heart desires to be filled, it fears nothing so much as emptiness, and this leads it ardently to desire the possession of something capable of fully satisfying it. It is hard for a traveller to find nothing after having wearied himself the whole day. Something like this happens to these lovers of self; for remaining separated from God, and unable to obtain from Him refreshment or nourishment, they find themselves alone, and, as it were, in a barren and desert land; for there is nothing more naked or more poor than man, who cannot be filled with self, except as animals are filled with wind. But in God we find all. Wisdom is an inexhaustible treasure; and what is wisdom but God Himself, possessed and enjoyed by the soul? *Riches and honour are with Me,* says she, *yea, durable riches and*

righteousness. Prov. viii. 10. One who belongs wholly to God cannot fail to be very happy, for he possesses God by all the faculties of his soul, chiefly by the understanding and the will, which nothing created can fully satisfy. Besides, God is pleased to enrich with His gifts those who seek Him. He gives Himself to them under the appearance of food, because they need nourishment to live; He serves them in some manner for raiment and abode. He is their treasure, and in Him they have a source of light, and of those joys which make the whole happiness of the pure in spirit here below.

If a man seeks not the Supreme Good, but has temporal advantages in view, what will he then obtain? Nothing but inward suffering, vain imaginations, evil habits, everlasting poverty and hunger. The worldly labour vainly to find something capable of satisfying them. They desire good; but they seek it on earth, and it is in Heaven. If they sought it where it is to be found, if they thought only of loving and serving God, He would give Himself to them, and they would be abundantly satisfied; but, seeing them attached to their own interests, He leaves them in want; thus they die poor and famished. There are none in truth so ill provided for, as those who seek themselves; while, on the other hand, there are none so well rewarded or so rich, as those who renounce self to devote themselves wholly to God.

CHAPTER VII.

(On these words)—" If thou dost more rely upon thine own reason or industry, than upon that power which brings thee under the obedience of Jesus Christ, it will be long before thou become illuminated." B. i. c. 14.

QUESTION.—What man is illuminated from above?

ANSWER.—He who knows truth in its origin, and not by its effects alone. He who has the true light in himself, differs widely from those who have it only by communication or reflection. For although the latter are neither ignorant nor misjudging, with regard to the truth, yet they know it only through the instruction of such as are directly taught of God, and see things as they are, without obscurity, without clouds, without those false lights and human interpretations which illumine them on one side, and darken them on the other.

The purest light is that which God communicates to the humble spirit in prayer. And it has this advantage, that it bears in itself the testimony of what it is, and makes itself known; so that those who receive it, though they are not obstinate, but humble, docile, and obedient in all things to their Director, are yet so firm in their belief of the things thus discovered to them, that it is impossible for them to doubt, so fully have they the air and the character of truths emanating from above. By means of this Divine Light, which is a ray of the Eternal Wisdom, the soul knows all that concerns her salvation, and the practice of the Christian virtues, and sometimes even many things simply moral and natural. This light is also a great assistance to her in all her doubts, whether with regard to her own conduct or to that of others; and having this, we may say of that soul that she is truly illuminated.

QUESTION.—What are the things which can render her unworthy of this heavenly light?

ANSWER.—In the first place, vice and sin, self-love, and all disorderly passions. But we are not now considering these things; we are considering only the hindrances to which even spiritual persons are subject. Our Author says, that the thing which deprives them of the true light is, that they trust too much in their own weak reason.

There are some people of good intention and true virtue, who yet put much trust in knowledge acquired by great application and profound meditations on the mysteries of religion. God being pleased to illuminate their minds with regard to these things, because after all they desire His glory, they value this kind of learning so highly, that they think it impossible to imagine anything better. But it is certain, nevertheless, that the purest light of God is that which He communicates to His perfect servants; and this is not the fruit of study and speculation, good as they are at the beginning, it is an effect of Divine Grace and Illumination, received in prayer and in the other exercises of the inward life. The Book of the Imitation of Christ is full of this doctrine. It repeatedly points out the difference between the wisdom of one illuminated from Heaven, and the knowledge of a man of letters. It attributes the latter to the man himself, the former to God alone; and says, that in one instant God raises up the humble mind to understand more of eternal truth, than if one had studied ten years in the schools[a].

Yet are there many people possessed of great learning, and in many respects deserving of praise, who are so fond of their own ideas, that all which does not agree with them appears to them doubtful or insignificant. In truth, the Saints were far better instructed in spiritual things by the light infused into them, than we can be by long and painful meditations. I do not deny that it is good to reason about the truths of the faith, nor that learning is very useful: reasoning and reflection are most necessary to beginners, and in times of dryness. St. Theresa

[a] B. iii. c. 43.

says still more: she says that not only beginners, but those who have made some progress, and even the most perfect, have need of them.

Yet the masters of the spiritual life are agreed, and this Saint often says, that the supernatural light which comes by contemplation is preferable to that which comes by study and by discourse. Those, then, who value reasoning more highly than these illuminations with which God favours the greatest Saints, and which are of free grace, will never be perfectly enlightened; for, whatever advantage they may obtain from human reasonings, they should fix it firmly in their mind, that that which comes immediately from God is far better, proceeding simply from Grace, and that in truth it is by contemplation that we learn to know the Truth in itself.

QUESTION.—How can we obtain this Divine Light which is so useful to the soul?

ANSWER.—By means of virtue, which brings the soul into subjection to Christ, as our Author says, and as he expresses still better in another place, where he says that all our knowledge must pass through the fire of Divine Love, and be purified thereby. St. Paul, speaking of that love which unites us to Christ, declares that it *passeth knowledge.* Eph. iii. 19. By love, then, we must submit our understanding to our Divine Master, so that love may apply and sanctify our learning.

There are two ways to fill ourselves with supernatural light. The one is to learn by meditation, and by reading many things which remain impressed on the memory: the other to instruct the understanding through a will attached to God by humble and ardent love. The latter is neither natural nor common, and it is not by this way that man ordinarily and directly attains to the knowledge of

Divine things; but when he has once entered it, the love with which he burns, which is all fire, illuminates his understanding, and fills him with sublime knowledge. It was thus that St. Bonaventure and St. Thomas became more learned at the foot of the Cross[a] than by the study of the Fathers.

What our Author means, then, is, that a man who trusts in the powers of his mind and of his reasoning, will never be illuminated from above, or that it will be long before he is so; and that the only means of being so quickly is to subject his reason to the grace of Christ, Who will bring it into the light of the Saints, according to these words: " Far more noble is that learning which floweth from above, from the Divine influence, than that which is painfully gotten by the wit of man." B. iii. c. 31.

QUESTION.—Wherein consists the practice of this doctrine?

ANSWER.—In three things; 1st, We must be persuaded that, though study is useful, we profit far more by the Divine Illumination than by our own labour. This thought will produce in the soul a great contempt and extreme distrust of her own wisdom,— a matter in which those who think they know all offend greatly.

2nd. We must humble ourselves, whether in prayer or in study, and yield our own knowledge to that which comes from Heaven. By thus abasing itself before God, far from the mind being weakened and made less fit for learning, it becomes, on the contrary, more quick and more penetrating.

3rd. Whatever progress we make in learning, we must accustom ourselves to make all an offering to the Divine Wisdom, and believe that to It we owe the knowledge, not only of supernatural things, but

[a] Du Crucifix.

of every truth whatsoever. Moreover, we must beware of ever giving too much liberty to our spirit, but keep it in continual dependance on Grace, that we may do those things on the principle of the love of God. Thus we shall become spiritual; we shall apply ourselves to the study of human learning, without losing the spirit of Grace, which must be ever preserved, after the example of the Fathers and Doctors of the Church, and of many great persons of these latter days, such as the Cardinals Baronius and Bellarmin, and innumerable others no less illustrious for sanctity than learning.

CHAPTER VIII.

(On these words)—" A true lover of Christ, and a diligent follower of virtue, does not fall back on comforts, nor seek such sensible sweetnesses." B. ii. c. 9.

QUESTION.—What is it to fall back on comforts?

ANSWER.—Not to receive comforts, but ardently to seek them, and to rest in them; to act like a man pressed with hunger, who throws himself on his food, and is not master of his appetite. We will explain how this is done.

A man truly spiritual, and strongly attached to the Divine Will, in whatever necessity he finds himself, and whatever favours he receives from Heaven, finds support only in virtue, and does nothing but what God requires of him, persuaded that to do otherwise would be to seek himself, and not God. But if, through natural inconstancy or violent temptation, he quits that support, and falls from the high state of perfection at which he had arrived, he must necessarily sink to the earth. If he remains firm, being supported by love alone, he tries to desire nothing but God, renouncing his own interest, and even all the comforts and spiritual joys that the Holy Spirit pours on his soul.

Not that he rejects them, unless he is strongly drawn and inspired to do so. He knows that there are occasions on which they are necessary, or at least useful, to enable him to love and enjoy God more; but he comports himself so wisely, and depends so little on these comforts and sensible joys, that when he is entirely destitute of them, he still preserves great evenness of spirit, and is never cast down or dejected but when he feels his own fervour diminish; for then, fearing to fail in fidelity towards God, he trembles, mourns, and implores aid from above with his whole heart.

On the contrary, a lukewarm and imperfect man, who knows not what is meant by simple love, feasts himself on these passing pleasures; and if God tries him as He tries His most beloved, he is afflicted, uneasy, and troubled. Unable to endure, he sighs for that which he regards as his only refuge, his supreme good. But when our Lord sees fit to comfort him by a fresh visit, immediately he forgets himself, because his great object is not to please God, but to satisfy himself. He thinks only of enjoying the pleasure that he receives from sensible comfort: on that he dwells and reposes himself; instead of imitating those holy persons who, when filled with spiritual joy, and favoured with the gift of tears, hardly bestow a thought on it, or think of it only sufficiently to give thanks to the Divine Goodness, because they go straight to God, and seek only to do His pleasure in all things.

QUESTION.—How is this done?

ANSWER. By lifting up the spirit to God in such manner as to love Him Alone, and only for Himself. To this disinterested love leads us; and when we have arrived at it, we offer ourselves courageously for all sorts of sufferings and labours; we even desire them, and wish ardently for nothing but to render God some considerable service for the motive of love alone, in which consists true integrity of heart.

When a soul is not yet fully detached from the earth, her natural weight, joined to her evil habits, hinders her from rising, and attracts her towards herself; so that she likes no place where she does not find her own comfort and advantage: she seizes upon things which please her, and in them sets up her rest. Thus those things which God has given her to be used as means of salvation, become the instruments of her ruin [a]; whereas, if she were disengaged from all earthly affections, she would look to God Alone; she would love none but Him; she would rejoice in no other; she would receive and use His gifts without attaching her affections to them.

This is difficult to practise, and of a great perfection; for perfection consists in this, that the soul, looking simply to God, not only gives the preference to the Creator over all creatures in her esteem, but in truth wishes and desires nothing but Him; has no other care than to be faithful to Him, and passes through visible things without delaying till she reaches that Divine Object, and begins to taste the ineffable delights of simple love. One who has thus learned not to look superficially on God, but, if I may dare to say so, to look into His depths, does not suffer himself to be carried away by excessive joy when comforts come; he remains firm, and is at all times equal: unlike the feeble and imperfect, who think rather of enjoying the benefits of God than God Himself.

This pure and disinterested love is not difficult to

---

[a] Ps. lxix. 23.

obtain, when we have acquired true poverty of spirit; for then we may enjoy all blessings and pleasures, whether natural or supernatural, that are given by God and approved by reason. We can make use of them without any diminution of Divine Love, which is but inflamed when we use them rightly; for in this case we lose nothing of that perfect indifference which we ought to feel with regard to the good things and joys of this life; we are no less insensible to them than if we were already dead; and at the very time that we are enjoying them, we are quite ready to renounce them. We always prefer the Cross and shame to glory and pleasure, in the hope that by this means we shall be more closely united to the Saviour, for Whom Alone we feel esteem, attachment, and love.

CHAPTER IX.

(On these words)—" O happy minds and blessed souls, who have the privilege of receiving Thee, their Lord God, with devout affection, and in so receiving Thee are permitted to be full of spiritual joy!"

" O how great a Lord do they entertain! how beloved a Guest do they harbour! how delightful a Companion do they receive! how faithful a Friend do they welcome! how lovely and noble a Spouse do they embrace!" B. iv. c. 3.

QUESTION.—What are the offices that our Lord exercises with regard to the just in the Eucharist?

ANSWER.—The four which our Author has noted. Jesus is, then, in this Sacrament, our Guest, our Companion, our Friend, and our Spouse. But it must be understood, that we do not now speak of the common effect that He operates in all the just, but of a particular effect which He produces in those whom He honours with His familiar intercourse. For although all the just being in a state of grace receive Him worthily, and He fulfils in them all the functions of a Guest, a Companion, a Friend, and a Spouse, it is yet true that those sanctified spirits that have the privilege of discoursing familiarly with Him, feel His presence in a singular way, of which others are incapable. They feel that He is present with them as a Guest Who has taken up His abode in them, and will go forth no more; as a Companion Who converses sweetly and continually with them; as a Friend Who ceases not to load them with benefits; as a Spouse Who embraces them tenderly, and lavishes on them a thousand endearments.

We have said elsewhere that the true happiness of this life consists in the union of the soul with God by simple love: this takes place whenever God wills it, but especially in the Communion, wherein, as was said by a great theologian, the spiritual marriage is completed.

1. We say, then, that the soul which attains in the blessed Sacrament to be united with Christ, not merely by Faith, but by a living Faith; a Faith so enlightened, that she believes she sees the Divine Guest Who abides within her, this soul participates, as far as is possible, in the happiness of the Saints who see Him openly in Heaven. She feels that He is truly in her, and this experimental knowledge of Him causes her such joy as not only fills all her powers, but overflows, and penetrates her very substance. Thus she feels the truth of that promise of the Saviour, *I will manifest Myself to him that loveth Me.* John xiv. 21. She has such convincing proof of it as to cry out with assurance, God is with me, Jesus is in me. And this proceeds from what our Saviour has also told us; *He that eateth My Flesh, and drinketh My Blood, dwelleth in Me, and I in Him.* John vi. 56. Would it be possible to have

a surer pledge of the presence of the God of mercy and love? She sees at last how truly He said, *We will come unto him, and make Our abode with him.* John xiv. 23. He comes, He abides; and by the grace of the Sacrament He unites Himself to the soul in such manner, that if He were not in all the rest of the world, He would dwell in her. Therefore our Author exclaims, "O how beloved a Guest do they harbour!"

2. But it is not only as a Guest that the soul receives Him, she possesses Him also as a Companion; and this is a favour which all men may hope for in this Sacrament, if they use It rightly. Those whom our Lord thus admits to familiar intercourse, not only have Him within them, but enjoy His conversation, and are in close fellowship with Him; a blessing which St. John wishes to all Christians, when he conjures them to lead such holy lives, that their fellowship may be *with the Father, and with His Son Jesus Christ.* 1 John i. 3. Thus they have always One to converse with, One to Whom they may unburthen their hearts, and Whom they may consult in their doubts; they are never alone, but always in the most pleasing and delightful company possible; they discourse familiarly with Christ; and in this sweet communion, weariness is impossible, because He is ever teaching them something new, or giving them fresh illumination on the same subject; and, in short, He so fills them with light, that they are able to dispense it to others.

It is then that they feel the streams of grace flowing in their hearts, and that they drink with pleasure of that excellent water "that springeth up into everlasting life[a]." It is then, also, that having lost their former thirst for temporal blessings, they think only of obtaining union with the Eternal Wisdom Who

[a] John iv. 14.

gives Himself to them with abundance of good gifts in the Eucharist. After this, what wonder is it that, having such a Companion Who never leaves them, they are always glad and perfectly happy? For if He sometimes hides Himself to try them, it is only to return again with a delightful surprise; it is only to make them feel His presence more than ever, by new and unhoped-for kindnesses; it is only, in a word, to restore to them that joy of which His absence deprived them, and to bring them into such a state that they may hope to lose sight of Him no more.

3. Moreover, He is not only their Guest and Companion, He is also their Friend, and in this quality He so gives Himself to them, that, not satisfied with conversing familiarly with them, He assists them in their necessities, He loads them with benefits, and through His extreme love, imparts to them the merits of His Death, communicates to them His Wisdom, and applies to them His Virtues.

4. But when to these tokens of friendship He joins the caresses of a Spouse, then the soul, wholly inflamed, and transported with love, feels within herself things that she cannot tell, and will communicate to none. These are, as it were, the kisses of the Divine Lover, of which St. Bernard says, that it is vain to ask what they are, because experience alone can make them known, and because the loving-kindnesses of God are proportioned to His Infinite Greatness. When Ahasuerus leaps from his throne to take Esther in his arms, who faints at beholding the great splendour with which his majesty is surrounded, when he calls her his sister, and comforts her, she falls into another kind of swoon, occasioned by love, not slighter than the former, but accompanied with unspeakable delight[a]. Thus some of the devout,

---
[a] Esther xv. 7—16. Vulg.

after receiving the Body of the Saviour, lose the use of their senses, are ravished and out of themselves, and, as it were, absorbed in God, and in this extasy they hear Him say things that no tongue can express.

It is then that the Celestial Spouse shows them kindnesses which may, in some measure, be called infinite; for although man has a very limited existence, we may say, that by means of the intimate alliance which he contracts with the Lamb of God in the Eucharist, there is formed in Him something incomprehensible, and surpassing all created beings.

But who will be found worthy to share this favour? We have said it often; he who has courage to deprive himself of all things for the love of God; he who quits, either in deed, or in will and affection, all that he possesses, and who renounces not only temporal but also spiritual blessings, and, in general, all things but God. This perfect deprivation prepares the soul to receive God, and to be transformed into Him. A man who is attached to a thing of no importance, though he is ready to part with all the rest, is as far below another who despises this trifle, and who has no attachment whatever, as the finite is below the infinite; at least with regard to the consequence: for though a created being is very limited in himself, he is not so in his desires; and when he is able to desire nothing, he becomes capable of receiving infinite good.

I own that for a small thing God does not absolutely break with us, yet we do not enjoy His blessings in all their fulness; He does not visit us, He does not draw us to Him; and we remain ever afar off from Him, unless He prevents us with His Grace, and we then oblige Him to draw near to us, by denying ourselves every thing, and banishing from our heart all affection for created things. This general self-denial is the way that it is necessary to take to arrive at the state of which we speak. And the cause why our Author says that there are so few contemplative men to be found is, that there are few who can wholly withdraw themselves from things created and perishing [a]. Not that it is required that they should quit the world, to confine themselves to a desert, or to a cloister; it is enough if they withdraw their affection and interest from it, desiring and seeking nothing but God.

If I were asked then, why of so many who consecrate themselves to the service of our Lord, so few are seen to arrive at a high degree of sanctity, I could easily reply to this question, and I would take my answer first from the Gospel, where the Saviour says: *If any man will come after Me, let him deny himself*, Matt. xvi. 24; and, secondly, from our Author, who says, that rarely is any one found so spiritual as to be stript of the love of all earthly things [b], and that there are few who put their whole trust in God, and study not to provide for themselves [c].

God desires sincerely and efficaciously, not only to save man, but to cause man to unite himself to Him by love. But the disproportion between them renders this union difficult. Man is little, and God is great; man is low, and God is lofty; man is impure, and God is holy. Thus God and man are directly opposed. To remove this opposition, man must make such good use of the liberty of God, that loving Him with his whole heart, he may prefer Him to all besides, not merely by speculative opinion, but by an effectual attachment of the will leading him truly to value only God, and that which comes from God. But because most frequently people value creatures, and think to find satisfaction in them, they do not give their whole heart to God,

[a] B. iii. c. 31. [b] B. ii. c. 2. [c] B. iii. c. 37.

and this it is that prevents Him from uniting Himself with man.

Let us conclude the whole discourse with the words of our Author. "For a long while shall he be small, and lie grovelling below, whoever he be, that esteemeth any thing great, but the One only Infinite Eternal Good." And he adds, "Whatsoever is not God is nothing, and ought to be accounted as nothing." B. iii. c. 31. On this is founded the whole of the spiritual life; and because few are convinced of this, there are few Saints. For if every individual were persuaded that there is nothing great in this world, nothing estimable but God and the will of God, they would think only of pleasing Him, and would try in all things to obey Him. But people prefer to yield to the low inclinations of their corrupt nature, and do not walk by the bright light of faith. Thus they cannot be united with God; they are excluded from familiar intercourse with Him; they cannot enjoy in the Eucharist that sweetness which the great Saints found in it. But when we know how to put in practice the fundamental maxim which has been explained, immediately God draws near, and brings back light; afterwards He pours out on the soul His treasures, which He does not give to those who love the good things of this world, and who say, in their extreme ignorance, that the just are rewarded in Heaven, but not on earth: for although this is true of glory and perfect blessedness, it is not so of the delights of Divine love, which make the happiness of the kingdom of God upon earth.

BOOK IV.

CHAPTER I.

(On these words)—"For a long while shall he be small, and lie grovelling below, whoever he be, that esteemeth any thing great but the One only Infinite Eternal Good." B. iii. c. 31.

QUESTION.—Wherein consists true greatness?

ANSWER.—In approaching as closely as possible to God: for God alone being truly great, and the origin of all greatness, if there is anything in man deserving of esteem, it is the resemblance and relation which he may bear to God. We desire, then, to know how man must approach to God, in order to become great; for, amongst many people who embrace virtue, very few are seen to rise from their low estate to any eminent perfection. Most of the servants of God find great difficulty in renouncing creatures, and totally forgetting themselves. Now he is small, according to our Author, who esteemeth any thing great that is less than God.

That which causes us to love God feebly, and to show incredible littleness of mind and heart in His service, is, that we do not know Him sufficiently to desire to be His Alone. Those who have true greatness of soul are persuaded that God is all, and that all that is not God is nothing. Every man protests that he firmly believes this truth, and that he is ready to sign it with his blood, if necessary;

but the many who say so are very far from showing by their works that they are perfectly convinced of it. Let us see, then, in what manner we must believe that God is all, and that the rest is nothing: let us see afterwards what we must do when we are persuaded of it, and how far we must go in order to become great, in such a manner as to acquire that most glorious union with God.

This sort of greatness consists in this, that the man who has conceived a high idea of the Divine Majesty thinks nothing important which does not bear some relation to the will of God or to His glory; consequently he sets no value on any thing human, however great, however lofty it appears, since it is but a created thing; therefore he proposes no design to himself, moves not his foot, writes not a single letter; in a word, does nothing with reflection and deliberate purpose which does not bear some immediate relation to God, or to God's service. If this were thoroughly understood, nothing more would be wanting to raise man to a high degree of virtue. Such are the sentiments of our Author, as may be seen at book iii. chapter 31, from whence I have taken the words which I have placed at the head of this discourse.

In fact, one who is too eager, who speaks or acts precipitately, who does not detach himself from all human interests, who likes to gratify himself, though he avoids the grosser faults; such a man, I say, has a low mind, and only crawls on the earth; his thoughts do not ascend to Heaven; he is subject to a thousand weaknesses, which keep him far off from the sublime perfections of the children of God, whose only care is to tend continually upward, and to be doing so every instant of their life. This is true greatness: a man is great when he suffers in himself nothing abject or earthly; when walking in the presence of God, he deems it unworthy of himself to think of anything besides Him.

This doctrine appears impracticable to some; others think it chimerical. I, for one, am persuaded that all who have rightly read the book which we are explaining, and who know what is meant by the spiritual life, judge quite otherwise; for the sentiments of spiritual persons are far from being agreed with the ideas of those who are little in the habit of prayer. I say, then, that a soul earnestly desiring perfection, and fully resolved to break through all the obstacles which she may find in the way that leads thither, will never feel more esteem or affection for any created thing, than what arises from the principles of faith, hope, and charity; for if she once gives some human affection admission to her heart, she will become as little and as bounded as the object of her love.

It is a folly for those who wish to become perfect, to run eagerly to see rare and curious things. They go under specious pretences, but after all they seek only to satisfy their curiosity; and not having God in their heart, they desire to fill it with creatures. For this reason they praise highly what they have seen, and speak of it with much exaggeration. The more gross praise natural talents, eloquence, a lively imagination, and other such natural advantages, which they often value more highly than the advantages of Grace. The cause of their error is, that they have not a high idea of these Divine gifts, and having besides but little minds, when they come to compare themselves with those who shine in the world, they cannot refrain from admiring and lauding those qualities of which themselves are destitute. It is on the same principle that they value so highly the dignities, the riches, the fine palaces, the superb train of the great; that they hurry to see the pompous entries of princes and other such magnificent shows, and are vexed if they lose the opportunity of being present at one of these sights. All this shows clearly the littleness of the heart of man, who has neither light enough to perceive God, nor strength and virtue to draw near to Him.

As for those who are somewhat more spiritual-minded, truly they do not entirely forget to praise the Author and Dispenser of these natural advantages; but as for enjoying God, they are very far from it, judging of things only by their senses, and according to the false ideas of the world. Those, on the other hand, who hold themselves close to God, and discourse familiarly with Him, and who know by their own experience how gracious He is, despise in their hearts all those things that the others value and exalt excessively. Thus a man, illuminated by Heavenly light, and governed by the true Spirit of Grace, thinks only of God, rejoices in none beside Him, and regards all other things as nothing. Not that he is unwilling to converse with his fellow-creatures, but he is led to do so only by the high value that he sets on the salvation of a soul, and on the Blood of Christ Who redeemed it by His Death. He praises nothing, he proposes nothing to himself, that does not either come purely from God, or lead to God.

The man who acts otherwise finds himself, as it were, surrounded by thick darkness, which he cannot disperse but by the exercise of prayer; for it is by that we are filled with a supernatural light, whose principal effect is to open and enlarge the heart, that it may raise itself towards God, and love and esteem eternal things alone. God having then given us by His Grace the means of labouring for the acquisition of the good things of eternity, we cannot lose our time in seeking others without making ourselves miserable; for from the instant that we conceive a high idea of human things, our mind becomes darkened, and our heart narrowed. For this cause we are sensible to the smallest occurrences, and are troubled with little reason; whereas, if our souls were great, God would be always present with us, and knowing Him as He is, even enjoying Him frequently, we should feel only a distaste for all besides, and thereby should extinguish in ourselves our natural passion for seeing all, knowing all, possessing all.

What is the reason that a lady takes so much pleasure in adorning herself? Why does a man rejoice so much to see himself caressed by a great personage, or praised by men of talent? These things proceed only from littleness of heart; for if this man and this woman comprehended how wonderful is the greatness of God, how precious the good things of eternity; if they had even in some sort made trial of these good things, as those do who are closely united with God, they would carefully avoid attaching themselves to anything so contemptible as the vain splendour and false honour of the world. This is a general rule. The man who cannot accustom himself to remain unmoved by passing good and evil, will always crawl on the earth and in the dust; he will never rise above visible things; he will turn with every wind, and receive all kinds of impressions; he will be vexed for three days by one annoying word spoken to him; in a word, he will be in perpetual agitation and trouble,—an evident token of a little mind and a feeble spirit.

CHAPTER II.

(On these words)—" If thou dost walk spiritually, thou wilt not much weigh fleeting words." B. iii. ch. 28.

QUESTION.—What are fleeting words?

ANSWER.—Those which are said of us either in praise or blame, which those who are devoted to the inward life feel very little, as our Author remarks. We have elsewhere explained what is meant by the inward life; it is enough now to say, that an interior man is one who maintains in his soul a close and continual communion with God.

Those who are unacquainted with this Divine converse, and who avoid meditation, are very sensitive to the smallest word spoken to them. We often see that a word spoken inconsiderately causes them feelings of irritation which they cannot overcome for whole days and weeks. Whenever they are alone, they employ themselves in musing and reflecting on what such an one said to them, and his intention in saying it. A worldly man will never be at rest till he has had an explanation; he excites himself to vengeance, and seeks for an opportunity of destroying him who has offended him. Another who does not live according to the maxims of the world, but who is yet weak and imperfect, cannot help feeling a small insult; he reasons with himself about it, and foresees evil consequences; he is uneasy and vexed, desirous of receiving just satisfaction; in short, he bears about with him a stock of bitterness, a subject of trouble, distractions, and useless thoughts.

Let a man, on the contrary, receive some praise and some token of esteem, his joy is inexpressible. No sooner is he returned home than he shuts himself up to occupy himself with his vain imaginations. This word of praise comes back on his mind; he thinks of it, and thinks again; he finds marvellous pleasure in it; he deduces consequences to his advantage, which, like wood put into the fire, serve for food to his vanity, and increase his good opinion of himself. All such are fleeting words; they fly through the air[a], and, like arrows, make deep wounds in feeble souls susceptible of the impressions of self-love.

The remedy for this great evil is to embrace the inward life, to love retreat, to establish ourselves in the faith, to enjoy everlasting truths.

QUESTION.—What is the first principle and foundation of the interior life whereof we speak?

ANSWER.—It is the doctrine laid down in the preceding chapter; it is a strong conviction that there is nothing great but God; which causes us to have Him ever in our heart, and to bear constantly with us the only Object of our joy, our fear, our hopes, and our desires. A man of a wandering spirit, incapable of dwelling at home, is constrained to go forth and pour himself out on external things, to occupy himself vainly with the things that he sees and hears, and those that flatter his ruling passion. He is not accustomed to meditate on the truths of the faith, nor inwardly to hold familiar converse with God, and therefore he burns with a desire of knowing all that is said and thought respecting him; he is extremely careful of what concerns his own honour, and these idle dreams keep alive his attachment to outward things. But when he seriously reflects that death is inevitable, and that at the hour of death there is no comfort except that of not having departed from God; when he considers that at that terrible instant all

[a] B. iii. c. 46.

those things that make the happiness of this world will vanish from his sight like smoke, then he comes to himself, and begins to value that which will then give him assurance and joy. He perceives that there is no folly equal to that of the worldly, who attach themselves to things which they cannot keep long: his whole study is to understand the maxims of the Gospel, and by them to regulate his affections and his actions.

He thus learns to retire within himself, and to become interior, and in this disposition he seeks nothing outward; he troubles himself no more to dwell in one place rather than in another; he thinks no longer of acquiring friends, or of amassing the trifles, the nothings, which he formerly sought so eagerly. He sighs only for spiritual and eternal treasures; these he makes his happiness, thither tend his desires, his designs, and his labours. Thus, whatever he hears said of him, though on the one hand he be extolled as a genius, or on the other considered ridiculous and foolish, all is equal to him; these arrows fly through the air, but reach him not, and he receives no wound either of pleasure or vexation. The solitude that he has formed for himself in the depth of his heart shelters him from all. He is above created things. As he values nothing but that which comes from God, he lets the world talk; whatever may be said moves him not. Therefore he listens calmly to those who insult and calumniate him; he restrains himself, and does not take fire at a small injury, like others, who, having no control over their passions, become heated and impatient, and are unable to hinder their resentment from breaking forth.

The quickest means of attaining to moderation in these circumstances, is to renounce self entirely, in order to be conformed to Jesus suffering; it is greatly to despise every thing merely human, to accustom ourselves to seek God fervently, to employ our prayers, our examinations of conscience, our communions, to form this habit, and to labour at it unceasingly, till we have attained to complete detachment from worldly things, after which we shall no more have any thing to desire or to seek in this life. Let men think, speak, and judge, as they please; their words, thoughts, and judgments, however unjust and disadvantageous, will be but like the heavy rain of a storm which falls on the house-roof without abiding there.

To excite ourselves to this holy practice, let us be fully persuaded that it is on the judgment which God passes on us that our everlasting happiness or misery depends, and that at the hour of death we shall have no other to fear. Let us say then, when we are praised, What avails this praise if God's judgment is different? And when we are blamed, What harm can the words of men do me, if God judge otherwise? Let us remember that the judgment of God is the rule of all equitable judgment. Let us consider that before God all men joined together are but as a grain of sand compared to the loftiest mountain; and then let us beware of being troubled by their judgment. If all mankind were on one side, and God Alone on the other, we need not fear all mankind if God Alone were for us. One who is fully penetrated with this sentiment may be called truly great, and all besides must appear small in his eyes. For all who are thoroughly united with God participate in His greatness: and as in order to arrive at this Divine union it is absolutely necessary to embrace the inward life, we must so attach ourselves to it as to show the truth of this saying of our Author, "If thou dost walk spiritually, thou wilt not much weigh fleeting words."

CHAPTER III.

(On these words)—" For that is the cause why there are so few contemplative men to be found, for that few can wholly withdraw themselves from things created and perishing."— B. iii. c. 31.

QUESTION.—Who are to be called contemplative men?

ANSWER.—Not those who live a retired life in a desert or in a cloister, but those whom God has favoured with the gift of contemplation, whatever their state or condition may be. This gift is most excellent: but God communicates it only to a few; and of this we must now enquire the reason. To comprehend it rightly, it must be understood that there are four sorts of people who apply themselves to prayer.

1. The first are those who succeed not at all, either because they know not how to continue it, or for want of finding pleasure in it, although their profession obliges them to its frequent exercise. Of these we may say, that what prevents them from obtaining much fruit from prayer is, that they have not the disposition necessary for it, and that giving too much licence to their imaginations, they cannot have that collectedness and attention that are necessary to profit.

2. The second are those who acquit themselves of this exercise with care and fervour, who find in it a sweet repose, who converse peacefully with God, and whose fidelity God rewards with great abundance of grace, whether they have much or little capacity and talent.

3. The third are learned people, who have facility in prayer, but a natural facility, because being accustomed to subtilize and reason on all manner of subjects, they can always find enough to occupy their mind. Their desire of serving God, and obtaining salvation, makes them love prayer; they continue in it easily: but after all they profit but little, because giving much less time to the affections of the will than to the discourse of the understanding, they are filled with innumerable thoughts and subtle reflections on the subject of their meditation, which serve only to dry up devotion; besides, that the grace of devotion is often wanting to them, because they are wanting in fervour: and thus all ends in vague and fruitless speculations. These people have not a very high or very exact idea of virtue; and this makes them think that all is going on as well as possible, because they imagine that the disposition in which they find themselves is the best to which they can attain, without some extraordinary grace that they do not comprehend; so fully persuaded are they that it is not to be obtained, and that it is not their own fault that God does not raise them to the most sublime contemplation.

Those who confine themselves to such small things are little illuminated; at best they are very destitute of that supernatural light which is the principle and foundation of all spirituality. They have that light which may be obtained by means of study, but which does not suffice to render them holy. Thus they are very far removed from true contemplation, and do not even seem to care much for it, because they think that their learning can supply the place of that supernatural light which God communicates to the simple and ignorant, and which produces, as they think, some pious affections, but little solid knowledge. Therefore they never become truly contemplative.

4. By this word contemplation I do not mean visions, revelations, extasies, and other such graces which we admire in the Saints: I mean only an elevation of spirit towards God, a state in which the mind, illuminated and strengthened from above, has no difficulty in conceiving mysteries, and the heart burns at the same time with love to God and extreme ardour for perfection. This kind of contemplation belongs to the Saints, who are the fourth order of those who give themselves to prayer. They join to abundance of light great freedom of spirit, and by virtue of this light, rather than by force of reasoning, they penetrate into the things which concern God and salvation, as well those of pure speculation as those of practice.

There is much difference between these and those whom we have placed in the third class. Their manner of prayer is the best of all; it is called contemplation; and to this God often raises those who love ordinary prayer, who practise it carefully, and who strive, as far as lieth in them, to co-operate with Grace. Therefore those deceive themselves who imagine it possible to supply the place of the gift of contemplation by acquired knowledge. This also is the cause that we see so few truly contemplative men, who are persons dead to the world and to themselves, full of right feelings, and closely united with God. Our Author gives the reason when he says that there are few who have resolution to embrace mortification; for it is not enough to keep ourselves in such a degree of innocence as leads us to avoid the grosser faults, and to render ourselves acceptable to those with whom we are obliged to live. Neither is it enough to be strict and regular in the Religious Life, nor to acquit ourselves worthily of certain employments by which we gain the esteem of the world: we must also mortify ourselves continually, and in all things; we must renounce all pleasure that is to be found in creatures, as an essential hindrance not only to Grace, but far more, to that supernatural life in which the soul, detached from all, seeks and breathes after God Alone, and does nothing for her own interest, whether in regard to the satisfaction of the mind or the pleasures of the senses. We must even carry mortification so far, as to die wholly to ourselves by a mystical and moral death.

Without this many good people, principally among the learned, who exercise themselves in prayer, rise from it quite cold after many subtle reflections. It is for this cause too that they often show so little amendment and so little fervour. They speak of the things of God, and appear to understand them; but their knowledge is only the fruit of study, and has little power to touch their hearts. To judge by their discourse, you would say that they were perfect in spirituality, and yet they know nothing of contemplation. And why? Because, though they are learned, and moreover not devoid of probity, they have still many human views, and much secret attachment to their own interests; which shows that they have not yet learned to yield themselves into the hands of Divine Providence. They do not like contempt; they are very careful to maintain their own credit; very delicate with regard to their reputation; little inclined to deprive themselves of the enjoyments and pleasures of life, and to afflict their flesh. What they apprehend most is ill success in their employments, and to draw on themselves reproaches from those on whom they depend; not so much because God might thereby be offended, as because they would be put to confusion. Thus they have but little love for JESUS Crucified, despised, abandoned; it is not by the way of humiliation that they desire to follow Him. Yet this is the way to approach Him, and to be enabled to contemplate His Greatness.

They deceive themselves much too, when they say that this exalted degree is only for a small number of elect souls, and that it is a free gift of God; that they desire it with all their hearts; that they would rejoice to have it, but cannot obtain it. My answer is what I have already said elsewhere, that there are two ways of arriving at contemplation; the one depends absolutely and solely on God, the other depends much on our own cares and labour. Not that I would propose a plan for contemplation, nor that there is a road that leads directly to it, but we may tend thither by a way which, though indirect, is yet sure; that of mortifying our appetites, correcting our faults, and depriving ourselves, as far as possible, of all the pleasures of life, even of those which appear innocent, but yet hinder the operations of Grace. St. Ignatius, for this reason, most particularly recommended to his disciples continual mortification in all things. This is not a plan, it is simply a means to obtain this gift of prayer, so necessary to all who aspire to a high degree of sanctity: and our Author says expressly, that the reason why there are so few contemplative men is, that there are few who embrace mortification [a].

CHAPTER IV.

(On these words)—"As to be void of all desire of external things produceth inward peace, so the forsaking of ourselves inwardly, joineth us unto God." B. iii. c. 56.

QUESTION.—What assists us most to obtain union with God?

ANSWER.—Two things particularly; the first of

[a] B. iii. c. 31. 1.

which is, to put away all outward things which may serve as a wall of separation between God and us; the second, to feel no attachment even to things within us. Without this perfect disengagement and entire freedom of spirit, we must not hope ever to be fully united with God.

QUESTION.—How does detachment from outward things avail to this union with God?

ANSWER.—It avails not a little, since it gives peace to the soul, and preserves it; for one who often and ardently desires something external to himself is always uneasy, because he is always finding some obstacle to the accomplishment of his desires: therefore there is no surer means of enjoying true repose than to desire nothing.

This is not difficult to one who seeks God with his whole heart, who regards Him as his Supreme Good, his only Happiness, and who knows assuredly that all created things, of whatever nature, are very little; for having conceived a true idea of the infinite Greatness of God, and being persuaded of this fundamental truth, that there is no solid joy but in God, he will find pleasure in desiring nothing besides Him. If it is difficult for him to do so, it is only because he has been long accustomed to seek for satisfaction in God's visible creation.

This evil habit causes a dangerous sickness of the soul, which is a constant uneasiness, and, as it were, an unappeasable hunger. Within the soul is a devouring fire, which demands fuel to feed it, and this fuel is some good thing either sensible or spiritual. Sensible things present themselves with powerful attractions, hard to be resisted; the inclination of nature is to that side, and thither she has ever allowed herself to be drawn from childhood. Those things which faith offers are invisible, they are not within the scope of the senses, and by meditation only can any knowledge of them be acquired; but at length Faith perceives them through a cloud. God reveals Himself to the soul, and with Himself brings peace to her. But if He withdraws, and she feels His presence no more, she hastens instantly in search of created objects; and then her uneasiness is renewed, according to the saying of St. Augustine, that our heart is always in a state of agitation till it reposes in God, and that it can therefore have no peace separate from God.

It is a very common delusion among those who desire to live happily, to be everywhere seeking occasions of rejoicing and amusement; for experience shows plainly that worldly pleasures, in proportion as they increase, augment, instead of diminishing, our thirst for them. Even the philosophers teach us not to accumulate riches, but to retrench our immoderate desires. The great maxim of the Saints is to desire nothing, but to be so indifferent to all things as to will only what God wills, and to will it through the motive of love; and even if that love be not accompanied by any sensible tenderness, never to cease to perform its acts, and to excite themselves to it by faith. He who walks after the light of Faith will find peace. We must try to unite ourselves to God, by wholly conforming ourselves to His Will; for it is by this union, which is the sole happiness of devout souls here below, that we begin to feel and enjoy Him.

QUESTION.—How is this sweet union of the soul with God formed?

ANSWER.—In the way that our Author says. As the means of obtaining peace, and taking away the very root of uneasiness, is to forsake all outward things, so the means of obtaining union with God is absolutely to renounce ourselves. How is this?

Figure to yourself that God stands at the door of your heart, and that when you open it by entire self-abnegation, immediately He will come in. It takes place thus.

A man who is engaged by his state of life in exterior functions, who cannot dispense with seeing the world, who has business, and who is obliged to discourse with all sorts of people, finds satisfaction in these employments, he attaches his affections to them so far as to make them a pleasure; and he has no scruple, because he sees no sin in them. But yet this pleasure takes the place of God in his heart, and He will not have a place already occupied. Thus too great an attachment to outward things hinders him from enjoying God. He is contented with a certain repose arising from the harmless life led by the generality of good people, for whom it is enough not to be guilty of great faults. But an interior man who seeks God simply, is not contented with a moderate degree of virtue; he will not rest therein. He renounces this satisfaction, which he thinks too merely natural; he deprives himself of it voluntarily; he strips himself of all, and makes in his soul, as it were, a void; and because he makes it for God, God immediately fills it. Thus is the Divine Union formed.

Certainly nothing can be more pitiable than the ordinary disposition of the generality of those who profess to serve God. They love to distract themselves, and to go out of themselves; they become attached to vain amusements, and remove yet further from their true repose. God offers them all real and solid good things which satisfy the mind, but very few receive them. They have none to blame but themselves; for all the evil arises from their desire of satisfying themselves without God, and from their attempt to silence their conscience, by saying, that God is not angry, under which pretence they go in search of human consolations which hinder the Divine Union.

Some are entirely unacquainted with this wonderful union; it appears to them a fanciful idea, or an invention of the mystics, on which the mind should not dwell. The truly Faithful, say they, do not seek to enjoy God, but to serve Him on earth; it is not in this life, but in the next, that they hope to possess Him, and to receive from Him the reward of their services. This objection is very weak, and easily answered. I acknowledge that simple love is not eager for pleasures, above all for those which may be enjoyed here below; but these people are not consistent with themselves, and their actions are very different from their maxims. They take no trouble to taste in prayer how gracious God is; and yet they have so little aversion to their own satisfaction, that they seek it in all circumstances. There is nothing that they will not do to please men, to attract their esteem, to obtain their praise; and they are delighted by some testimony of affection, some good office done to them, some sign of gratitude shown to them. It might be said to them, Despise these consolations and passing joys which come from creatures; and if the Lord refuses or withdraws His, at least for a time, bear this privation as faithful and zealous servants, who care only for their Master's concerns. But that you should be resigned to lose the consolations of Heaven, and at the same time anxiously seek those of the earth, is very strange, and entirely contrary to reason.

People are much deceived in their judgment with regard to this supernatural union of God with man. It aids us extremely to know, love, and serve Him. None can know better how to conform themselves to the Divine Will, than those who depart from outward things in order to converse more freely with the Lord in prayer. For by this they lift up their heart and mind to heaven, and conceive ardent desires of being for ever faithful to God. But those of whom we speak, and to whom we are now replying, think that such unions of the soul with God are nothing more than certain spiritual affections, more fit for women than for men, and ordinarily accompanied by some tears of devotion. They say that very common feelings are concealed under very specious words; that they have the same feelings themselves, but do not make much of them like the mystics, who express the most well-known things in terms full of affectation and emphasis. In this there is much error and ignorance; for the supernatural union, often spoken of by our Author and by all who have treated of the mystic life, this union, I say, is, as it were, a participation in the Divine Nature; it is that perfect *fulness of God*, Eph. iii. 19, which the Apostle desired for the faithful of his time; it is *the hidden manna*, Rev. ii. 17; it is an inestimable treasure for the pure in spirit; it is a source of grace and truth, from whence comes far other light than can be acquired by the disputes of the schools, and in which are found far other joys than those which God sometimes bestows on the imperfect, when He is pleased to testify to them that He approves of their good works; in fine, it is the shortest of all means of arriving at perfection.

Thus the most important truth to impress on the minds of those who profess to serve God is, that man being unable to exist without some pleasure, and God Himself having created him to be happy, he must necessarily find his happiness either in God or in himself; that there is none but God able to satisfy him, but that God Who is Purity Itself, cannot dwell with any thing impure; that he must then seek to purify himself; and that as this cannot be done but by renouncing himself, he must so watch over himself, that whenever any thing pleasing to the senses presents itself to him, he should immediately turn away, in order thus to show how much he loves Him Who Alone is worthy to possess all hearts.

By labouring constantly thus to mortify ourselves, we become more and more united with God, we participate still more in His Divine Perfections, and the union at length becomes so intimate, that we may say with the Apostle, *I live: yet not I, but Christ liveth in me.* Gal. ii. 20. It is this that makes Saints; for it is certain that the height of sanctity is so completely to conform our will to that of God, as to feel God Alone acting and reigning within us. This should be continually preached to those who aim at perfection, above all to those who are engaged by their state to aspire to it. And it is to this that every man should try to attain, instead of satisfying himself with an ordinary degree of virtue, which is in general only a low, natural life, full of imperfections.

CHAPTER V.

(On these words)—" He that loveth God with all his heart, is neither afraid of death, nor punishment, nor of judgment, nor of hell." B. i. c. 24.

QUESTION.—What is it to love God with all our hearts?

ANSWER.—It is to do that of which we have spoken in the preceding chapter; to give entrance into our hearts to God Alone, to rejoice in no other, to feel attachment to none but Him, to desire nothing but to serve Him, to seek only to accomplish His most Holy Will, to be interested only in what concerns His glory. This is to love God with the whole heart. When a man has arrived at such a state as to be moved only by what concerns God, then is he free from all those fears that torment most men.

How many do we see who have the fear of God, who hate sin, but who, not contented with the necessaries of life, require many more things which they might do without, and which serve only to nourish the delicacy of the flesh, or the curiosity of the mind! They desire to be well treated; they like applause, places of public resort, cards, the conversation of merry persons; and, if they pique themselves on talent, they like to read curious and diverting books, poetry, history, and other such works, without seeking any thing but their own satisfaction, though they try to persuade themselves falsely that they do all with reference to God.

These people are, in general, very apprehensive of the sorrows which may befall them. They grieve for the loss of their relations and friends; they have themselves a strange fear of dying: death is to them a terrible object, and they think of it as little as they can; or if they do at times think of it, it is a new subject of fear[a]. These persons are often strongly drawn towards perfection, and are not wanting in good desires; but they are subject to very great weaknesses, and so much attached to their little comforts, that they cannot be said to love God with all their heart; for the perfect love of God would free them from all their disquietudes, as well as from all their attachments.

QUESTION.—How then can we place ourselves above all these things?

ANSWER.—By practising that which we have taught hitherto, which ought to be repeated a hundred times. I mean, by voluntarily renouncing our

---

[a] Omission.—ED.

own interest for the love of God; by resigning ourselves absolutely to God's Will; by mortifying our appetites; by despising all that is pleasant and delightful in creatures; by so thoroughly overcoming our passions as to love nothing, to rejoice and grieve for nothing but with reference to God only, and, under all circumstances, to think of nothing but loving and serving Him.

This is too much for the weak and imperfect, who say complainingly, Why require such hard things of us? Is there any harm in innocent amusements, in a promenade, in passing a few hours at cards, in hearing or telling news, &c.? Can God impute this to us as a sin? I reply, without much dwelling on the injustice of their complaints, that the least which can be said, and which they must acknowledge, is, that while they take too much pleasure in these vain amusements, they do not love God so much as they might, for their heart and their love are divided; they are reserving a part for themselves, and for innumerable other things which they seek passionately.

So thought St. Augustine, who said, Lord, it is not loving Thee enough to love any thing with Thee, and not to love it for Thee. We must not be surprised, then, if our Lord does not exercise His whole bounty towards them: for it is not just that when they give Him not all, He should refuse them nothing. Therefore, as long as they use caution and reserve towards Him, He will not deliver them from their fears, and they will still tremble at the thought of death, judgment, and hell. But if they are fully resolved to desire none but Him, and to rest in Him Alone; if they wish to die to all the things of the world, in order to possess Him, and to be united to Him by love, then will they find themselves raised, by virtue of this very love, above all fear, and will be tranquil as a child in its mother's arms.

One, therefore, who desires to follow the way of mortification and of the cross, will undoubtedly find a little trouble at the beginning; but he will at length arrive at this state of tranquillity and peace, unless God, by a special providence, for his greater good, permits his mind to be always agitated by some fears—a thing of rare occurrence. For one who despises the good things of the earth, who renounces all that he may have God for his inheritance[a], and who, in all that he does, only proposes to himself the glory of the Divine Majesty, this man truly loves God with his whole heart, and is in general so full of joy, so convinced of His goodness, that, throwing himself into His arms, he casts his whole burden upon Him[b], and abandons to Him even the care of his salvation, not through negligence, but through confidence and love. Then he experiences in his own person what the Prophet said: "His abode is in peace[c], and his dwelling in Sion."

It is vain to preach this in the world; those who feel it in themselves may repeat it for ever, they will persuade only a few, who, after their example, will reject all that serves only to flatter the senses, and to divert the mind; who will seek God simply, and who, to go straight to Him, will tread in the steps of His Son. This Man-God constantly followed the hardest and narrowest way, which is that of mortification and privation of all things; and He taught it to the world no less by His words than by His example. This is the only way that leads to the most exalted holiness. The misfortune is, that the greater part of the righteous do not enjoy those advantages of which we speak, and are never exempt from fears,

[a] Deut. xviii. 2.
[b] Ps. lv. 23. 1 Pet. v. 7.
[c] Ps. lxxv. Vulg. lxxvi. 2 (Heb.) E. V. "Salem." The Vulg. gives the interpretation and drops the word.

though they try perhaps to assure their consciences, and to fortify their minds, by reasons of little weight, drawn rather from philosophy than from the Gospel. Wherefore is this? It is because they do not go far enough. I mean so far as to free themselves from all attachment to honour, to pleasure, even to study. It is that often they desire to inhabit this place and not that; to live with such and such persons rather than with others, purely to satisfy their self-love, which always desires the things that are most pleasing and most convenient.

What they say and repeat constantly is, that there is no harm in this, that they see no sin in it; that God is not a hard Master, Who forbids innocent pleasures to those who serve Him. It is true that God is full of goodness, that He is very indulgent to His servants, but yet He is a jealous God, Who requires them to be His Alone: He can suffer no division in hearts which belong absolutely to Him, and which were only made for Him. He says, by the mouth of our Author, "Forsake thyself, and thou shalt find Me," B. iii. c. 37. Forsake all, and thou shalt find all. It would be far better to resolve to follow the way in which the Saints walked, than to seek so much for vain pretences for dispensing with doing as they did. By imitating them we should become worthy of a share in the promises of Christ: we should obtain perfect peace; we should be filled with confidence in God; we should rise so far above created things, as to be inaccessible to fears and disquietude.

CHAPTER VI.

(On these words)—" Give all for all ; seek nothing ; require back nothing ; abide purely and with a firm confidence in Me, and thou shalt possess Me." B. iii. c. 37.

QUESTION.—What is it rightly to enjoy and to possess God?

ANSWER.—We truly possess God when our mind and heart are attached to Him. But it is to be observed, that we speak not now of full possession, which is reserved for the Saints in Glory, nor of that imperfect possession which is common to all the Just, and which consists simply in being in a state of grace, but of another, which is the fruit of the union of the human heart with that of God; a union so close, that it may be said with truth, that man possesses God, that he is full of God. Yet it is not equal in all who share it. It is excellent in some, as in persons of consummate holiness, who, by virtue of Divine love, and by the illumination of Faith, truly enjoy God, from which they gain marvellous blessings, which we have noticed in many places. In others it is less perfect; but always sufficiently so to give them an exquisite sense of the presence of God, with a high idea of His Majesty; and in this state they live fully contented, entirely free from those disquietudes and fears that are common to other men. They feel the presence of God, and enjoy its infinite sweetness.

Now God thus communicates Himself in a greater or less degree, according as the soul has more or less love for Him, and attachment to creatures. Therefore the devout are always trying to secure themselves in the possession of God; they learn to feel His Presence within them; and the means of which they make use for this are prayer, the frequent use of the Sacraments, and other pious exercises. They study principally to practise thoroughly the two things recommended by our Author. The first is, to build on God Alone; the second, to attach themselves to Him constantly and for ever. By these means they attain at length to possess God, in a manner more or less perfect, in proportion to their fervour.

QUESTION.—What is it, then, to build on God alone?

ANSWER.—It is to regard God with a single eye; to look to Him with an upright intention, without ever turning aside to creatures. But this is not done by those who act on impulse, and who follow the inclinations of nature. When I speak of following the inclinations of nature, and thereby losing the possession of God, I divide mankind into three classes.

1. The first consists of those who are resolved to keep themselves from deadly sin, but who care little for anything else. These fear God, but they have little thought for His Glory, because nothing touches or occupies them but their own salvation.

2. The second sort go much further; for, not content with avoiding deadly sin, they avoid, as far as they can, those slight faults which are committed with reflection and deliberate purpose; yet they are not always watchful over their actions; they are not always careful to do nothing but what pleases God, and thus they fall into many imperfections; much self-love mingles in their conduct, for want of light, and of application to that which is their duty. In truth, when they perceive a thing to be forbidden, they abstain from it, although they think it but a venial sin; but they are deceived in thinking that

that will suffice to render them perfect. It cannot certainly be denied that by an innocent life we acquire much merit; but this will not bring them to the full possession of God, because though they commit few sins with full consciousness and evil intention, they fall into many through frailty and precipitation: and thus they never enter that way that leads to perfect purity, in which men rarely fall even into faults which are committed through inadvertence. I say rarely, for I do not pretend that we can ever subdue self to such a degree as not to sin at all.

Thus there are three distinct degrees of perfection. Those who have attained to the first avoid mortal sins; in the second, they keep themselves from venial sins; in the third, they are exempt even from many slight faults into which men fall without much consideration, and purely through frailty. In the last alone can they obtain that purity of soul which is necessary to possess God. Further, we do not now speak of singular graces and extraordinary gifts, but only of what a man may do by applying himself as he ought to the ordinary exercises of the inward life. For it is evident that, with the assistance of grace, it does not surpass human powers, first, to avoid the greatest crimes; secondly, to abstain from the smallest faults, when we reflect on them, and are not taken by surprise; thirdly, to be so watchful over ourselves, and so careful in all things, as to guard ourselves against the slightest failures.

QUESTION.—Teach us more particularly how this is to be practised?

ANSWER.—By being always watchful over themselves, and trying to do nothing on natural impulse, nor by a secret movement of self-love, which it is impossible to discover without careful observation.

Interior and fervent men are not thus deceived, for they apply themselves most diligently to examine their very smallest actions, to consider what spirit moves them, what motive leads them to act, what is the end at which they aim. What they principally desire is, to make the Glory of God their great end, and to be mortified in all their works, without any mixture of vanity, curiosity, or sensual pleasure.

This is rightly called seeking God in every thing; but it appears impracticable to those who are not spiritual: yet many devout persons find nothing in it but sweetness, tranquillity, and peace.

Those to whom we are now speaking, and whom we wish to instruct, are those who content themselves with a moderate degree of virtue; who desire good, and abhor evil, but who do not strive sufficiently to arrive at the lofty state proposed to them, or who regard it as imaginary, or cannot do themselves violence enough to approach it, and who consequently dispense with this salutary practice recommended to them in these words, "Attach thyself solely and continually to Me."

Not that God will not recompense them for their good works, as He does in general all the Just: He does not refuse them His consolations; He gives them peace of heart, and that repose which accompanies a good conscience; but He does not communicate Himself much to them, and they possess Him but imperfectly. Those, on the other hand, who carefully follow our Author's counsel, obtain the true possession of God which is promised to perfect purity of heart. *Blessed are the pure in heart*, said the Saviour, *for they shall see God*. Matt. v. 8.

2. The second condition of this holy practice is, that we should apply ourselves to it incessantly, and without intermission. Many are deterred by the difficulties with which they meet: for that we may

be capable of possessing God in the manner of which we speak, to have a share of His Illumination, and be filled with Him, there must be no void in the soul; she must be entirely filled with Him, and so closely attached to Him, that nothing can separate her from Him; and if through frailty she quits Him for a moment, she must return to Him quickly, and beware lest through slothfulness she remain long parted from Him. This is a point of so much consequence, that we may call it the beginning of all spirituality. Without this we can never reach perfection, and with it we shall infallibly attain to it. The reason, then, why there are so few perfect men is, that for want of courage, a thousand pretences are found for dispensing with that holy and salutary practice which the Son of God recommends when He says, *Knock, and it shall be opened unto you.* Matt. vii. 7.

CHAPTER VII.

(On these words)—" He to whom the Eternal Word speaketh, is delivered from a world of unnecessary conceptions." B. i. c. 3.

QUESTION.—Who is he to whom the Eternal Word speaketh, and who is able to hear that Divine Voice?

ANSWER.—We render ourselves capable of hearing It in three ways. First, when we keep ourselves silent inwardly; and the superior part of the soul enjoying a complete calm, resembles the sea when it is not agitated by winds. Now this calm can arise only from a perfect mortification of the passions, when we desire nothing temporal and perishable. and look to God Alone. For all is then so tranquil, that the Uncreated Wisdom, the Divine Word, the Image of the Majesty of God, is depicted easily and faithfully on this calm and peaceful sea. And thus it is that the Word speaks to the soul, which, having nothing in the inferior part to trouble her, without difficulty receives the Divine impress. Then are we in a peace which passeth all understanding, and which is called *the peace of God.* Phil. iv. 7.

It is not then, as our Author remarks, with "noise of words," B. iii. c. 43, that God speaks to the soul, and teaches her many truths; it is by applying Himself to her, and impressing His own Image on her. But before that, she is troubled, and incapable of seeing the light clearly, or of hearing distinctly the Voice of the Uncreated Word. Those, then, who have not yet learned to master their imagination, to moderate their desires, to repress their passions, and to regulate the motions of their sensual appetite, are always restless, and hear but imperfectly, and with difficulty, the instructions of the Divine Spirit. It is the same with those who are not wholly indifferent, and resigned to the Will of God : for they are easily troubled, and can hardly comprehend His words, when He speaks in whispers to their heart.

2. The second means of rightly hearing the inward Voice of the Word, is to subject our reason entirely to It. People full of an opinion of their own sufficiency generally fail here; though many of them are gentle, and willing to be familiar with the little ones, they yet trust much in their own wisdom, and are vexed even when they do not receive all the deference which they desire. The consequence is, that their presumption keeping them at a distance from God, they never approach Him sufficiently near to hear His Voice aright, Which makes little noise, and is but faintly heard in silence. Their good opinion of themselves goes so far, that without well-knowing what

they are doing, they in some sort despise this Divine Voice. Not that God, if they are sincere, refuses them His Illuminations; but undoubtedly the secrets of Celestial Wisdom are hidden from them, and they know nothing of what is properly called spirituality, till, humbling themselves before the Lord, they acknowledge their own littleness, and begin to distrust themselves and their own wisdom; for then they become capable of entering into the meaning of the Divine teaching.

3. The third means or the third condition necessary to a profitable reception of the teaching of the Word is, to act little from ourselves, and much by the Spirit of God, Who is the Father of lights[a]. Those who have acquired learning owe it to their talent and industry. If they are Theologians, they make use of that knowledge which Faith gives them, and join to it their reasonings; and from these beginnings they draw conclusions very useful to the Church, which supports and defends herself against heretics by means of the doctors. God Himself confirms their decisions in the councils, where the assistance of the Holy Spirit Who presides there does not fail them. Thus when the general good of the Church or some point of faith is concerned, He teaches them what to believe, and assists their reasonings; but in other cases the judgment of each doctor, in spiritual matters, is not very certain, unless it is supported by long practice in the things of God. Profound erudition is less profitable for this than the light that God gives to the humble spirit in prayer. For this light is not acquired by study and reading: the Holy Spirit Himself pours it on the soul; and He sometimes imparts it to doctors of eminent virtue, not on account of their learning, but of their sanctity. If we speak then of

---

[a] James i. 17.

the assistance to be obtained from learning with regard to the inward life, it is nothing compared with that which proceeds from Grace, and from the gifts of the Holy Spirit.

Yet there are some who think that, because they are learned, they must be judges of spiritual things, and who reject as visions all that they are unable to comprehend by force of study. This is an error; for mystic theology is a science apart, and has its own principles, conclusions, and proper terms, independently of all other sciences. To speak of them learnedly, we should have studied them. But there are many, who, without having read much of those authors who treat of the mystic life, think proper to criticise and even to condemn it. It is surprising that in all sciences people listen willingly to the masters of each, and that in this alone every one thinks himself a master, for want of having well considered what our Author so frequently says, that "there is great difference between the wisdom of an illuminated and devout man, and the knowledge of a learned and studious clerk [a]." The difference is, that the latter is acquired by our own labour, the former is the gift of God.

We may judge justly of interior things, when we have learned to command ourselves, to live in peace with ourselves; when we are humble, and well prepared to receive the Divine Impress under the guidance of the Holy Spirit; for then there is nothing to hinder us from hearing the Voice of the Eternal Word when He speaks to the heart.

QUESTION.—What advantage is obtained by the soul which fulfils all these conditions?

ANSWER.—Our Author tells us that she is thereby delivered from an innumerable multitude of different

[a] B. iii. c. 31.

thoughts, opinions, and feelings, which keep her in constant restlessness. In fact, all those who have no knowledge but what they have gained for themselves, are now of one opinion and now of another; they have nothing fixed and certain, whereas those who are led by the Divine light in the manner of which we have spoken, are not subject to these doubts and hesitations, and changes of feeling, because they always tend towards Unity, and are firm and immoveable as their object. The right understanding of this truth so strengthens the mind, that it can no longer be carried away by the torrent of vague and uncertain thoughts, which trouble those who follow any other light than that which comes from Heaven. Woe unto them that trust too much in their learning! for the Lord speaks to them but little in secret, because He is not hearkened to, when the mind is distracted by objects of various kinds.

CHAPTER VIII.

(On these words)—" If it were well with thee, and thou wert well purified from sin, all things would fall out to thee for good, and to thy advancement in holiness." B. ii. c. i.

QUESTION.—Of whom may we say that he is entirely purified?

ANSWER.—Of him who has past through all the ways and all the trials by which God leads a soul to perfect purity.

QUESTION.—What are these ways and trials?

ANSWER.—We may form a just idea of them by representing to ourselves the way in which a house infected with the plague is cleansed. All impurities are removed, and incense and other perfumes are burnt; it is whitened; a fire is lighted, which consumes the bad air; lastly, it is furnished, and then it is considered clean, and no one fears to inhabit it. God does something resembling this in a carnal and worldly man, when He is pleased to convert him. The man illuminated by the Divine Light, is careful first to cleanse his soul well by penitence, and by a general confession, accompanied with bitter regret for his faults; then he tries to take away the odour of sin by many good thoughts, by different pious considerations, and above all, by the recollection of the good example of the Saints; afterwards, he whitens it by the exercises of an austere and penitent life; lastly, he completes its purification by the fire of Divine Love, which, being thoroughly lighted in his heart, drives out the pestiferous air of worldliness and vice; after which, the soul becomes perfectly clean. Those who saw her sullied with crimes, have no difficulty in perceiving the change; she sees and feels it herself, humble as she is, and is not unconscious of the miraculous effect which the Holy Spirit has designed to work in her by His Grace. This gives her that inward peace which accompanies her everywhere, and which she never loses.

Souls may also be purified in another excellent manner, which resembles that in which plate is cleaned. Ashes and water are taken, it is rubbed and soiled with them in such a manner, as seems only intended to make it dirtier. Yet the very contrary is intended; for on being washed with fresh water, it appears more beautiful and bright than ever. God sometimes deals in like manner with the souls that He is pleased to raise to a high degree of purity. He permits them to receive from the evil spirit, or from corrupt nature, violent suggestions of all kinds of wickedness; the temptation is often so extreme, and the feeling so lively, that they dare not assure themselves that they have not consented. There arise in them furious movements of pride, hatred, impurity, anger, and sometimes even of despair, with such thick darkness, that they do not know themselves, but think themselves very unpleasing to God, and, at last, become unendurable to themselves.

By this knowledge of evil, which does not go so far as consent, and which serves only to purify them more and more, they return to that happy state of perfect innocence in which they were after Baptism. Who, seeing the plate rubbed with ashes, would not say, that it was done on purpose to dirty it more? Yet it is but in order to make it more clean. Who would not think, in like manner, that a soul filled with abominable thoughts and feelings, must resemble the evil spirit who inspires them? Yet this very thing serves to purify her, because, loving God truly, and having always in the depths of her heart that Divine love, which is hidden and kept alive under the ashes, the more she is pressed by temptation, the more violence she does herself to surmount it. As opposite qualities gain strength by combating and clashing with one another, so the ardour of the celestial flame, with which she burns, inwardly augments in proportion to the opposition she meets with.

Nothing, then, contributes more to purify a soul thoroughly, than the great efforts which she is obliged to make, and constantly to reiterate, in order to resist the enemy, who uses all means to induce her to sin. From these attacks of the evil one she gains also a great advantage, that of satisfying the Divine justice for all her past faults; for[a], can we doubt that violent temptations, nobly endured, serve even in this world to purify those whom God tries so severely?

---

[a] Omission.—ED.

QUESTION.—What then befalls a soul which God has been pleased to purify in this manner?

ANSWER.—The reward of its patience and fidelity in the troubles of this life, the fruit of so many confessions made, so many penances and good works done, above all, of so many acts of love to God performed, is, that all things issue to its advantage; for when we see people exceedingly fearful of the evils which seem to menace them, and irresolute through anxiety and trouble, we may be sure that the cause of their disquiet and dejection is, that they are not yet completely purified from their sins and vices.

A man who shrinks from being in a certain place, or with some person to whom he has an aversion, shows plainly that he is not master of his unregulated emotions; for when his interior is once well regulated, that which formerly was to him a cause of vexation, becomes a subject of joy; and he often wonders to see that Providence has so well disposed all things, that he profits wonderfully by those which formerly caused him nothing but trouble. Thus in all circumstances, good and evil, sweet and bitter, contribute to his salvation; and then it is manifest that the great Apostle said rightly, *that all things work together for good to them that love God.* Rom. viii. 28. This is a powerful motive for the devout to aspire to perfect purity of heart, and to grudge nothing in order to its attainment.

CHAPTER IX.

(On these words)—" A perfect contempt of the world ... will give us great confidence we shall die happily." B. i. c. 23

QUESTION.—What is the best preparation for death?

ANSWER.—As regards those who have long ago set

their conscience in order, and who aspire to perfection, it is to try to purify their heart in such manner as to have no remaining attachment or affection to present things. Now there are different degrees of purity and inward separation from all things, according to which the preparation for death will be more or less perfect.

The first degree is to have such a horror of deadly sin, as to avoid all occasions of it, and to fear nothing so much as sullying the conscience. The second is to avoid even venial sins, and especially those which are committed of deliberate purpose; so that neither through a self-indulgent spirit, nor through human considerations, nor through passion, should we ever permit ourselves any thing which we see plainly to be evil and unpleasing to God. This purity is great; it is the distinctive character of the children of God; this it is also which will give the most assurance in the hour of death. But the third degree, that of which we would now speak, adds to the two others a firm resolve not to allow the slightest attachment to any creature whatever, neither to places, persons, or employments; in a word, to nothing which nourishes and foments self-love.

When a soul has made a general renunciation of all, when, after the labour of many years, she has at length arrived at such a state that nothing in the world is capable of giving her pain, or of attracting and charming her, then is she free; she is able to fly like the dove sent forth from the ark, and to rise to Heaven, to repose there in the arms of her Creator. When death draws near, God not only liberates her from all fear, but He gives her also a sure hope of salvation. She has become so pure, that she appears to have regained her original purity, since, with the ornaments of grace and virtue, she now remains only that simple substance which she had when she came forth from the hands of God.

Naked came I out of my mother's womb, and naked shall I return thither. Job i. 21. These words may be applied to the soul when truly purified and freed from all earthly affection. She came forth from the baptismal font perfectly clean, adorned with the Grace and the gifts of the Holy Spirit, pleasing in the eyes of the Lord, free from all evil habits, in extreme ignorance of evil, in perfect innocence, and in a state to go directly to God. But innumerable pleasing objects having been since presented to her eyes in the intercourse of the world, she has begun to know and enjoy them; has suffered herself to be taken by them, and lost her first purity. At length, having resolved to turn to God, she has so completely renounced herself, and all created things, that she has regained her freedom; her bonds are broken, and nothing now hinders her from returning to the bosom of God; for if the weight of her sins had, as it were, pressed her down and bound her to the earth, she has set herself free by penitence; she has liberated herself from all. God has restored to her His Grace, and has anew inflamed her with His Love, and this Divine flame draws her with it to Heaven. A man thus purified and detached from creatures, finds himself even in this life perfectly free, and hindered by no obstacle from mounting to God.

Many feel in themselves an indescribable weight which presses them down, and fills them with languor and weakness of which they cannot imagine the cause; they feel themselves inclined to be remiss, to satisfy their desires in many respects, to throw themselves on outward things. This is because they have wearied themselves in the pursuit of many objects incapable of satisfying them, and because the accomplishment of their desires has become a heavy burthen to them. When a soul, noble and faithful to God, has broken her attachments, when she has freed herself, she begins to breathe an air so pure and so sweet, that none can speak of it but those who know it by experience. It is this which fills her with confidence when she thinks of death; and when the hour is come, far from fearing, she feels inconceivable joy.

It is related in the life of the famous doctor Francis Suarez, of the Company of Jesus, that when his last hour approached, the abundance of consolations with which his soul was filled, caused him to say these words, "I had not thought that it had been so sweet to die." This sentiment proceeded from the admirable purity which he had acquired by entire privation of worldly things.

Serenity and joy are ordinarily depicted on the faces of the Saints when they are about to die. Not very long ago I was attending a monk at his death, and being alone with him, I heard him suddenly utter so loud a cry, that I feared some violent pain had come over him. I approached his bed to see if I could relieve him; but I found that it was only an exclamation caused by joy proceeding from the sure hope of that everlasting happiness to which God called him. This holy man throughout his life had proposed to himself to seek God Alone in all things. And therefore when he felt his end near, he passed some hours in such transports of delight, that his heart in very deed suffered from them, and he appeared like a man whose breath was impeded by pain. The weakness of his body could no longer endure the excess of his joy.

I remember also that in my youth I was in a place where an ancient Religious, very spiritual and much mortified, was dying. His illness was a violent colick, which quickly carried him off. Directly he was alone, he conversed with Jesus Crucified in so tender a manner, that all in the house were much affected, and they quitted all to come and hear him at the door of the infirmary. I then reflected that such perfect joy, peace, and tranquillity, with so much devotion, could be the fruit of nothing but the purity of a soul entirely dead to the world, and having no love but for God Alone.

Every one thinks thus on these occasions; but there are very few who do not yield to the tendency of corrupt nature, and who, for want of resolution, do not return to their old habits, and crawl on till death without ever liberating themselves from those bonds which will then be broken without their consent, and which the desire of liberty should have led them to break long before.

BOOK V.

CHAPTER I.

(On these words)—" Desire to be unknown." B. i. c. 2.

QUESTION.—How can we hide ourselves, and be unknown in the world?

ANSWER.—In three ways. The first is, to retire entirely from the society of men, and to be in the world as if not in it. This has been done by innumerable solitaries, who buried themselves in deserts far from their kindred and their country. This history records of St. Paul the Hermit, of St. Arsenius, and many others, who made it their perfection and their security, to be as dead while yet on the earth, and to bury themselves alive. These without doubt literally followed the counsel of our Author, to "love a retired life."

2. The second is to follow an even course of conduct in the world without any affectation of singularity, leading a life outwardly common, but containing inwardly rare and extraordinary virtues. Those who do thus, wish to be known to none but God, Who searches the heart; they discover themselves to Him Alone, and in this they admirably observe this rule, " Desire to be little esteemed of[a];" for, in fact, no-

---

[a] B. i. c. 2.

thing is known of them that it is in their power to conceal. We read in the life of St. Ignatius, the Founder of the Company of Jesus, that God granted him extraordinary favours, and honoured him with very particular and frequent visitations; but that he confided them to none but his Confessor, a Father of the same Company, named James Eguia. This Father used to say, that if he survived Father Ignatius but three hours, he would declare things that would surprise the world. But the Saint, who loved obscurity rather than renown, so prevailed with God by his prayers, that he survived Eguia three days; and thus this treasure remained concealed. He afterwards appeared to a person of great piety, with his face entirely covered by a cloud[a]. This was to denote, as he gave him to understand, that the most singular part of his sanctity was his carefulness to conceal it as far as possible, even from those who approached him most nearly.

QUESTION.—What is the third way of practising this precept, Desire to be unknown?

ANSWER.—It is practised when we are exposed to the sight of men, but in such a situation as to be in some manner hidden from their eyes, appearing before them blackened, disfigured, covered with shame. It was thus that the Son of God appeared before the Jews during His Passion and Death; and we may affirm He was never more hidden, more difficult to recognize, than at that time. He was truly the King of the Universe; He possessed all the treasures of the wisdom, knowledge, and holiness of God; and yet in the mind of the people, and even of the priests and pontiffs, He passed for an im-

---

[a] This vision does not seem to be authenticated. See Boudon, Life hid with Christ, Pref.

postor; He was treated as a malefactor; He was crowned with thorns, with a reed in His hand for a sceptre; they bowed the knee in mockery before Him; they saluted Him as a pretended king; they spit on His Face. Who in such ignominy could have recognized His Greatness and Power? Could He have been more hidden in the wildest desert?

Thus, to disguise ourselves for the love of Christ, and to deceive the eyes of the world, is something heroic, and a sign of great perfection; it is a secret of the Gospel which has been revealed to Saints only, that is, to those who burning with the desire of resembling the Saviour, of being despised, rejected, calumniated, and condemned, as He was, perfectly imitated the first Christians, whom St. Paul represents as *being destitute, afflicted, tormented; of whom the world was not worthy*. Heb. xi. 37, 38. They not only practised this themselves, but also recommended it to all the faithful as the most heroic thing in the world. But no one has done so in stronger terms, and more expressly, than St. Ignatius, who will have his children desire nothing so much as to wear the livery of their Divine Master; that is, to suffer, after His Example, outrages, false witnesses, and injuries. He will have them desirous even to be accounted fools, yet never giving occasion for it, and by this shame to obtain great merit with God. This is to practise admirably our Author's precept, "Desire to be unknown." For we must not imagine that it is enough to admire it as excellent, and of sublime perfection; we must desire it, ask it earnestly of God, and omit nothing to obtain it. This is what is required of a true disciple of Christ, and of one who professes to follow the Saints.

CHAPTER II.

(On these words)—" From that One Word are all things, and all speak that One." B. i. c. 3.

QUESTION.—How is it that all creatures hold the same language, and speak but one thing which is contained in the unity of the Word?

ANSWER.—It is, that souls illuminated by God look solely and with a single eye to the Divine Word, Who manifests His infinite Perfections to them in all things, and enables them to comprehend them by a sovereign reason by which alone they are guided.

To explain this better, it must be understood that the pure in spirit look at all things in their principle; that they regard God Alone; and that whatever charms, whatever beauty or goodness, may be in creatures, they pay no regard to them; that is, that in all they see, in all they propose to themselves, in all they undertake, they make no difference between high and low, little and great, but consider solely the relation that all things bear to God. The way in which they preserve this purity of intention is this: they practise three things, called by the masters of the spiritual life— conformity, uniformity, Deiformity.

QUESTION.—What is conformity?

ANSWER.—It is a holy habit of conforming ourselves in all things to the will of God, and of taking precisely so much of all things as pleases God. Thus a secular man, who has a wife, children, and property, must look only to the Divine Will with regard to these things; he must leave all the events of his life to the care of Providence, and be able to say with the Saviour, *I do always those things that please Him.* John viii. 29.

QUESTION.—What is uniformity?
ANSWER.—It is the disposition in which the soul finds herself, when, having exercised herself in doing those things that please God, all things appear to her but as one through their relation to the Divine Will; because she does not examine her own particular reasons for loving or hating each thing, proposing to herself only this general reason,—God desires it, God wills it, God commands it. This is rightly called uniformity; for this one consideration effaces all others, and makes all things alike; so that abasement is loved as much as elevation, because the soul is convinced that it is the Divine Will which gives a value to all things; and, in fact, all motives are united in that one—the Will of the Supreme Master, Who Alone is worthy of our love and service.

QUESTION.—What is Deiformity?
ANSWER.—It is another and more excellent disposition, in which a soul, already accustomed to look only to that general reason which makes all things equal and indifferent to her, becomes lost in God, and incapable of seeing any thing but God in all surrounding objects. As then by long striving she has effaced all images of creatures from her mind, so far at least that they no longer make any impression on her will, all her views and desires tend towards the Creator; she sees Him in all things and in all places; she discovers Him in His works; and when she thinks of created things, it is as if she thought not of them, because she is completely filled and occupied with God, and loves Him Alone. This view of God, so universal and so simple, teaches her

far better, and makes her know things far more thoroughly than they can be known by those who regard them in themselves, and not in their First Cause. This is what our Author means by these words: "He to whom the Eternal Word speaketh, is delivered from a world of unnecessary conceptions [a]."

CHAPTER III.

(On these words)—"Thou oughtest to give all for all, and to retain nothing of thyself." B. iii. c. 27.

QUESTION.—What is it to give all for all?

ANSWER.—It consists in refusing nothing to God, in obeying Him in all things, and parting with all for the love of Him. What He demands, and we must sacrifice to Him, is, in the first place, all outward things that we love too much. Thus, we must have no attachment to any particular place, to little comforts, to things, or to persons, nor to any thing that pleases the flesh or the mind. It is, secondly, all offices and employments in which nature delights. Lastly, it is all joys, all graces, all supernatural gifts, which must be delivered into the Hands of Him from Whom we received them; so that we may be always ready to renounce them, and that there may be nothing which we will not readily quit to obtain the possession of God, and to do His Divine Will, which should fill the place of all. A man who reserves for his own satisfaction but one of the things of which we have spoken, and becomes attached to it, is very far from the perfection contained in this maxim of our Author.

[a] B. i. c. 3.

QUESTION.—What is the all that we promise to give to Him Who gives all?

ANSWER.—It is the entire disposal of all good things, even those which are spiritual. This God demands, and it concerns us much to offer it, for He refuses nothing to one who gives Him all. The liberality of God is proportioned to that of man. One who offers little receives little; one who gives all, gives all; but one who reserves but a single hair, does not give all. And in these dealings between God and man, there is a very great difference between much and all. We must try them according to the counsel of St. Paul, to be *perfect in every good work* [a]. But, besides this abundance of spiritual and supernatural good things, we acquire another Good of infinite value; it is God Himself, the Most Holy Trinity, Who gives Himself to the soul, to dwell with her in true union—a favour not to be obtained by those who give not all.

QUESTION.—What must we do to retain nothing of ourself?

ANSWER.—The soul must forget herself, so that her whole affections may be given to God. This can be done in three ways: firstly, by turning away her eyes from her own interests, and abandoning to the disposal of her Lord and her God all that concerns her property, her health, her life, with all that may befall her, not only in time, but even in eternity. This absolute freedom from all private interests makes her careful to be led only by the purest motive—that of pleasing our Lord. Not that the desire of recompence is not a good motive, or is to be blamed; but the most praiseworthy and perfect is that of disinterested love, whose only object is to give glory

---

[a] Heb. xiii. 21.

to God. With this we may hope all from the Father of mercies, for Whom we renounce all.

2. The second way in which we may forget ourselves is, by following in all our actions the guidance of Grace rather than the motions of nature. Many fail on this point in that they give way too much to temperament and disposition, and obstinately refuse to change their way of proceeding, as being in general natural and disinterested.

3. The third way of retaining nothing of self, is so to love God, and to let Him so absolutely rule all the powers of the soul, that she should no longer feel herself[a], as our Author says. This is a practice of great perfection, and depends far more on the operation of Grace than on the efforts of the creature. Thus a man, moved and excited by the Spirit of God, feels within him no longer his own inclinations, but those of the Holy Spirit, Who is the principle of all his movements, according to the saying of the Apostle, *As many as are led by the Spirit of God, they are the sons of God.* Rom. viii. 14. A soul thus guided by God, is no longer conscious of its own actions, and knows experimentally that one who gives all, retains nothing of himself.

CHAPTER IV.

(On these words)—" The more thou canst go out of thyself, so much the more wilt thou be able to enter into Me." B. iii. c. 56.

QUESTION.—How can we go out of ourselves?

ANSWER.—In three manners particularly. First, by combating self-love, that vicious or too merely natural love, which enters every where, and disguises itself

---

[a] B. iii. c. 21.

by a thousand artifices. How many people do we see, who are reputed virtuous, and who, when called on, do many good works, but who yet cannot rid themselves of a certain affection, a natural tenderness for what concerns themselves, and above all, for their own person! They avoid every thing painful; they love their ease and repose; and if they feel ever so little pain, they cannot speak of it without bemoanings, and great signs of compassion for themselves. To combat this delicacy, so contrary both to the severity of evangelic precepts, and to the nobleness of the true followers of the Cross, is to go out of ourselves, in order to draw nigh unto God.

2. But we may also go out of ourselves in another manner, when we discharge our employments without looking to ourselves in them, without becoming attached to them, being too much interested in them, and giving them too much application and care. For most people who have business to do, who are to speak in public, who are in high stations, or important employments, think of nothing else day or night: they are uneasy about the success of their labours, and the judgment that will be formed of themselves; this occupies their whole mind.

Figure to yourself a Sister in a religious house, who, after having long been Superior, is deposed from her station, and reduced to a level with the others. She feels as if transported into a new world, or a great desert. This does not happen to Sisters alone; it happens also to men, who stand quite amazed when they are removed from government, or from the management of affairs. The only cause of their trouble is too passionate a desire of succeeding in their employments: for their mind would be at rest, and they would be always tranquil, if they looked only to God: because, being filled with God, He would be always present with them, and they would enjoy His sweetness. It is, then, a means of going out of ourselves to try to fulfil our duties well, with the sole view of pleasing our Lord; and to do so, we must never propose to ourselves those low and human motives which self-love commonly suggests. We must not be very anxious either to please men, or to receive their praise; we must despise all that the world can say, and desire nothing but to please God. This is indeed renouncing ourselves, and being truly interior.

3. But the third manner of going out of ourselves, and forsaking ourselves entirely, is undoubtedly the most difficult, and few have courage to embrace it. It consists in hating and maltreating the body by penitence, in order, as it were, to separate the soul from the flesh in which it naturally reposes. Many people, spiritual by profession, know not the value of this holy practice; and for want of exerting themselves to combat corrupt nature, they can neither leave themselves, nor be united to God.

When a man has quitted sin, and renounced all the natural satisfaction which he might find in his employment, he has not yet wholly given himself up to God: he must complete this going out of self by treating himself roughly, by forcing the soul, so to speak, to abandon the sweet repose that it finds in the flesh; he must deal with his body as men do with certain animals which they wish to accustom to stay in some place where their master needs them: they are beaten every where else; and when there, they are caressed, and made to feel that it is their only place of rest. In like manner, when we wish to constrain the soul to abide in the superior part, which is the spirit, we must persecute her in the inferior, which is the flesh, and give her no rest till, wearied with so hard and continual a war, she mounts at last to that lofty region where God calls her to gladden and comfort her.

It is with this view that the most fervent practise great austerities. They seek to oblige the soul, by force of macerations, to quit the flesh, that she may ascend towards God, Who, being a pure Spirit, takes pleasure in spirit alone [a]. We have already remarked, that many good persons are quite at rest with regard to this, because they think they stand well enough with God, and, contented with their state, they do not think a more austere manner of life ought to be required of them. But their fervour might go much further, and they would not stay there if, following the leading of Divine love, which is strong and courageous, they made war upon themselves by the mortification of the body, which the Saints esteemed so highly, which they praised so loudly, and of which they tasted the fruits, sweeter than can be told, and to be known only by experience. To reduce this to practice, every man must offer himself to God as a burnt-offering, without seeking in any thing to flatter or spare himself, and must pray Him earnestly to make known to him His will respecting it. Having done this, he has reason to hope that our Lord will enlighten his mind, and give him the strength necessary for the execution of his good designs.

CHAPTER V.

(On these words)—" He that endeavours to withdraw himself from obedience, withdraweth himself from Grace; and he who seeketh for himself private benefits, loseth those which are common." B. iii. c. 13.

QUESTION.—Why is it that he who withdraws himself from obedience deprives himself of grace?

ANSWER.—Because obedience is necessary to pre-

[a] John iv. 24.

serve the gifts of Heaven, as rain is necessary to make the trees shoot and the flowers open. There are souls, undoubtedly, who have received great gifts from above, and to whom it is easy to rise to a high degree of sanctity, and to an intimate familiarity with God: but if once they trust too much in their own illumination, if they rest too much on the great things that the Spirit of God works in them, immediately they fall into delusion, and these graces, no longer supported by humility and faith, their sole origin, soon cease to exist.

It is quite otherwise with those who are entirely submissive both in mind and in will to their superiors: for when they seem, by obeying, to renounce the favours of the Divine Spouse, then they secure them to themselves more abundantly. And by this very thing it appears manifestly that we cannot withdraw ourselves from obedience, without depriving ourselves of Grace. We read of St. Simeon Stylites, that he lived in a surprising manner, on a pillar forty cubits in height. He had taken up his abode there, not by the order or advice of any man, but by the inspiration of God; and yet he so thoroughly retained the spirit of obedience, that when the Bishops, to try him, sent him word to come down from his pillar, he immediately prepared himself to obey their command: it was thus that he preserved the wonderful gift that he had received from God. Those, then, in whom the Holy Spirit works great and uncommon things, must be always ready to obey, for otherwise they will infallibly be abandoned by Grace.

QUESTION.—Wherefore is it that those who seek for themselves special gifts lose those which are common?

ANSWER.—For the reason that I have just said; for of spiritual gifts, some are common, and some private gifts. The common are necessary to all, as the virtues founded on faith, humility, obedience, charity, &c. The private are certain feelings of devotion, sublime thoughts, illuminations, and other free graces, which God gives to whoever seemeth Him good, and which must be pleasing to Him, though far less so than the common graces, since these last serve as a basis and foundation for the others.

Many people so attach themselves to their private devotions, that they find no pleasure in those exercises of piety that are common among the faithful. If you speak to them of the Passion of the Saviour, of His sacred Wounds, of His Childhood, or of the judgments of God, and the rules which the Saints have given us to live as Christians, they are hardly at all moved. This delicacy in spiritual matters is very dangerous, and carefully to be avoided: for those who affect special gifts too much, lose the fruit of the common; and those who, desiring, through a spirit of singularity, to distinguish themselves from others, practise devotions which they alone enjoy and esteem, depart from true devotion, and sometimes even from the Faith; there being nothing easier than to pass from singularity to delusion, and from delusion to error.

Persons of solid piety, although God discourses with them familiarly, and grants them great favours, cease not to approve of those holy practices which the Church recommends in general to all her children; but those delicate souls, which will have nothing common, cannot read any thing but the Greatness of Jesus, and other such works. St. Francis de Sales they do not think sufficiently elevated: nothing pleases them in Grenada, in Rodriguez: they are not satisfied without something more subtle, more strained, and less easy to understand. Not that there is not much to learn, and much to be profitably studied in the books which treat of the mystic life; but one who is truly spiritual takes pleasure also in reading those which explain the best known things; and nothing is more to his taste than the book of the Imitation of Christ, simple and intelligible as it is.

It is related in the life of Sister Mary of the Incarnation, a Carmelitess of great sanctity, that the simplest preachers touched her much, and that little was required to inspire her with devotion. Souls thus disposed are like those who, having their stomach in a good state, digest everything, and benefit by the coarsest food; but the others may be compared to people who live on dainties: when they accustom themselves to these delicacies, by degrees they lose their taste for bread and ordinary food, and are in great danger of destroying their health.

There is an important remark to be made here, that those souls whom God leads by common ways, must not envy those whom He conducts by extraordinary paths, and whom He is pleased thus to sanctify; and that these last, for their part, must beware of resting too much on the particular favours that He gives them, for it is both best and safest to attach themselves to those practices of devotion which are most customary in the Church, to seek to please God, and particularly to love humility and obedience. For if they make their virtue to consist in those extraordinary things which the Holy Spirit works in them, it is to be feared that in time they may lose the common graces so necessary to a right performance of the essential duties of the Christian life. St. Theresa appeared after her death to one of her nuns, and told her to admonish all the Provincials of her Order to exhort those whom they should receive, and over whom they should bear rule, not to be too desirous of visions, revelations, and other such favours, but rather to labour for the acquisition of solid virtue;

that for herself, if God had been pleased to have mercy upon her, it was not on account of such gifts, but for other and far better things which He had deigned to teach her, and by means of which He had conducted her to that glory which she was enjoying.

CHAPTER VI.

(On these words)—" There is great difference between the wisdom of an illuminated and devout man, and the knowledge of a learned and studious clerk." B. iii. c. 31.

QUESTION.—Wherein consists this difference?

ANSWER.—In three things principally. The first is, that the wisdom of a man of prayer cometh from the Father of lights [a], and that it "floweth from above," B. iii. c. 31, while the knowledge of a man of letters is but the fruit of study. Whence it follows, that this wisdom, emanating from above, cannot be without truth, seeing that it comes from the Fountain of all light, the Uncreated Truth. Therefore is it always firm, always certain, without clouds or darkness; whereas that learning which is acquired by reasoning, has much of the weakness of the human mind, naturally subject to doubts and self-deceit. Even the pagan philosophers acknowledged that those thoughts which come to us unsought, and as of themselves, are more valuable than all the productions of our mind. If this is the case even with profane learning, how far more must it be with supernatural things which are above our reason, and can be discovered to us only by the Divine Light.

2. The second difference is, that the wisdom which God communicates to man in prayer easily enters his mind; while human learning costs him much trouble, and cannot be thoroughly obtained without long

[a] James i. 17.

labour. Supernatural and Divine Knowledge has this property, that it relieves, consoles, and enlarges the heart, but that which requires study and meditation wearies the mind; as the wise man says, "*He that increaseth knowledge increaseth sorrow.*" Eccl. i. 18.

3. The third is, that the knowledge which is given by a ray of the Eternal Light, is always, or almost always, suddenly impressed on the soul, and that which is introduced into it by means of speculation, enters slowly and gradually, as the Author on whom we are commenting remarks, when he makes our Lord say, " I am He that in one instant do raise up the humble mind [a]." We feel ourselves, in fact, more enlightened in this one instant, than we should be after ten years of study in the schools. This is done by the operation of the Holy Spirit, and by the infusion of a light which is quite simple, with no variety of objects, but which contains within itself the essence and abridgment of a thousand distinct truths.

To comprehend this rightly, represent to yourself two men, of whom one writes, and the other prints a discourse. The first requires much time to form every letter, to arrange and join them together. The second, by a single movement of the press, can complete a whole sheet. So a studious man may in time acquire some knowledge of the things of God; but one who is taught by supernatural Light is at once so enlightened, that he is able to speak long and in a Divine manner on the most spiritual subjects.

But that which distinguishes him most above the other is, that God communicates His Spirit to him, according to the promise of the Saviour, Who said to His Apostles, *The Spirit of Truth, which proceedeth from the Father, will guide you into all truth.* John xv. 26; xvi. 13. Thus, as we daily see, are

---

[a] B. iii. c. 43.

the words of Scripture accomplished, that *a man's mind is sometime wont to tell him more than seven watchmen,* more learned than he, *that sit above in a high tower.* Ecclus. xxxvii. 14.

This has been proved in very many instances, and particularly with respect to St. Theresa. Fifteen learned men were assembled at Avila to judge by what spirit she was led. When the examination was finished, they concluded that the astonishing things that God worked in her were the operations of the devil. But a holy monk, of the Order of St. Francis, passing by, perceived and declared, that it was the Spirit of God that governed her; and St. Francis of Borgia, more illustrious for the gift of contemplation which God had given him than for his learning, confirmed this declaration.

It is written in the life of St. Clara of Monte-Falco, that she discovered a concealed heretic, who was universally regarded and revered as a Saint. God has worked many other wonders in His servants. He sent St. Bernard to destroy many errors, and to 'undeceive many heretics. Yet the Saint in his youth had given but little time to study, and with all his talent, what he had learned could not have sufficed to write the many admirable works which he has left us.

Even women, as St. Catherine of Sienna, St. Theresa, and some others, have discoursed so well on the Mysteries of the Faith, that their works cannot be read without admiration. St. Ignatius, the Founder of the Company of Jesus, had received such light on the Ineffable Mystery of the Trinity, that he undertook to write a book on it without having studied. St. Francis of Assisi, when consulted on many difficult passages of Scripture, instantly replied so clearly, that learned men were surprised at him. You have only to read the Chronicles of his Order to see some remarkable instances of this; and all this proceeds, not from the strength and penetration of the human mind, but from Divine Illumination. Therefore it is more fitly called wisdom than learning.

CHAPTER VII.

(On these words)—"If thou hadst but once perfectly entered into the secrets of the Lord Jesus, and tasted a little of His ardent love," &c. B. ii. c. 1.

QUESTION.—How can we enter into the secrets of the Lord Jesus?

ANSWER.—By penetrating and learning experimentally what is most inward in Him. Three things are most particularly so. 1st. The tender love which He has always felt for His Father and for us. 2nd. The moral precepts which He has most recommended to us, and on which He dwelt the most. 3rd. His inward pains and sorrows.

QUESTION.—What are the tenderest feelings in the heart of Jesus?

ANSWER.—Towards His Father they are: a generous love for that Father so worthy of love, a constant waiting for His orders, an ardent desire to see His whole will done. *I do always*, said He, *those things that please Him*. John viii. 29. And elsewhere, *My meat is to do the will of Him that sent Me*. John iv. 34. Towards us they are paternal affection, and a most ardent thirst for our salvation. One who desires to enter into the secrets of the Lord Jesus must be acquainted with His feelings, and try to produce some resembling them, that thus he may be bound very closely to Him, and that, according to the Apostle's precept, *this mind may be in him, which was also in Christ Jesus*. Phil. ii. 5.

QUESTION.—What are the moral precepts most proper for Christian souls?

ANSWER.—The principal points of our Saviour's teaching, in which He has comprised its spirit. They may be reduced to a thorough practice of humility and gentleness, patience in the evils of this life, love of the Cross and of mortification, charity towards our neighbour, evangelic poverty, and a desire above all of being despised and humiliated as He was during His Passion; for this is to be His, to wear His livery, to enter even into His secrets. This mystery is hidden in Him, and is known but to very few.

There are many who have a regard for Jesus; they adore Him, they bow the knee before Him as before their Lord, and yet they retain a secret aversion to the most essential parts of His system. They know the exterior of Jesus, His Sovereign Power, His Greatness, His Majesty, His design of saving men, and other such things, but not the more hidden things, and those which are nearest His Heart. Therefore we might say to them with our Author, "If thou hadst but once perfectly entered into the secrets of the Lord Jesus," &c. And as He says in another place, "He that hath the Spirit of Jesus will find an hidden manna." B. i. c. 1. This heavenly manna is nothing else than the abundance of graces, illumination, comforts, and spiritual delights, which Jesus bestows on those who enter into the full meaning of His precepts.

QUESTION.—What is the third thing to be observed among the secrets of the Lord Jesus?

ANSWER.—His Sufferings, which we must try to impress on our minds, by constantly meditating on them with tenderness and affection. If any man, then, desires to know and feel what passes within Jesus, oppressed with sadness and grief, he must have His Passion constantly before his eyes, and dwell thereon, not only in thoughts, but also by a feeling of sympathy which penetrates his heart.

2. Another and more efficacious means of feeling the Sufferings of Christ is, in some measure to experience them. "No man," says our Author, "has so cordial a feeling of the Passion of Christ, as he who hath suffered the like himself." B. ii. c. 12. St. Bonaventure teaches us, that this is done by looking to this Divine Model of patience, and trying to feel in ourselves the rigour of His Tortures; and thus, that we may know in ourselves what He suffered at the pillar, we must, says this holy Doctor, discipline ourselves to blood. One who sincerely loves our Lord, and who desires nothing so much as to participate in His Sufferings, can thus best judge how cruel His Scourging was, and how great the pain caused by the nails which pierced His Hands and Feet. Many pious persons of the present day, falsely persuaded that it is enough to care for the interior, might learn by such experience that the exterior exercises of virtue are of no little service to the soul which desires to be hid with Christ in God[a]. I may add, that very many in the religious life, who have not much outward occupation, and who have but too much leisure to spend in their cells, ought to think themselves happy to have it in their power to hold familiar converse with Jesus Crucified, instead of losing their time in reading curious books or profane histories, or in thinking of their health, and of the means of preventing and curing imaginary infirmities. This would be infinitely more useful to them; their mind would become more fervent, and their body more healthy and vigorous.

3. It is very sweet also to the soul to share in the inward Sufferings of Christ. If she sometimes feels that desertion, that pain and anguish, of which we

[a] Colos. iii. 3.

have elsewhere spoken, she should profit by them, and believe that they are as doors to enter into the secrets of the Lord Jesus, Who suffered in Soul as well as in Body; and that in this way the union is formed between the holy soul and her Divine Spouse. For this reason also, St. Bernard had constantly before his eyes Christ on the Cross, and never lost the recollection of His Death, as he testifies in many parts of his writings, particularly on Solomon's Song.

The same is told us of Saint Francis, and it is related in the Chronicles of his Order, that a passer-by once hearing him cry aloud, imagined that a murder was being committed, and ran hastily towards the place from whence the voice came; but when he arrived there, he was much surprised to see St. Francis lying on the ground covered with tears. He knew him, and asked him why he wept. "My Saviour has died," replied he; "He suffered so much, and you ask me the cause of my tears!" This vehement grief proceeded from the love with which he burned, and by which he had entered far into the secrets of the Lord Jesus. All those who, after the example of these Saints, make the sufferings of their Master the subject of their meditations, will, like them, be much affected by the evils which this Man-God deigned to suffer, when He immolated Himself for their salvation and for that of all sinners.

CHAPTER VIII.

(On these words) —" Drink of the Lord's cup heartily.... As for comforts, leave them to God." B. ii. c. 12.

QUESTION.—How can we drink of the Lord's cup heartily, and with regard to comforts leave them to God?

Answer.—In three manners; the first of which is, following our Lord in the narrowest way, when we think it better than a wider path, in which we can neither follow nor serve Him so perfectly. There is nothing more common than to see people who make a profession of virtue, corresponding but little to the good feelings which God gives them, though they seem to receive them rightly, or at least do not entirely reject them. Spiritual progress no way consists in this, but in putting into execution those good desires with which God inspires us; in living a life under rule; in loving meditation, silence, and prayer; in mortifying the appetite; in hearkening attentively to the voice of God within the heart; and in doing all these things with extreme carefulness and fervour.

This path, which is that of perfection, is not easy to follow; it is a thorny path; few walk in it, and much courage is required to enter it. We cannot too earnestly exhort most men to combat sensuality, to resist the tendency of nature, not to seek their own ease, to live as children of the Cross, and, above all, to practise what Jesus says to all, *If any man will come after Me, let him deny himself, and take up his cross.* Matt. xvi. 24. This is the first way of loving the sufferings of the Saviour.

Question.—What is the second?
Answer.—It is not only to strive to keep the Law of God, but truly to love suffering, knowing that there are hidden treasures in the afflictions and labours of this life. The great advantage obtained from this is, that we learn to avoid self-indulgence, and grow stronger day by day in virtue, and in the love of our Lord. The best portion of the heirs of the Cross is pain and grief; and, when all is well considered, he who suffers most may be called the

richest. But few know the value of this great treasure. Our Author, who knew it well, counsels spiritual persons to place their satisfaction and happiness in self-denials. We have elsewhere spoken amply of sufferings, and of the good effects which they produce.

QUESTION.—What is the third manner of embracing the Cross of the Saviour?

ANSWER.—It is not only to embrace mortification and contempt with our whole heart, but to love them principally with the design of being made like unto our Lord, according to the rule which St. Ignatius gives us in his exercises, that if we could glorify God equally in adversity and in prosperity, we ought to prefer the former state to the latter, through the sole desire of resembling Jesus, and of showing Him that we love His Person infinitely more than His Gifts and Favours. Love, which, by attaching our hearts to the Son of God, fills us with all manner of things that are good, makes us know what He is, and what He suffered, better in proportion as we try to feel His Sufferings in ourselves, in the manner spoken of in the preceding chapter.

Our Lord ordinarily joins Himself to those whom He loves, because it is natural for love to tend towards union; and according to the different states in which He was during the course of His mortal life, He unites Himself to them; now as a Child, impressing on their soul the character of His holy Childhood; now as glorified and transfigured on Mount Tabor, communicating to them some ray of His Glory; now as suffering, causing them inwardly to feel His afflictions; now as dying on the Cross, causing them swoonings and mortal agonies. Thus He unites them so intimately to Himself, that it might be said that henceforth they are but one with Him. A soul which has found this hidden treasure renounces all to obtain it[a]; takes tribulation for her portion, loves it, delights in it, and regards it as the means of drawing nearer to her Saviour and her God.

QUESTION.—How can we renounce comforts, and leave them to the will of God?

ANSWER.—By doing nothing to obtain comforts, but always, on the contrary, desiring crosses, like that pure lover of Christ, St. Catharine of Sienna, who once seeing her Beloved offer her two crowns, the one of gold, the other of thorns, left the first, and taking the last, fixed it on her head. Every faithful and generous soul should do as much. With regard to joy and sensible comfort, she must leave all to that Gracious Saviour, Who, seeing her thus resigned, will give her a hundredfold more than she would desire. *If so be that we suffer with Him*, says the great Apostle, *we may also be glorified together*. Rom. viii. 17.

CHAPTER IX.

(On these words)—" God will have us perfectly subject unto Him, that being inflamed with His love, we may transcend the narrow limits of human reason." B. i. c. 14.

QUESTION.—How is it that ardent love may be said to rise above natural reason, and far to transcend the powers of the human mind?

ANSWER. — First, because one who enjoys God by love, knows God more clearly by experience than by all the penetration and intelligence of the mind. The reason of this is, that man, under the veil of faith, is able to attain to God, and to be united to Him by love immediately, and with no void between, as the mystic theologians say. Thus love

---

[a] Matt. xiii. 44.

is far superior to natural reason, because it goes straight to God, not indeed seeing Him as He is, yet believing Him as He is. Therefore we say that Faith, dim as it is, surpasses all notions that we can have of the Essence and perfections of God, except the intuitive vision. Even the faithful, who believe though they see not, have God present with them, as well as the blessed, but with this difference however, that the blessed see Him as He is; and that, although the faithful believe Him as He is, they are very far from having as clear a knowledge of Him as those who see Him.

After all, when by virtue of pure love, which enables us to feel and enjoy Him, we have the happiness of embracing Him, we are united to Him immediately, as the blessed are; and in this close union we conceive an idea of Him incomparably more perfect than all that the most skilful doctors can form. Figure to yourself a learned and eloquent man, coming from a northern country, who, without having ever drunk wine, undertakes to discourse of it in public, and collects for that purpose all that has ever been written on the subject. What would be thought of him? Those who heard him would certainly think that he understood nothing in comparison with the simplest peasant who had drunk it, although this last might be unable to speak on the subject in well-chosen language.

QUESTION.—How can it be said, secondly, that love surpasses knowledge?

ANSWER.—Because we approach closely to God rather by the way of affection than by that of reasoning; for it is certain that by this means we reach God more easily and more surely, than by any speculation, however subtle. Picus of Mirandola, more illustrious for his learning than for his high birth, after having read and written much, protests, finally, that it is great folly to study so much in order to attain to the Supreme Good, because It may be attained more easily and with less trouble by affection than by meditation, nothing being easier than to love.

This way is it which St. Ignatius recommends to his children, to whom he requires that a year should be given after their studies, to learn to unite themselves more closely than ever to God; and this he calls a school for the feelings and affections of the heart. His design is, that after having long laboured to attain to the knowledge of God by learning, they should try to approach Him by the exercises of pure love. Before all things, then, we must study to grow in humility and charity, to seek God with a childlike simplicity, and to lose ourselves in Him, without being too anxious to search into Divine things, but contenting ourselves with what we know by faith, yielding our own reason, blinding ourselves, so to speak, and following in all things not our own guidance, but that of Heaven; keeping ourselves ever in dependence on a Director, in order to go to God in the same manner with the simplest persons. True devotion consists not in reasoning, nor in forming fine ideas of the truths of the Faith: it consists in humble submission of the mind and heart, in a holy affection, which, while it attaches the will to God, enlightens the understanding. In truth, Divine love is a fire which gives light no less than heat: so that those in whom it is kindled, though otherwise ignorant and untaught, have sublime thoughts and lofty feelings respecting its mysteries, sufficient even to impart to the best instructed. It is useless then to wear ourselves out with watchings and labours in order to acquire much knowledge by dint of study, since love is like an ever placid river, which noiselessly brings into the soul the inestimable treasures of wisdom and knowledge.

QUESTION.—How may love be said, thirdly, to rise above knowledge?

ANSWER.—Because it subjects the intellect, however unwilling, to the light of faith, and ever prefers ardent love to sublime knowledge. This way does not differ much from that of which we last spoke; it only adds to it a certain constraint, and a species of violence done to the understanding, to suppress its natural vivacity. Some people say: Our devotion is not like that of the ignorant, it is wise and reasonable. If they mean by this that it is founded on good principles and sound doctrine, this is very good, but if they mean only that in the things of God, they reason and argue like philosophers, they are in error. The devotion of St. Bonaventure was not of another kind than that of Brother Giles[a]; but there was this difference, that that of Brother Giles proceeded wholly from God, and that of the holy Doctor was supported by his acquired learning. Yet when St. Bonaventure discoursed with God, he did so with as much simplicity as Brother Giles. The devotion of Father Suarez was of the same nature with that of Brother Ximenes; what distinguished them was, that Father Suarez could rest his on the principles of theology, and that this advantage was wanting to Brother Ximenes; but in the exercise of prayer he did not yield in humility to this simple brother. He even valued his theology far less than the remarkable gift of prayer which God had communicated to him; and he said that he would rather have renounced all his

---

[a] The third who joined St. Francis, and remarkable for the ecstasies into which the mention of God or His love cast him. A. Butler relates (Life of St. Bonaventure) that Brother Giles asked St. Bonaventure, "Can a dull idiot love God as perfectly as a great scholar?" St. Bonaventure, "A poor old woman may love Him more than the most learned master and doctor in theology." On which Brother Giles, meditating, fell into an ecstasy.

learning, than have lost a single hour of his ordinary conversations with God.

There is a very great difference between the light proceeding from charity and grace, and that which comes by study. Therefore are they grossly deceived, who think they can reason about piety as they do about learning, and that the same means must be used to become a spiritual man as to become a good theologian or a good philosopher. This is a dangerous delusion, which prevents very many learned men from advancing far in the way of perfection. Our progress in that way depends less on the thoughts of the mind, than on the affections of the will, and on a blind submission both to God and to those who are in the place of God. This saying of Scripture should be always remembered: *If ye will not believe, surely ye shall not be established* in those truths that are taught you, Is. vii. 9. Many people read the writers on the mystic theology in the same way as those on the scholastic, not considering that the principal end of the former is not to enlighten the understanding, but to inflame the will. In consequence, far from finding pleasure in their works, they are disgusted with them; whereas, if they read them in the same spirit in which they were composed, they would not only find no obscurity, but they would comprehend their mystery, and would be inwardly touched with a real desire for perfection. Thus, much more is gained by ardent love than by profound erudition.

CHAPTER X.

(On these words)—" He is truly learned, that doeth the will of God." B. i. c. 14.

QUESTION.—What must we do to accomplish the Divine will.

Answer.—Two things in particular are necessary: one is to do nothing which we do not think entirely conformed to the Divine will; the other, to do all, only because God commands it. As to the first, the greatest difficulty, when we are determined only to do God's will, is to know wherein it consists, so that we can certainly say, This is God's will. For a good man, who knows how important it is to do what God desires of him, will easily resolve to do so, if only he knows what it is; but this is the difficulty.

It should be known, then, that there are three things by which we can distinguish with certainty what is the Divine will, and what is not so. The law of God is the first, the disposition of Providence is the second, and obedience the third. To these may be added a fourth, more hidden, and more difficult to discover, inspiration.

1. By the law of God we mean all that is contained in the Decalogue, and all ordinances emanating from a legitimate power, whether written, or authorized and confirmed by custom. We comprehend also the statutes and general regulations made by prelates and ecclesiastical superiors. To accomplish all these things faithfully, is to submit and conform ourselves to the Divine will.

2. The dealings of Providence, such as events which depend in no manner on the will of man, are evident tokens of that of God. Amongst these we must class sicknesses, misfortunes, bad weather, unforeseen accidents, loss of property, persecutions, all things, in a word, which God does not leave to our own disposal: for if we examine these things well, though the malice of men may have a part in them, it is manifest that they are inflictions of God's Providence, and effects of His will.

3. There remains only the obedience due to those whom we are lawfully bound to obey. Now we can-

not doubt that in executing their orders, we execute those of God. For the Saviour said to the Apostles, and in their person to all His ministers, *He that heareth you heareth Me*, Luke x. 16; and St. Paul orders all the faithful to *obey them that have the rule* over them. Heb. xiii. 17. Those who live in a community, under a head who governs them, have this advantage over those who are free, that they are sure of doing God's will in practising obedience.

4. With regard to inspiration, people are sometimes deceived; and the difficulty of distinguishing between the true and the false, leaves the mind in great uncertainty as to the will of God. But it is certain that one whose intention is perfectly pure is not exposed to grievous doubts, because acting sincerely, and desiring to do whatever is best, he can hardly be deceived; and in any case he will be excusable, if before acting he examined the inspiration, and, for greater security, consulted with persons experienced in the spiritual life. Moreover, those who have long been led by the Spirit of God, are in the habit of following the drawings of Grace and the direction of the Holy Spirit, and consequently cannot then fail of doing His Divine will.

The greatest difficulty regards those things which are not of obligation, and which God leaves to our choice: for it is easy to mistake them; and while we think we are doing God's will, to do our own. This happens to the weak and unmortified. All in their conduct is human and mere nature, and they act through self-love alone: or, if they seem to perform some action on the principle of faith and for a Christian motive, nature often seeks herself in it, and has generally as large a share in it as Grace.

It is no wonder, then, that there are so few perfect men, since there are so few who apply themselves as they ought, to know the will of God in those things that are free to them. We see but too many of a holy and religious profession, who, except in the things prescribed by their rule, and those expressly ordered by their superiors, follow the inclination of nature almost entirely, without taking any trouble to discover what is most pleasing to God. If they form some design, attach themselves to some study, practise some exercise, it is not because God inspires them with the thought, but because their inclination leads them to do so, and that they regard therein only what is material and sensible; because, in short, they find pleasure in it, and they think that none can blame them when they have said that God does not forbid it, and that they see no harm in it.

QUESTION.—How, then, can we know what is the Divine Will?

ANSWER. — First, we must beware of acting like men in general, who love themselves alone, and have nothing less in view than to please our Lord. They generally act on three bad principles: caprice, passion, and interest. Thus they depart widely from the will of God, Who discovers Himself only to peaceful, gentle, and disinterested souls. Before all things, then, they must labour to destroy in themselves these three causes of disorder; which is the first means of rightly knowing and afterwards of doing the things that God requires of them.

2. The second means is prayer, in which we entreat the Lord, if it be but by a simple aspiration, that He will be pleased to lead us in the way of His holy Commandments. Thus we obtain from Him some light to know His Will, and the soul thus illuminated, infallibly makes the right decision, and is at rest with regard to her duties.

3. The last means, when we doubt which of two things to do, is always to incline rather to that which

mortifies than to that which flatters the senses; for, as the Saviour assures us, that the way to Heaven is narrow, he who chooses that which is most contrary to the flesh and to sensuality, may hope that he is entering the way of God, and that he is doing that which is most pleasing to Him. Besides, as thus he shows more virtue, and does not act from self-love, God will not refuse him light.

By this whole discourse it appears how difficult it is to know what is the Divine Will in those things which are not of strict obligation, and that this grace is never granted save to those who seek God sincerely and in all things; for as they aim at the highest perfection, and God, Who regards good-will more than anything else, always wills that which is most perfect, it is to be believed that they easily discover what pleases Him most.

QUESTION.—What is the second thing necessary for the complete accomplishment of the Divine Will?

ANSWER.—For this it is not enough to do precisely what God wills; we must do it because He wills it, and never resolve or even incline to any thing whatever, except because He desires it. This is a very important point, and cannot be sufficiently recommended; for, in the first place, this motive is so excellent, that it increases exceedingly the merit of our good works; in the second place, it is so pure, that no selfish consideration mingles in it; lastly, it is so sublime, that it leads directly to perfect love. When the soul is enabled to comprehend what is God's will, and is thoroughly imbued with it, she little values all besides.

But it is to be observed, that if this is noble, it is also very spiritual, and that few but those who walk simply in a spirit of faith are capable of it; for of things not commanded, men in general regard only what is great and striking. But those who set before themselves only the will of God, consider the substance of the action but little in comparison of the motive. It is for the motive that they care; that is the only thing they value; and they are so indifferent to all besides, that gold and straw are alike to them. They think only of obeying the precepts of God, and in that alone they find their satisfaction and their rest.

One of them may perhaps have an opportunity of hearing a famous preacher, or of going to see something rare and extraordinary, when it is proposed to him to perform some action, small indeed, but apparently more pleasing to God. If he is a religious, for instance, his superior may appoint him to accompany another who is obliged to go out for some good work. Persuaded that God requires it, he leaves all to go where he is sent, and thinks no more of the sermon which he wished to hear, or of the rarity which he desired to see. But if he feels repugnant to mortifying himself, it is a certain proof that he has never rightly understood how important a motive is the will of God, and that he knows not what is meant by simple love. Thus, however he may strive, he will never do any thing great, since he prefers his own will to that of God: and all the excuses by which he persuades himself of the contrary are complete delusions.

It remains only to be observed, that when we have resolved to act on this pure motive only, and to humble ourselves to every thing which God desires, we do not at first find much pleasure in it, because we have been accustomed to employ ourselves in ministrations of distinction. Not having yet known or felt the sweetness contained in the Divine will, we find ourselves with no enjoyment in many humiliating employments, particularly in those which are hard and painful. But after having persevered for some time in this holy practice, we then begin to enjoy what before appeared very insipid, and find full satisfaction in it. Thus we make it so great a pleasure to sweep a room in obedience to the will of God, as to prefer this low action to the highest employments in the world, if we are not called to them by God. This pleasure often increases to such a degree, that feeling over ourselves the special guidance of Providence, we arrive in time at the highest degree of uniformity, in which we see, feel, and enjoy God Alone in all things, which is that happy state which may rightly be called a paradise on earth.

Those who embrace the spiritual life must therefore be warned, not to be disheartened by the first difficulties: for it will be like the manna with which the Israelites were at first disgusted as insipid, and not nourishing [a], but in which they afterwards found the flavour of all the most exquisite food [b]. Let them persevere in this exercise, and they will find it a sure way of arriving at what they seek, which is perfect repose of heart, and the most intimate union of the soul with God by true charity.

CHAPTER XI.

OF THE FOUNDATION OF THE WHOLE SPIRITUAL LIFE, WHICH IS HUMILITY.

(On these words)—"A man's worthiness is not to be estimated by the number of visions and comforts which he may have, or by his skill in the Scriptures, or by his being placed in a higher station than others; but the proof is, if he be grounded in true humility." B. iii. c. 7.

QUESTION.—What is the foundation of the whole spiritual life?

[a] Numb. xi. 6. 8.   [b] Ex. xvi. 29. Wisdom xvi. 20, 21.

ANSWER.—That on which rest all the exercises necessary to become solidly virtuous. But as the spiritual life may be considered differently with regard to different states, it may be said, in general, to be established on two foundations, the one further, the other nearer, to that which we call perfection.

The remote foundation, as we have said elsewhere, is the first step to be taken in the way of holiness, which consists in a firm resolution to refuse nothing to God, and to spare nothing in order to please Him. Whatever we do before this, though good, cannot properly speaking be classed as belonging to the spiritual life. Thus those who repeat long prayers, who perform some penances, and even do many good works, without being entirely resolved to do all that is required to satisfy God fully, have not yet made the first preparations towards acquiring perfection: for if they lived till the end of the world, continuing in the same state, and acting in the same manner, without any addition to their ordinary exercises, they would ever be imperfect; and although they might acquire some merits, they would still remain very far below what we call perfection.

But when once a man is resolved to omit nothing which he thinks will please God, from that time he enters the way which leads to perfect holiness. Yet is he only at the beginning, though often he imagines that he has already reached the end. This is the foundation of the spiritual life: but it is only the remote foundation.

QUESTION.—What then is the immediate foundation?

ANSWER.—The state of a man who, having learned by Divine illumination the great advantage of self-knowledge, is so led to annihilate himself before God and man, as to be completely indifferent to all that is said or thought of him; to desire no privilege, nor any token of distinction; instantly to forget all injuries done to him, without seeking to do himself justice; in short, to become, as it were, insensible to all that concerns his own interest. One who has been enabled to arrive at this state, whatever his merit, however great his age, joyfully suffers himself to be treated like a child; he does not complain; he does not even think that too little consideration is shown him: and if he is under obedience in the religious life, he is well satisfied that his Superior shall see all his letters, and send or retain them as he pleases: and though he may have preached in the most celebrated pulpits with the general applause, not only of the people, but even of princes, he is not reluctant to be humbled: far from that, he makes abasement his delight, and reposes on it as in his centre, ever as passionately desirous of contempt, as worldly men are of honour and of the highest dignities. When a soul is thoroughly established in this disposition, not by a mere yielding, but by a generous and efficacious love of humiliation, she may be said to know what is meant by true humility: and if she has not yet learned to practise it in full perfection, to have at least the thought and desire of doing so.

On this is founded the whole of the spiritual life: and this foundation may be called immediate, because, when it is once laid, we are able to build solidly, and to raise to its highest pitch the edifice of Christian perfection. With this a man is capable of filling all offices, of acquitting himself well of all sorts of employments; and God can entrust His gifts to him without risk. Without it, if God raises him to a high degree of contemplation, or men judge him worthy of the greatest honours, he may become the sport of fiends, and be carried away by the winds of pride and ambition. This is the cause why many, whom our Lord has been pleased to favour with extraordinary graces, overcome by temptation, fall into the abyss. Satan, accustomed to counterfeit an angel of light, blinds others to such a degree, that they are unable to discern him, and will listen to no one; so high is their opinion of themselves, and so full are they of their own sufficiency.

For this cause the Saints have so highly praised humility, and St. Ignatius, among others, calls the love of contempt a most valuable step in the spiritual life. He often recommended it to his first companions, and some of them, touched by his lessons, became eminent in that virtue. It is related in the History of the Company of Jesus, that Father James Laynez, the most learned Jesuit of his time, and a famous preacher, having been made Provincial of Italy, complained to his General, St. Ignatius, that he called all the best labourers of his province to Rome, and that for want of their assistance the colleges were ill provided. The holy man replied wisely, that it was right to prefer the common to private good, and that it was more important to religion that Rome should be provided with fit persons than the other towns. But Laynez, seeing that the General still persisted in taking away many of his evangelic labourers, thought it right to represent to him once more the inconvenience that this caused him. Then St. Ignatius could not refrain from testifying to him by letter his displeasure, that though he had sufficiently explained to him why he did so, he still continued his complaints, and thereby showed less obedience than he ought. Send me word, added he, if, on examination, you do not think that you have done amiss; and in case you find yourself guilty, let me know to what penance you condemn yourself. The reply of Laynez was a manifest proof of his profound humility, and his letter is preserved word for word in the history. He begins by thanking St. Ignatius for his goodness in warning him of his fault; then humbly acknowledging himself guilty, he asks his pardon for the trouble which he has caused him by his importunity; him, whom he honours as the father of his soul, and to whom he owes the utmost respect: and to the Saint's desire that he would inform him of what punishment he thought himself worthy for his want of obedience, he replies, that whatever he is pleased to order him, will be that which he will most willingly accept; but that since he must impose one on himself, the least of which he thinks himself worthy, is to be deposed from his office, forbidden to study, and deprived of all books except his Breviary, reduced for his whole life to teach grammar to little children; in a word, to be regarded as filth. He adds to all this many other penances, as fasts and scourgings; and to this he voluntarily condemns himself for a fault which others would have judged so slight, as hardly to believe it a real fault. But because he has been blamed for it by his Superior, he returns unto himself, and accuses himself with a humility which cannot be too much admired in a man of extraordinary merit, a man whom the Supreme Pontiff had chosen to be his preacher, whom he had sent to Trent to assist at the Council as his theologian, and who at length succeeded St. Ignatius in the office of General.

This is the Divine virtue, which should be regarded as the immediate foundation of all graces and all spiritual gifts. Therefore St. Ignatius, in his instructions for the examination of those who feel themselves called to enter the Company, directs that it shall be particularly enquired of them, whether they have humility enough to love and desire insults, calumnies, and outrages, as much as worldly people love and desire honours and dignities. On this must the spiritual edifice be founded, according to the words of St. Augustine, "Do you desire to raise your building very high? Be careful to found it well in humility." Serm. x. *De verbis Domini.* The Institutor of the Company, then, desiring above all things that those who should be received into it should aspire to a high degree of virtue, required this perfect contempt of self to be proposed to them, as the basis of all; and himself, as long as he lived, ceased not to exercise in it those whom he ruled.

QUESTION.—What must be done to arrive at this degree of humility?

ANSWER.—Three things in particular. The first is, to consider wherein consists the virtue of humility, and to comprehend of what importance it is to despise ourselves, to practise thoroughly all we have said thereon, to bind ourselves to it by firm resolutions, to beware, above all, in whatever vexation, that we never feel anger or resentment. The second is, whenever we think ourselves offended, to be careful instantly to arrest the angry movement which rises in the heart; and, in order to repress it, to arm ourselves with a lively faith, and to recall to our mind all the holy thoughts we have had in prayer. The third is, every time that we examine our conscience, to reflect particularly on this, as on a point of great importance, and if we find that we have failed therein, have spoken any harsh or disobliging word, to conceive sincere grief, to be ashamed before God, to chastise the body severely; and, in order to humble the spirit through the flesh, to study ever to speak with great reserve on those occasions on which we ought to show humility, modesty, and gentleness.

CHAPTER XII.

OF THE PERFECT USE OF FAITH.

(On these words)—" Endeavour to withdraw thy heart from the love of visible things, and to turn thyself to the invisible." B. i. c. 1.

QUESTION.—Wherein consists the perfect use of faith?

ANSWER.—In the effort we make to apply our whole mind, not to the things that strike our senses, but to those which God has been pleased to reveal to us. It is natural for man to turn to sensible objects, to dwell on them, and take pleasure in them; but to do this, is to act according to nature, not according to faith, which presents to our minds objects to which the senses cannot attain. Spiritual men attach themselves only to the things which God reveals to them by His instruments, the Apostles and Prophets, that is, to heavenly and eternal things; to the mysteries of the Life of Christ, and to His teaching. This is continually before their eyes; to this their affections are given; this occupies them no less than temporal affairs occupy those who are governed by the senses.

A worldly man, who follows the guidance of nature, or of human reason, thinks only of what regards the present life, of establishing his family, providing advantageously for his children, obtaining some important office; all his care, all his labours, are directed to these things. But one who is led by the spirit of faith tries only to know and to enjoy the good things of eternity, and the precepts of the Gospel. To these things he gives all the attention, the affection, and ardour, that others can bestow on perishing things. An instance will serve to make this truth clear.

Consider the life that St. Joseph lived on the earth. He was almost the only person to whom God had discovered the greatest and most sublime of all the mysteries. He had always in his house, and almost always before his eyes, a Virgin Mother of a Child, Who was God, and the only Son of the Everlasting Father, Who possessed all the treasures of the Divine Wisdom, and Who alone was able to teach men the way of salvation, and to save them from death. His knowledge of this mystery was certain, for he had received it by revelation. The thought of it had become to him very familiar and very sweet: for in him God had made the care of outward things accord so well with the consideration of things spiritual, that without much effort all the powers of his soul were inseparably attached to a Man-God and a Virgin Mother. Yet he was diligent at his work, and was not obliged to interrupt it, because however he was outwardly occupied, he was always inwardly attracted by the only Object of his love, Who was always present with him.

Thus those who practise the perfect use of faith, so give themselves up to the inward life, that they make all other things bear a relation to it and do it service. In consequence, they take but little interest in the concerns of the present life, and in what regards the satisfaction of the senses. Loss of property, the death of those whom they most esteem and cherish, and a thousand other such occurrences, move them but little in comparison with the work of salvation, because they give all the application possible to that important affair, and are very moderately careful for those of this world, according to the Apostle's precept: *It remaineth, that both they that have wives be as though they had none;—and they that use this world, as not abusing it: for the fashion of this world passeth away.* 1 Cor. vii. 29. 31.

QUESTION.—What must we do to arrive at this entire detachment from all things?

ANSWER.—We must exercise ourselves early, and long continue to employ all the powers of our soul, above all, our understanding and our will, to comprehend and to hold fast those things which we know by faith; we must repress the unregulated emotions of the heart, if it too eagerly and passionately desires present things. There is this difference between the just in general and St. Joseph, whom we have proposed as an example, that this great Saint found no difficulty in applying his mind to those objects of which all should think continually, but which are quickly effaced from our memory. He rarely lost sight of the two persons in this world most deserving of love, Mary his wife, and Jesus, Who passed among the people for his son; Jesus, Whom he loved with all the tenderness with which natural love can inspire a true father, or a true mother; happy in finding so much facility where others find so much difficulty. I say so much difficulty; for, without doing ourselves much violence, we cannot continually apply our minds to these objects, lovely and full of delight though they are, and we must strive much before the mind becomes thoroughly imbued with them.

For this there is no means more efficacious than the exercise of prayer and meditation; to which may be joined many things of which I have elsewhere spoken, and which are taught by religious books. But the feebleness of the human spirit is like a weight which drags it almost against its will to material things; so that it needs great firmness to support itself, and to rise ever higher towards the contemplation of the loftiest mysteries of the faith.

It is true, that among those who serve God, there are two sorts of persons. The first have received special graces, which serve extremely to strengthen their faith, and which make them in some sort partakers of the privilege which we have said St. Joseph enjoyed: for in these heavenly visitations they find themselves so enlightened, and so far above visible creatures, that they often feel within them the presence of Christ [a], which gives them marvellous openings to understand the truths of religion. The others have not this abundant light; they have only that which is common; and it is always with difficulty that spiritual things are impressed on their minds. What they have to do is, to study the precepts of the Gospel, and to labour with all their might for the acquirement of Christian virtues, according to the knowledge which they possess, without attempting to rise to God otherwise than by constant fidelity. At length, either He will open their minds, and make them understand supernatural and Divine things, according to His promise to the Disciples, that He *will manifest* Himself to them, (John xiv. 21,) or without any other assistance than that of ordinary faith, they will obtain perfect repose of mind, and will grow day by day in the knowledge and love of our Lord. For if they make so much progress as to be resolved to do all that God shall demand of them, He will undoubtedly give them what the Saviour has promised to those who keep His Word, *a hundredfold* in this life, (Matt. xix. 29,) so that growing in faith and in charity, their conversation will be in heaven [b], and at last they will enjoy God even here, in a manner in which, as the Saints testify, the just find a paradise on earth.

[a] An omission. ED.   [b] Phil. iii. 20.

CHAPTER XIII.

OF THE REMEMBRANCE OF THE PASSION OF OUR LORD.

(On these words)—" If thou canst not contemplate high and heavenly things, rest thyself in the Passion of Christ, and dwell willingly in His sacred Wounds." B. ii. c. 1.

QUESTION.—What are the fittest means of acquiring a perfect love of God?

ANSWER.—To set before our eyes the Sufferings of Christ, to think of them constantly, till our heart is penetrated with lively sympathy with a God, Who, to save the world, became a Man of sorrows. St. Francis said, that he was never weary in his illnesses, because he always found a sufficient and holy occupation in the consideration of the Saviour's Sufferings.

One who desires to acquire perfect devotion and simple love to God, must often recall to his memory the whole Life of Christ, but particularly the shame and pains of His Death: and, to conceive a lively idea of them, he should make use of some easy method; such as imagining a mountain on which are several chapels, which should be so many stations, and which should severally represent each Mystery of the Saviour's Passion. In the first He appears sad and in agonies as He was in the garden; in the second, insulted and smitten before the two High-Priests, Annas and Caiaphas; in the third, derided and treated as a fool at Herod's court; in the fourth scourged, crowned with thorns, and condemned to death at the tribunal of Pilate; in the fifth, dying on the Cross; in the sixth, dead and buried. By accustoming ourselves to meditate on these things, we do in mind what St. Charles Borromeo did in fact on the Mount Veraglio, where are many oratories like those of which we have given an idea, in which that holy Prelate performed his stations with much piety. In many parts of Christendom there are places thus consecrated to the memory of the Sufferings of Jesus: and this is the first practice to be used, if we desire thoroughly to impress on our minds the image of His Passion and of His Death.

2. The second is, in all the evils that we endure, whether sicknesses, misfortunes, persecutions, or voluntary penances, always to remember the wounds of the Saviour. Thus they are strongly impressed on the soul which is inflamed with love for Him Who suffered so much for her, according to these words of our Author: "No man hath so cordial a feeling of the Passion of Christ, as he who hath suffered the like himself." B. ii. c. 12. In like manner, in the sorrows, disappointments, fears, and disquietudes, which befall us in this life, we must think of the desertion, the sorrow, all the inward Sufferings which pressed upon our Saviour's soul, and become united to It by thought and affection.

3. The third is, to read some pathetic discourse or some pious meditation on the Passion of our Lord, in order to be fully instructed therein. Father Louis de Grenada is one of the best writers on this subject. It is also good in the holy week to hear some fervent and zealous preacher: for it is certain that a sermon, well composed and well spoken, on this subject, produces great effect on the heart; and that for three reasons. The first is, that we come with good dispositions, and with the design of profiting by it, because we are then thinking of confessing and being reconciled to God. The second, that the preacher may speak as long as he thinks proper without wearying his audience, because the people who usually

complain of the length of sermons, are determined on Good Friday to hear the whole history of the Passion of the Saviour, with all the reflections which should accompany it. The third, that there is no subject more beautiful, or more pathetic, than this. For these causes the preacher has a rich field to expatiate in, and to produce much fruit among his audience.

I can assert that I have felt this, and that I speak from experience; for in the year 1628, being at Paris, I had the privilege of hearing a famous preacher, who spoke for three or four hours of the Saviour's sufferings, with such force, and in so tender a manner, that I was much moved by it. I then comprehended the efficacy of a Passion-sermon well preached; and never since has it come to my mind, but the first impression was immediately renewed in my heart. The preacher was a Jesuit, at that time well known and much esteemed. This was his design, and the division of his discourse. In the first hour he began by exhibiting the Greatness and Dignity of Him Who died for us; which should serve as a preparation for all the rest. Then he simply related the history of the Passion, which he divided into several parts. In the second hour, after a pause, he continued, and finished the remainder of the history. In the third, after another pause, he took the crucifix in his hand, showed it to the people, and conjured all who were present to remark three things particularly in seeing the image of a Crucified God. The first was, the extreme rigour of that justice which the Father exercised on His Own Son; the second, the value of a soul for whose salvation this only Son of God did not spare His Blood; the third, the infinite love of God towards man.

All these things, well explained in this order, and at much length, with great zeal and in a touching manner, produced admirable effects on the heart:

above all, they excited a most tender affection for Jesus Suffering, Whose Image impressed on the soul is an inestimable treasure ; for when we have acquired the habit of thinking of Him and sympathizing with His Sorrow, we cannot do otherwise than love Him, for the sympathy we feel for Him is at once the principle and effect of His love.

CHAPTER XIV.

OF THOSE GOOD THINGS, FOR WHICH THOSE WHO EMBRACE VIRTUE MAY HOPE IN THIS LIFE.

(On these words)—" Great grace shall be given to those who shall have willingly subjected themselves to Thy most holy service."

" They who for Thy love shall have renounced all carnal delights, shall find the sweetest consolations of the Holy Ghost." B. iii. c. 10.

QUESTION.—What may he who embraces virtue hope for in this life?

ANSWER.—To attain the true happiness of which man is capable in this place of banishment.

QUESTION.—Wherein consists this true happiness?

ANSWER.—In being united with God and full of God, in an abundance of the most desirable things in the world.

QUESTION.—What are these good things more particularly?

ANSWER.—In the first place, that which Saint Paul, writing to the Ephesians, calls *all the fulness of God*. Eph. iii. 19. That is, that fulness of gifts and perfections which God pours forth on all the faculties of man, when, as a recompense for his endeavours to please Him, He thoroughly imbues him, so to speak, with Himself, and wholly fills him. In this state he possesses God; he is filled with Him, and his very body is wholly sanctified. Thus every man finds his good works abundantly recompensed even in this world, not to speak of the promise which the Saviour makes to those who persevere in His service, that after having filled them with grace in this life, He will give them also life everlasting. Of this He assures them in these words: *Every one that hath forsaken houses, or brethren, or sisters, or father, or mother, &c. for My Name's sake, shall receive an hundredfold, and shall inherit everlasting life.* Matt. xix. 29.

It is then certain, that the Good and Gracious God gives to those who exactly keep His Word, that is, His Precepts and Counsels, perfect contentment, and that this is the fruit of His Grace, and of the Love which unites Him closely with them; so that they may call themselves truly happy, since *neither death, nor life, nor sword, nor persecution, nor height, nor depth, nor any other creature, shall be able to separate them from the Love of God.* Rom. viii. 38. 35. 39. Now every love is not sufficient for this: it must be a love like that which burned in Saint Paul, like that of the Saints who felt God within them, and who were so full of Him, that Grace sometimes passed from the Spirit even to the flesh. Some persons, as we have already observed, apply to this the saying of the Apostle, that *eye hath not seen, nor ear heard, neither have entered into the heart of man, the things which God hath prepared,* not only in the future life, but even in this, *for them that love Him.* 1 Cor. ii. 9.

And truly, one who, in obedience to the words of the Son of God, entirely lays aside all affection for earthly things, becomes so filled with love for Him, and so transformed into Him, that all the delights of Royalty are nothing in comparison with the happiness and the sensible joys which the Presence of God produces in his soul. This is proved by many promises of the Saviour, of which we have already spoken. *If a man love Me*, says He, *he will keep My Words; and My Father will love Him, and We will come unto him, and make Our abode with him.* John xiv. 23. And elsewhere: *If any man hear My voice, and open the door, I will come in to him, and will sup with him, and he with Me.* Rev. iii. 20. And again, in another place: *There is no man that hath left house, &c. for My sake, and the Gospel's, but he shall receive an hundredfold*, Mark x. 29, 30; that is, inestimable treasures of Grace.

Let us then figure to ourselves the richest man on earth, the most prosperous, the highest in rank. If, for the love of our Lord, he renounces his wealth, his pleasures, his honours, *he shall receive an hundredfold now in this time*, even though he be in extreme necessity, and suffering *persecutions*. But what shall be given him? Though the Saviour seems to say that those things of which he has deprived himself shall be restored to him with usury, (and this does sometimes happen,) yet we must not, generally speaking, take this *hundredfold* literally and in the material sense, but in a spiritual sense, as denoting the inward peace which the Saints enjoy. For, in exchange for a father, a mother, a wife, a house which we leave, we must not imagine that we are to have a hundred; but we shall have perfect contentment, and abundant heavenly consolation, which will make us full amends for all things that we have left for God.

This is confirmed both by the experience of the Saints and by reason; for as God, Whose Liberality is unbounded, has given His Son to men for their redemption on the Cross, and for their sanctification in the Eucharist, and has moreover sent to them His Holy Spirit, it is not possible that He should have given them these great Gifts, without desiring that they should profit thereby; but He requires that they should make themselves worthy of them, and remove the obstacles which themselves oppose His Goodness. The light is seen, as soon as that is removed which concealed it. Let us put far from us all creatures which hinder our view of Heaven; let us free ourselves from the love of earthly things, and the love of self, and immediately God will be ours. In proportion as we put away sensible objects from our mind and heart, we cause spiritual things to enter. If God is Good, He is no less Holy; and no man is worthy to receive Him who is not pure as He is. Directly the soul has purified herself, He enters, and makes His Abode there.

If we have not those great gifts that He gives to some, the fault is in our own undeservings, we have none but ourselves to blame; for He created all men with the intention of discovering Himself and communicating Himself to them, in this world by faith, and in the other by the beatific vision. Thus all who are careful to mortify their flesh, and to purify their heart, may be assured that God is in them; that He fills all their powers, their understanding, their will, their memory, their sensitive appetite, even their flesh, and that He liberally pours forth His Gifts, which the Apostle calls *the heavenly gift, and the powers of the world to come*, Heb. vi. 4; in order that, thus assisted, they may live a wholly angelic life.

This, then, is the first thing that makes the happiness of souls purified by Grace. To come to more exact details, their understanding is full of light with regard to God and to themselves; their will is inflamed with love for the Supreme Good; their memory is so occupied with the sweet remembrance of God, that they think only of Him, and of rightly fulfilling their duties; their imagination presents to them none but supernatural objects, and even natural things are depicted in it in that situation and order in which they ought to be with regard to God; their sensitive appetite is governed by the Holy Spirit, Who so regulates all its motions, that they contribute not a little to their perfection; their very body is in some sort sensible of the pleasure of the Spirit, and with it rejoices in God: in short, the whole man is so amazed at the goodness which God shows him, and so charmed with His Purity, that he is enraptured and out of himself.

This is the case also with some who have not yet completed their purification, and whom God designs to raise to a high degree of virtue; but it is the ordinary disposition of those who have acquired perfect purity; and this also makes their blessedness in this world a firm and solid blessedness; for without visions, without revelations, without raptures, by a faithful co-operation with Grace, they arrive at an intimate union with God, from Whom they receive an infinite number of such good things as no man can take away: therefore they may be called truly happy; and if it is objected that if that were the case, there would be many more happy people than we see, or than there really are, this is notwithstanding the order established by God; and if all do not feel its effect, it is only for want of faithfulness to the inspirations of Heaven. For as it is God's Will generally to save all men, and yet an infinite number perish through their own fault, so many are called to perfection, and yet few arrive at it, on account of their too obstinate resistance to the Divine Call.

QUESTION.—What, then, can hinder the just man from arriving at this state of perfection?

ANSWER.—We have shown already that the smallest thing possessed with attachment is an essential hindrance to it, as a spot before the ball of the eye is enough to hide the sun.

QUESTION.—What is the second advantage of this state?

ANSWER.—It is a continual converse of the devout soul with God and with Jesus; a converse like that of a bride with her bridegroom, who never leaves her. We may say also, that the soul being detached from all, God deals with her much as a mother does with her child; she holds it by the hand, helps it to walk, teaches, warns, caresses it from time to time, and is careful of it in all its wants. Thus God, with His All-powerful Hand, supports the soul, speaks to her, teaches her what to do, gives her counsel, raises her up when she falls, and often causes her to taste His Sweetness in a way which experience alone can make known to us. The happiness of thus enjoying her God causes her infinitely more joy than a friend can have with the person he loves the best, or a king amongst his people by whom he sees that he is adored.

It is to be added, that this familiar intercourse with God and with Jesus is always accompanied with favours, gifts, caresses, and all possible tokens of affection and confidence. Having this, a man rests contented: he is filled and overflowing with blessings. Is. lx. 5.

QUESTION.—What is the third advantage of this blessed state?

ANSWER.—It is a thing very difficult to express. It is an immersion (if I may use such a word) of the essence of the soul in that of God; so that the soul, surrounded with light and flame, plunged in an Ocean of peace, is lost in God, as the fishes are in the sea. A fish, small as it is, has for its abode all the width and depth of the sea. There he roams where he will: all is his own, and he enjoys it in perfect freedom. Thus the just soul possesses all the Immensity of God, wherein to lose herself pleasurably at all times. She sings and leaps with gladness in that abyss of joy, delight, and pleasure, loving none but God, seeing none but God, abiding in God as in her element, and finding no satisfaction but in Him. Her whole life passes in this Abode of pleasantness, and whatever happens, nothing troubles her rest. All helps her to lose herself more in God; and as fire kindled in a forest is always increasing, because material is not wanting, so the love with which she burns is ever inflaming, and she is at the same time as if enclosed in an immense furnace, and in a bottomless sea: it is at once a fire which burns, and a water which refreshes her.

END OF THE FIFTH BOOK.

A SPIRITUAL LETTER TO A LADY OF RANK.

MADAM,—May the Cross of Christ be your portion, and His Love your treasure.

It seems to me that I must no longer write to you as a worldly person. Our Lord inspires me with other sentiments regarding you; and you must have forgotten the false maxims of the world, since you have begun to enjoy the truths of the Gospel. I will then answer the questions which you have asked me, and I will answer them in the Spirit of Christ, that is, quite simply, and according to His Principles.

You desire to know, 1st, how true poverty of spirit is to be exercised even amidst riches, and by what means this virtue is acquired?

2. If we ought to be so detached from all things, as in no manner to feel the most painful occurrences of life?

3. If we should suffer ourselves to be despoiled of our possessions without defending ourselves, without complaining, and even joyfully?

4. What is meant by inward detachment from all things[a], wherein it consists, and how it is to be practised?

5. In what manner, lastly, you may know whether in the things that you desire you seek God, or yourself, because self-love often disguises itself so artfully

---

[a] Dénuement intérieur.

as to have all the colour and appearance of Divine love?

To these truly holy and spiritual questions I cannot reply better than by my commencement. In that you will find a short explanation of all your doubts, and a resolution of all your difficulties. May the Cross of Christ be your portion, and His Love your treasure. If you knew the depth of this mystery,—if you well understood the dealings of our Lord with the souls that He calls to perfection,—you would see that nothing can be more opposed to a worldly spirit; you would know that His Kingdom is not of this world[a], and that all who worship Him in spirit and in truth[b] think it a happiness to share in His Poverty, His Shame, His Sufferings. It is bearing His Cross to enter into this fellowship with Him; and to be poor thus, is to be poor even in the midst of riches and plenty.

But that you may esteem more highly the Poverty of the Saviour, and may regard it as the foundation of Christian morality, the basis of the Gospel, the first of the beatitudes, the principle of perfect holiness, I pray God that He will enlarge your heart, enlighten your mind, and make you to see plainly what is the religion that you profess, and what a soul regenerated in Christ, and become by Grace *a new creature*. 2 Cor. v. 17. Gal. vi. 15. For on this are the evangelic counsels founded, and this is the beginning of all the paths that lead to perfection.

The morality which you have embraced is that of Christ. You intend to follow it,—you solemnly bound yourself to do so at your Baptism by a protest which you have often since ratified, and which you renew daily in the Sacrament[c] of the Eucharist.

[a] John xviii. 36.   [b] John iv. 24.
[c] "Des Sacremens de la Pénitence et de l'Eucharistie." Orig. The words "de la Pénitence" were omitted, because,

This protest must be sincere and efficacious; it must come from the heart, and not the lips; for not words but works are required of you. The Christian virtues are not virtues of speculation, but of practice. To love, to do, and to suffer, these are the discipline of a soul which aspires to the highest degree of holiness.

Consider, then, that the Eternal Wisdom, the Incarnate Word, willed to destroy the false wisdom of this world by the Mystery of the Cross, which was to some *a stumbling-block*, and to others *foolishness*. 1 Cor. i. 22. By this means He established His new Law; and if you consider Christianity in its whole extent, you will find that it is a Religion whose seat is in the heart, and which forms there, by means of Grace, that new man whom the Scripture calls *a new creature*[a] in Christ Jesus.

This being understood, you must firmly believe that the life of a Godly man, who professes to follow no other laws than those of a Crucified God, is wholly a life of faith, of self-denial, of suffering, a state of crucifixion and death. The Kingdom of the Saviour is a spiritual Kingdom, which we cannot know but by faith, enter but by mortification, abide in but by charity. Those, then, who have Christ for their King, who have had the blessing of regeneration through His Blood in Baptism, who are called to perfection; these must be in the world as if not in it; they must enjoy without attachment the things

although private confession and absolution are, under certain circumstances, recommended by our Church, and have been, and are increasingly, found a means of grace to individuals, they are not yet so common as such a statement presupposes; and to rank Absolution (although a Divine Ordinance and means of grace, and so, in the larger sense of the word, a Sacrament) at once with the Holy Eucharist, would have seemed contrary to our Church's teaching, and the exceeding greatness of the Holy Eucharist.—[ED.]

[a] 2 Cor. v. 17. Gal. vi. 15.

they must one day leave, and look only to the good things of Eternity. Thus their conduct must not only be different from that of the world, but must condemn and correct it; they must take pleasure in a simple, obscure, hidden life, because they think only of satisfying their Divine Master, Who invites them to a participation in His Cross.

In consequence of this, as in all their ways, they walk according to the Spirit (for the truly religious see all things with the eyes of faith); they must be entirely spirit; that is, their thoughts, their views, their affections, their works, must be spiritual, and the flesh must have no part in them. It is necessary that they should be crucified unto the world, and the world unto them[a], that they may live the life of Christ, Who is the Head of the Church, and the Pattern of the perfect.

But because it is to be feared that they may presume on their virtue, it is most important that they should be thoroughly convinced that of themselves they are weak and helpless altogether; that there is in them a fund of evil and corruption, from which they can never free themselves without strength from above; that their understanding is full of ignorance, their will depraved, their senses enfeebled, and their passions in disorder; in a word, that they are incapable of doing any thing that is good without that help which the Saviour obtained for them by His Death. Yielding themselves, then, to the direction of the Spirit of God, Who animates them in all their works, they labour for the destruction of their own corrupt nature, that they may become worthy of that Grace with which they cannot be filled till they are emptied of themselves.

Thus they live by faith; that is, they are led by

---

[a] Gal. vi. 14.

the light of faith, and of that faith which worketh by love[a]. They are easily convinced, as well by this Divine light as by their own experience, that the maxims of the world are directly opposed to those which they design to follow, since they all tend to the satisfaction of the flesh and the senses, whose desires are always contrary to those of the spirit. Therefore they detest and avoid them as obstacles to Grace, which teaches them to strip themselves of all, to acknowledge their weakness, their misery, and their nothingness; and to put at last their whole trust in the mercy of God and in the merits of Christ.

Being then of a religion which is wholly spiritual, and which looks only to eternity, they regard themselves while here as in a place of banishment, in a weary prison, where Divine Justice has condemned them to expiate their offences. Their hatred of the world leads them to break with it entirely and for ever, knowing that they cannot attach themselves to it without multiplying their crimes and increasing their punishment. The remembrance of their sins fills them with confusion; all creatures appear ready to avenge the Creator on them, and they punish themselves severely for their offences against Him; they humbly entreat His pardon; and in profound silence, with tears in their eyes, wait for forgiveness. They despise all that is delightful and charming in the world, and cling to the Cross as their only refuge.

The light of Grace enables them clearly to discern the precious from the vile, the true from the false, the absolutely necessary from the merely convenient. They prize things at their real value; they know that in the world there is nothing but disguise; that greatness passes away; riches have no solidity; honours are vain and imaginary; that with regard to

[a] Gal. v. 6.

the supernatural state, there is no inequality of station; that in this respect all men are brothers and all heirs, all children of one Father; all regenerated in the same manner by Baptism; all ransomed by the same price, the Blood of a Man-God; all called to the same inheritance, everlasting glory. From this they conclude, that no man is great by birth except he who is born of the Holy Spirit; that true nobility is that conferred by Christian virtue; that the most honourable of all ranks is that of the children of God; and that nothing is more consoling and more sweet than the hope of a happiness which will never end.

All that men esteem appears as nothing in their eyes, and they are ashamed when they see themselves devoid of virtue, exposed to numerous accidents, subject to all sorts of calamities. Then they lift up their eyes to Heaven, they admire the greatness of God, they contemplate Him in His glory; and, dazzled with the splendour of Its rays, they hide themselves in their own nothingness, and would descend, if it were possible, to the very centre of the world, to humble themselves more profoundly before His Supreme Majesty. On the other hand, considering the holy Humanity of Christ, Who offered Himself on the Cross, they consider their past ingratitude with bitter regret and extreme confusion; they accuse themselves of their unfaithfulness, condemn themselves to death, and give sentence against themselves, conjuring the Divine Mercy to arrest its execution by the merits of Christ, Who deigned to shed His Blood for the expiation of the sins of the whole world.

I. After well considering this, I think, Madam, that it is easy to reply to your questions, and to give you the desired means of advancing in the way of Christian perfection. You desire then to know how voluntary poverty is to be practised in the midst of riches.

Observe, first of all, that the riches of which you speak are only natural goods, and consequently imaginary goods, since they are perishable; that if they appear to have any reality or solidity, it is to those who judge of them by the senses, not by reason. You cannot properly call a thing your own, when you will be compelled to leave it, when death will deprive you of it, and it is impossible for you to keep it long.

Always distinguish the base from the precious, the true from the apparent; set a right value on every thing. Nothing is to be counted truly good which does not bear relation to eternity; and things which lead not thither are only deserving of contempt. The truly good things are supernatural gifts; they are sufferings, persecutions, the merit of good works; in a word, all those pious practices which the Saviour recommends in the Gospel. Of these He tells us to lay up treasures, Matt. vi. 20: they are figured by the talent of the good and faithful servant, Matt. xxv. 21; by the lamps of the wise virgins, Matt. xxv. 1, 2; by the wedding garment of those who are invited to the marriage of the Heavenly Bridegroom, Matt. xxii. 12.

If it is then true, as none can doubt, that in the order of Grace there is no inequality of ranks; that the care of Divine Providence is extended to all, whether rich or poor; that the earth is given to them for an inheritance; and that their portion is equal as regards the right of procuring and asking necessary things; it suffices us, according to the rule of the Gospel, to have wherewith to provide for our most pressing wants: all the rest is not properly our own; with regard to us it is a superfluity, and we are obliged to make a lawful use of it for the relief of our neighbours, since the Everlasting Wisdom, by an admirable disposition, has ordained that some men shall be rich, and others poor, in order that brotherly love may be exercised among them, and that they may know themselves to be all equal in the order of Grace. The rich have the inheritance of elder, the poor of younger sons: but all being brothers, all children of God and of Christ, the elder, by natural and Divine right, owe to the younger their lawful portion, that is, enough for their subsistence; reserving to themselves nothing more than is necessary. And here, Madam, you will observe some truths which God inspires me to propound for your instruction.

1. The first is, that in speaking of necessity, we do not exclude a certain propriety belonging to every station, for God Himself has distinguished different ranks among men. Now this sort of propriety must be measured according to age, sex, disposition, birth, dignity, without, however, being extended too far, but being always restrained within the bounds of temperance and Christian modesty. God ordained the powers of this world [a], and He is no less the Author of nature than of Grace. As in the order of Grace, then, there are diverse ministries subordinate the one to the other, so also, in the order of nature, there are many great differences: but the great of this world, whom the Lord has raised above others, are only His vice-gerents, and have only the administration of the things entrusted to them.

This being the case, we are permitted, and even in some sort required, to preserve our rank, and to support the honour of our ministry, whether in spiritual functions, like St. Paul, or in sovereign power, like St. Louis and many others, more venerable for sanctity than for royalty. But this propriety of which we speak must be regulated, not according to the feelings of nature, alway attached to its own ease, but according to the movements of Grace, which are

[a] Rom. xiii. 21.

easily distinguished when we are determined to follow the guidance of a disinterested Director: for light is never wanting to the humble and teachable spirit. I will add, that those who have some experience in the inward motions of the Holy Spirit, have no difficulty in distinguishing how far this propriety should extend, and determining it according to the rules of the Gospel. This is the first degree of the perfection of all stations in the world.

2. The second truth is, that we may employ all reasonable means to procure the things which we want, and which are suitable to our station, but without eagerness and without disquiet, forgetting nothing that depends on ourselves, and leaving the rest to Providence, firmly believing that unassisted all our cares will be useless.

3. The third is, that as far as regards secular people, they are not only permitted, but even obliged to provide for their maintenance, according to their station and quality [a]; that they must be moderately careful of their interests, take pains to regulate their families well, maintain their rights by the way of justice, defend themselves against oppression, even attack the usurper, if constrained to do so; watch over the education of their children, and try to provide for them [b]; protect their dependants, lay up enough to pay their debts, and do many other things of indispensable obligation,—I say of indispensable obligation, because they are acts of justice, and justice has a prior claim to charity. Not that all justice is not a sort of charity: for charity has its degrees, and that which is well regulated must begin at home: but, in short, we may say, it is commonly said, that works of charity yield to those of justice, because one of these two virtues is absolutely necessary, the other is not so, at least not in the same degree.

[a] 2 Thess. iii. 12.   [b] 1 Tim. v. 8.

Many of those who give themselves to prayer and works of charity are manifestly self-deceived; for they are very neglectful of their domestic concerns; as if the care which these require were an obstacle to good works and to prayer. Therefore, instead of thinking of satisfying their obligations, they apply themselves to easier exercises, more favourable to their self-love. Yet, since, properly speaking, they are only the dispensers of the things they have received from the Hand of God, they ought to be as careful of them as a servant of those which his master has confided to his administration. It is not for their own interests that they labour, but for those of God, Who has entrusted them with the administration of His property, of which another perhaps might give a better account. This appears clearly in the parable of the faithful servant and the Lord of the household [a].

I have long remarked, that there is a particular blessing from Heaven on secular people who apply themselves in this spirit to temporal affairs, and strive to acquit themselves well of the duties of their station. By this means they advance very far in the way of perfection, because they do the Will of God, and faithfully abide at the post where He has placed them; for Divine Providence having sanctified all stations, however different, gives Grace with equal liberality to all who are called to them; and sometimes in situations of great difficulty there is found greater contemplation, inward peace, and union with God, than in seclusion and the exercise of charity, in which vain-glory and self-love are mingled.

4. The fourth truth is, that every man must consider himself accountable, not only for his property, but also for all the talents that he has received both of nature and Grace, for health, strength, learning, repu-

---

[a] Matt. xxiv. 45. 47.

tation, time, and, above all, for the supernatural gifts of Grace. He must, therefore, be so careful of what he says, that no uncharitable, or even idle word, may ever escape him. His eyes must ever be turned towards Heaven, and he must have God Alone in view; all his actions must be performed with judgment and prudence, and he must be so careful of his time, as to fulfil all his duties, and satisfy all the obligations of his station.

I content myself with telling you these things simply, without going further, and explaining in detail what the Gospel teaches with regard to them. Know only that it is a great error, on the subject of devotion, to think ourselves very spiritual because we have given alms, or performed some other charitable work; for since we are called upon to love God with all our heart, with all our mind, with all our soul, and with all our strength [a], we must in consequence reserve nothing to ourselves, but offer Him all, and set no bounds to the love we bear Him.

5. The fifth and last fundamental truth is, that this distribution of our property and talents for the benefit of our neighbour, must be made without attachment and self-love, purely for God's sake, and in the Spirit of our Lord, of Whom the poor are members [b]. Observe that, under this word "neighbour" are generally comprehended all whom Providence directs to us for assistance. They are our brothers, and if Providence treats us as elder sons, it is on condition that we share with them the things bestowed upon us. We must assist them in all their wants, without ever suffering them to need anything, either advice, comfort, instruction, or anything else in our power; and it is good to do this ourselves, as far as possible, and not to leave the care of it to others; for it is a mis-

[a] Mark xii. 30. [b] Prov. xix. 17. Matt. xxv. 40.

take of worldly people to do their charities by the hands of others, in order to spare themselves the trouble. This sort of delicacy much diminishes the merit of the action, of which they have often but a very general and slight knowledge.

This proceeds from want of faith; for we are ordinarily more led by the senses than by reason, and our actions proceed less from charity than from natural compassion. Certainly, if with the eyes of faith we saw our Lord concealed and disguised under the appearance of a poor man; if we regarded this poor man as our brother by the Divine Adoption common to us; if we reflected that he even approaches more nearly than we do to Christ, Whom he much resembles in his poverty and his sufferings, we should respect in him the character of the Man-God Who died on the Cross for the salvation of all men; and there is nothing which we should refuse to do for a soul created in the Image of God, and called, like ourselves, to the possession of glory: we should enter into the feelings of the Samaritan, who knew how to discern his neighbour in the person of the Jew, robbed and wounded by thieves[a].

These truths being established, you will find it very easy, without quitting your property, to practise voluntary poverty. Consider that these are unreal goods, and that there are no true goods but those of Grace. Think that they have been given to you on the condition of giving account of them, and that you will be most severely punished if you misuse them; that you have no right to take more than is necessary for a person in your situation; that all the rest is not your own, but is the portion of your brethren, and that Christ reserves it to Himself for the nourishment of the poor. After that, shall you

[a] Luke x. 33.

think yourself rich, and the possessor of anything? Shall you think yourself the owner of a thing of which you must give account? Is it not ignorance and weakness, or rather, strange blindness, to attach ourselves to things which pass away, to love that which we do not possess as our own, and cannot long possess at all?

Where is the light of nature which teaches us that we are all born equal? Where is that of the Gospel, which shows us that we should use the things of the world as though we used them not; that we must love them without attachment, enjoy them without appropriation, and preserve them without passion? Where is the fervour and disinterestedness of the first Christians, who, being closely united in love, had all things common, and were of one heart and of one soul[a]? This is the pattern that I propose to you, and I cannot give you a nobler idea of the perfection of Christianity, of which I have elsewhere sketched the outline; for as the life of a Christian is one of charity, so also is it of practice, because charity, which looks at once to God and to its neighbour, is never idle; it is always in action, whether occupied in producing frequent acts of love to God, or employed in the relief of its neighbour.

6. Lastly, to show you plainly how to practise evangelic poverty, I have only to represent to you a thing which passes under your own eyes, and which you know by your own experience. Consider, I pray you, Madam, those whom you have entrusted with the care of the fine estates which your ancestors acquired, and which Divine Providence ordained that they should leave to you, that their great revenues should be in your hands a resource for the poor. Reflect on their way of proceeding. They

---

[a] Acts iv. 32.

obey your orders respectfully; faithfully acquit themselves of their duties; attend to your affairs without eagerness and without anxiety, being only stewards of the property which you have entrusted to their care. Unfortunate occurrences occasion them but little grief; it is enough that they render you an account of all, and punctually execute your desires. Their office is but for a time, and you may dispose of it as you please, for you gave it to them, and are free to take it away. Would not they be deserving of blame if they attributed to their own merit and address that which depends not on themselves? and would they be excusable if they acted as proprietors and masters, whereas nothing is at their disposal and in their power?

Apply this figure to yourself. You acknowledge that God is the Master and Proprietor of all that you possess: you have only the administration, not only of the riches, but of all the gifts, whether of nature or of Grace, that you possess and have received from Him. You are accountable for them to Him, and have no right to take or keep more than is precisely necessary for your station; and this you must receive as alms from the Hand of the Supreme Master of all, believing that by so often misusing His benefits, you have rendered yourself unworthy of them; and that others would have made a better use of them than you have done.

Possess them, then, without attachment; preserve them without uneasiness; dispense them with prudence and simplicity; be reasonably careful of them, as far as possible; and if you must lose them, do not afflict yourself; your loss will not be great; you will be relieved from a burthen; and if you choose, you will but be the more at rest. Perhaps, too, the Lord will be pleased to try your virtue, to see if you are thoroughly detached from creatures; for self-love creeps in everywhere, and is found not only in the enjoyment, but even in the distribution of temporal things.

Let the Will of God be done both now and for ever. One who desires to be perfect must so conform himself to the Divine Will, as not only to will only what God wills, but to make it as it were a necessity to himself to desire no other thing. By this you will easily comprehend how being rich, we can exercise voluntary poverty; and persuaded of the excellence of that first beatitude, to which the Kingdom of Heaven is promised as a recompense, you will inwardly renounce all your possessions, you will strip yourself of them, and restore them into the hands of Him from Whom you received them; and will offer them to Him within your soul as a sacrifice for a sweet-smelling savour. You have begun too well, not to complete the offering. After your separation from the world, and your resolution of avoiding even the most lawful pleasures and the most innocent amusements, can you have any remaining attachment for earthly things? Can a holy spouse of Christ desire any other treasure than Christ Himself? If your love for this chaste Spouse has caused you to embrace the Cross, and nobly to despise all worldly grandeur, what remains but that in your heart you offer to Jesus all your possessions? The Bride must be in the same estate with her Bridegroom; and what are the riches of Him Whom Alone you love, but perfect poverty, and general privation of all things?

II. We now come to your second question, which regards the way in which we may love the Saviour's poverty. Once more I wish that His Cross may be your portion, and His love the only passion of your heart. If you love Christ Suffering and Dying for you, and if you love Him Alone, as it is your duty to do, you will also love those things which were nearest to His heart, and which accompanied Him as long

Y

as He lived, poverty, shame, and pain. This is truly bearing His Cross, entering into His Feelings, being crucified with Him to the world. If you have well considered Him deprived of all, if you have rightly reflected on His conduct and His precepts, you must undoubtedly have remarked, that He voluntarily renounced temporal things, and reserved to Himself nothing but the simple use of the things necessary to life, often even living on alms. You will have found that He did even more, so desirous was He of leading men, by His example, to the highest perfection.

In fact, He so loved obscurity, that though He was of the blood of kings, and of the greatest kings in the world, He concealed His nobility, and appeared a poor carpenter. He never desired either countenance, or credit, or a reputation for wisdom and knowledge in the world. He sought to pass for an ordinary man, and was distinguished from others by nothing but the sanctity of His actions, and the purity of His doctrine. Add to this the continued persecutions, the indignities and shame that He suffered to the very end of His life, of which I omit many circumstances, to avoid wandering from my subject, which principally regards voluntary poverty.

Only consider in general how He made Himself the lowest of men, and the outcast of the people[a]: see His Head crowned with thorns, His Body covered with bruises, torn and pierced with wounds. He dies naked on a Cross, in ignominy, like a malefactor, between two thieves, with none to help Him, overwhelmed with suffering, unable even to obtain a drop of water to give any relief to His thirst, having no soundness from the sole of the foot even unto the Head[b], so maimed that He could not have been recognized, and to say all in one word, *a Man of sorrows.* Is. liii. 3.

[a] Ps. xxii. 6.   [b] Is. i. 6.

What say you on beholding so sad an object? Are you not amazed? Is not your heart touched? Does not this inspire you with love and esteem for poverty, contempt, and sufferings, even if you have not sufficient courage to seek them?

But unawares my zeal is carrying me too far, and I am insensibly going beyond the precise answer your question requires.

We wander pleasantly and happily, if indeed we may be said to wander, when we find Christ in the noblest and most perfect act of His love to man. But since you love a God supremely deserving of all love, Who gives His Life for you, love Him in such a manner that your love may be said to be crucified. Unite yourself with Him, not only by a feeling of tenderness, but by a generous desire of bearing His Cross. Love must bind you to God, and mortification to Jesus. The love of the Cross is inseparable from self-abnegation, and both are necessary to a perfect and constant union with the Saviour. Is it not right to live and die like Him, to love what He loves, to do what He teaches? *The disciple is not above his master.* Matt. x. 24. He has set us the example of entire detachment from all things; we must follow His steps, and teach others to do so[a]. Entreat Him humbly to grant you that grace, be faithful to Him; having deigned to enlighten your understanding, He will excite your will; for illuminations are followed by affections; but they must be distinguished from one another.

Learn then now the secret of the inward life. Illuminations serve to enlighten the mind; they are rays of the Sun of Righteousness, which, suddenly falling on the soul, enable her to perceive in a wonderful manner and with extreme pleasure, the mysteries of

---

[a] 1 Pet. ii. 21.

the Faith, the beauty of Heavenly things, and the greatness of the Divine perfections. Affections are movements produced by the Holy Spirit in the soul, which, of themselves, without any reasoning, arouse the will, excite her to good, and gently engage her to put in practice those holy maxims which the understanding sets before her. This is purely spiritual, and is done by the operation of the Holy Spirit in the superior part of the soul. A passing remark is enough to show you the beautiful order and the admirable œconomy of Grace. You will know then by the following tokens whether you sincerely despise the riches of the earth, and love poverty.

See and consider, as in the presence of God, if these unreal and apparent goods are a burthen to you ; if you feel their weight; if you groan under this heavy load ; if you have more unwillingness than inclination to retain them; if you look with fear on the obligation to dispense them faithfully, and according to God's intention ; if you are thoroughly persuaded that the things of this world are deserving only of contempt ; if your heart has no attachment to worldly greatness; if you know the value of the good things of eternity, not by force of reason, which the pretended wise men of this world may have as well as you, but by an inward consciousness and feeling, which proceeds simply from grace ; if you are entirely indifferent to all that may happen to you which is pleasing or otherwise ; if you enjoy great inward peace amidst the most painful occurrences of this life ; if you seek for humiliation, and sigh after sufferings.

Examine yourself on all these points ; and if you find that you have gained one, know that it will suffice to produce in your heart a love of poverty, and a holy desire of forsaking all. With this you may possess great riches without renouncing the Cross of Christ : you may be rich and poor at once ; may *know*, like the Apostle, *how to be abased, and how to abound.* Phil. iv. 12. Many honour alike God in the possession of His gifts, and Christ in the participation of His Pains. It is unnecessary to say more to induce you fervently to embrace these holy practices, for the Grace of the Holy Spirit has already disposed you to do what the Saviour teaches, and to follow His example. As for me, I only follow His direction, and am hardly master of my pen; for without intending it, I am writing a book rather than a letter. But we must yield to the Spirit Who moves us, and Who will inspire us with nothing but what is good. This, however, is enough, both to throw light on your doubts, and to serve for your guidance. These truths firmly established will contribute not a little to satisfy you respecting your other difficulties, which are, as it were, contained in the former. I have yet, however, some instructions that I think it right to communicate to you.

III. Impatience to arrive quickly at perfection, makes you desire to know if we ought to be detached from temporal goods to such a degree as in no manner to feel their loss, far from grieving and lamenting over it. This view, Madam, is very elevated, and shows a noble disposition to practise fully the evangelic counsels; but it is not always necessary to take things literally; it is enough that we accomplish them as far as we can, according to necessity, or the propriety of our station.

These counsels have different degrees, according as they are regarded in themselves, or with relation to the different dispositions of persons. Perfect abnegation begins by great detachment from the things of the world; it is augmented when we can bear losses and misfortunes with calmness; it grows still more when we are able to bear them with joy; but it is in its greatest perfection when we leave all, and leave it willingly to follow Christ[a]. This is the great sacrifice of a soul regenerated by Grace. But it supposes a contempt for perishable things, a spirit of contemplation and retirement, the love of the Cross, union and resemblance with Jesus Crucified. Yet the retired life is but little conformed to the common and civil life which our Lord sanctified by His example, and in which we require some means for the subsistence of our family and our own maintenance.

All are called to perfection, both in the intercourse of the world and in seclusion. Therefore the Saviour said to His Apostles: *What I say unto you, I say unto all.* Mark xiii. 37. Thus spake He Who is *the Truth and the Life.* John xiv. 6. Is it not in our power to navigate the sea of this world without making shipwreck? Cannot we, by Divine Assistance, preserve angelic purity in a mortal body? Is it impossible in the secular life to serve God, and to live according to the Spirit of Grace; to observe exactly the precepts of the Church, and the salutary counsels of its Pastors; to use the creatures only for the service of the Creator? Is this out of the power of a man Whom Jesus forcibly draws to Himself[b]; Whom the Holy Spirit governs inwardly, and to whom It beareth witness that he is of the number of the children of God[c]? But if there is no impossibility in this, does it not follow, that a person living in the world, and called by God to perfection, may attain to it while living in a manner suitable to his state? When defence is necessary, it must be lawful. Reason requires then that every man should preserve his property by just means, in the sight of God, because, as we have said, he is but the steward of it; of which the Gospel sets before us an excellent figure in the parable of the faithful servant and the lord of the household.

[a] Matt. ix. 28.   [b] John xii. 32.   [c] Rom. viii. 16.

But if, after all our care and all our faithfulness in rightly fulfilling this trust, Divine Providence withdraws it from our hands, and deprives us of this administration so pleasing and so satisfactory to nature, then is patience necessary to us, and we must try to remain calm amid the tempest. If nature revolts, we must at first yield a little to its weakness, and not harden ourselves too much against it. Virtue is gradually perfected by combat; and the harder the strife, the more glorious the victory. If these first movements are violent, they are not voluntary: we may resist them with the assistance of Grace, but we must not hope to be altogether free from them. They are a continued cause for humiliation, because they are so ordinary and so natural to us, that even those who live in solitude, far from all occasions, are not exempt from them. It is sufficient then to yield no consent to them, and to subject our will to the Decrees of Providence. Whether the loss is felt or not, is of little importance, provided that it is received with submission, respect, and love.

IV. But the greatest difficulty is not this; it is to die entirely to self, to acquire absolute empire over self, and to have no more will or judgment of our own. This is the subject of your fourth question, of which you feel that it is difficult to comprehend the extent and the greatness. It is the most heroic and sublime of all things, the height of perfection; and when I spoke to you of it, it was not so much to require you to practise it, as to give you some slight notion of it. How could I venture to try to explain that which I do not understand myself, and of which I hardly know the first rudiments? Always to live, yet ever die; always to combat, and ever conquer; to have a body and senses, and act only according to the Spirit; to be subject to the corruption of nature, and only follow the movement of Grace; to be endowed with reason, and guided only by faith: this demands entire and absolute detachment from self.

Thus, to speak plainly, if you desire to arrive at this high degree of perfection, you must resolve to offer to the Lord as a sacrifice your body and your soul, your illuminations, your affections, your desires; so that all your senses, both interior and exterior, may be attached to nothing but what leads you to God. This would take long to explain. To do it shortly, I say that your eyes must never rest on beautiful objects, except in order to know and admire their Author; that your ears must hear only such things as are useful to you, and suitable to your state; that your palate must never taste good food to find pleasure in it, but solely to support and strengthen nature; and so with other things; that your imagination must be full of the Mysteries of the Faith, of the Labours and Sufferings of the Saviour, of the good things of eternity; that your memory must have these same objects always present, and forget all worldly things which are neither suitable to your profession, nor necessary for your salvation; that your understanding must not trust in its own knowledge, and that the most learned must humble themselves to believe that all their learning is but ignorance, and all their wisdom but folly; that, lastly, your will must break all its attachments, and change so much in inclination and taste, that sweet things may become bitter to it, and bitter sweet. Let then your whole happiness be in the Cross, your whole joy in suffering, and be thoroughly convinced that of your own you have only impotence, helplessness, evil, disorder, and corruption. This is, in truth, a state of death to all sensible things. It is, as St. Paul says, *the dividing asunder of soul and spirit* (Heb. iv. 12), of nature and grace: it is the extinction of the old man; it is the production and life of that new creature in Christ Jesus, of which the same Apostle so often speaks.

For the rest, however difficult, however impracticable what I say may appear to you, think not that it is impossible, nor that this is a pattern of perfection given you to admire, and not to imitate. The Gospel proposes it to us as imitable: though it is very difficult to attain to it, all is possible to Grace[a]. I acknowledge that they are only some chosen spirits whom God leads in this path, and that the number is much smaller in these latter days than it was in the first centuries. Yet I venture to say for your comfort, that I know many who have arrived at this, and even proceeded further, who, transformed by love into Christ, live rather an angelic than a human life, acting only according to the impulse of Grace, beginning already to taste the joys of Paradise, and being able to say with St. Paul, that they live in Christ, or rather that Christ liveth in them[b].

You ask me how it is possible to live in this excellent manner. This I cannot explain to you; for, as this life is wholly Divine, God Alone is able to teach it to you. I have shown you the way to die; it is for the Holy Spirit to teach you to live. It is for Him to shed His Heavenly Unction on your soul, and to lead you in His Ways; to discover to you the profound mysteries which are hidden in Christ, and to give you grace, not only to believe in Him, but also to suffer for His sake. Entreat Him humbly and confidently to grant you this favour. You have built on His Promises; He never refuses anything to those who have faith, and who trust in His Divine Mercy.

V. But it is time to conclude. Your questions lead me too far; and I should never have finished if

[a] Matt. xix. 26. Mark x. 27. Luke i. 37.   [b] Gal. ii. 20.

I undertook to answer them. You ask how you can know certainly whether the object of your desires is the Glory of God, or your own satisfaction: if your works are pleasing to God, and such as He would have them; if nature has no share in them; in a word, if you are truly faithful to Grace. I think that I see in this a little curiosity, and somewhat unsuited to Christian simplicity, which is always supported by living faith, and averse to so much thought, subtlety, and reflection on self. But as your conduct appears to me sincere, and I am convinced that you seek after the greatest perfection, I will communicate to you in few words the thoughts which God gives me on this subject, and I will add some directions which will be a great assistance to you in self-knowledge.

Examine, then, the movements of your heart; see if you are resolved to die rather than to sin against God; if you have a real desire of pleasing Him, and Him only. If you have nothing to reproach yourself with in this respect, doubt not that your actions and thoughts are pleasing in His sight; for this is the surest mark of a right and Christian conduct. But to augment considerably the merit of your good works, do them on the principle of the love of God, with a single eye to His Glory, and in the spirit of our Lord. An action is truly holy and perfect when these three things meet in it.

But I must stop. These sentiments are very elevated, and belong only to souls above the common order, and many volumes would hardly suffice to explain them. It belongs only to the Holy Spirit to impress them on the heart. It is enough that you know what they are.

With regard to that vain complacency which insinuates itself among good works, I advise you to maintain yourself against it, but without being disquieted. It is not at all to be feared when actions are performed in the manner that I have said; and whatever discomfort it may cause, the will is always free to resist it. We must suffer from it: this evil root is not easily extirpated. Man is composed of flesh and spirit. If the spirit is strong, the flesh is weak, and unfortunately the weaker part often carries away the stronger. It is a combat that will continue throughout our life, and at the same time a cause for humiliation, to serve as a counterpoise to extraordinary favours received from Above[a].

Walk always with great simplicity and uprightness; avoid those reflections which tend to scrupulousness, and which serve only to trouble your conscience. Think only that of yourself you are incapable of every thing good, unfit for all, and that in every thing you depend on the Divine Mercy. Entreat the Lord to teach you what to do, to give you courage to undertake it, and to help you in its accomplishment, because the whole work is His; He is its Author, and He its Finisher, and in you He finds only obstacles to His Grace.

After this, can you feel any self-complacency, or any attachment to your own will? Shall you still find it difficult to distinguish between the movements of Grace and those of nature, which are so contrary, and produce such different effects? But do you wish thoroughly to know your inward state? Do you desire to know if your conduct is pleasing to the Divine Majesty, if your feelings and desires proceed from Grace, if you are acting in the Spirit of our Lord? Examine if you preserve peace of heart in the tumult of the world; if you avoid applause and praise; if you despise the honours and good things of the earth; if you have a true hatred for yourself,

[a] 2 Cor. xii. 7.

and sincere charity for your enemies; if you love sufferings; if you are indifferent to all that may befall you; if you seek nothing but God; if you feel His Presence, His Gifts, His Loveliness, which cannot be rightly known but by experience; if your own conscience makes you no reproaches; and if the Holy Spirit bears witness to you that you are in a state of Grace, and of the number of the children of God[a].

Examine all these things thoroughly; and if you have them all, or at least have some of them, I dare not say with certainty that you are in a good state, for, according to Scripture, we can never be certain on this point[b]; but I say that it is very probable that you are so, and that to you may be applied the words of the Prophet: *Say ye to the righteous, that it shall be well with him.* Is. iii. 10. As long as you are in this disposition, doubt not that The Cross of Christ shall be your portion, and His Love your treasure.

I end where I began; and in this you will observe that it is always the same Spirit Who guides me. The sentiments which He has given me, and with which I seek to inspire you, are very pure and spiritual: profit by them. Read this Letter often: you will find directions for your conduct in the state to which God calls you. It is written for you in a spirit of simplicity. Represent my necessities to our Lord that He may be pleased to remedy them: ask of Him pardon and mercy for a sinner, who is in the union of His Spirit,

    Madam,
      Your most humble, &c.

[a] Rom. viii. 16.   [b] 1 Cor. iv. 3—5.

THE END.

GILBERT & RIVINGTON, Printers, St. John's Square, London.

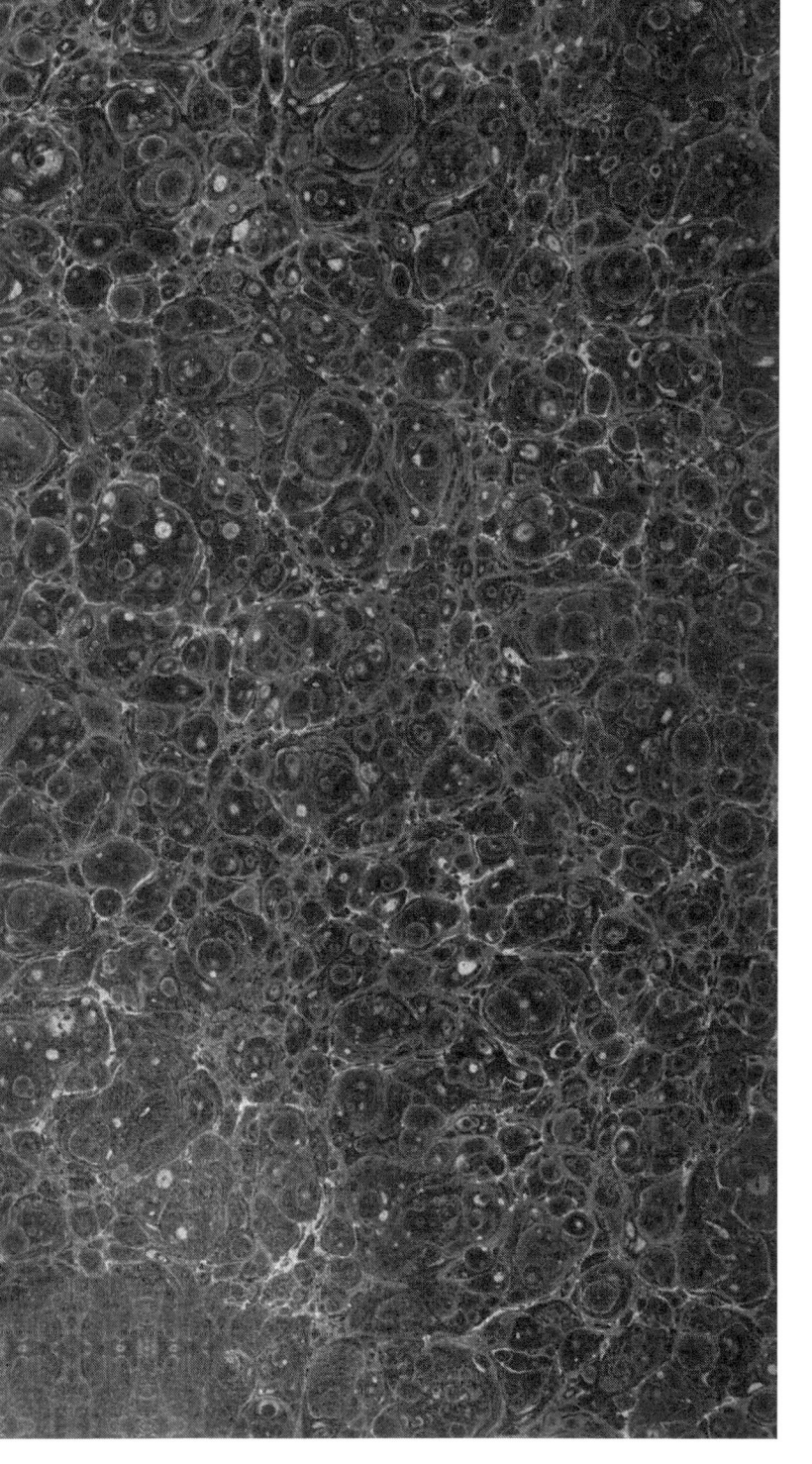

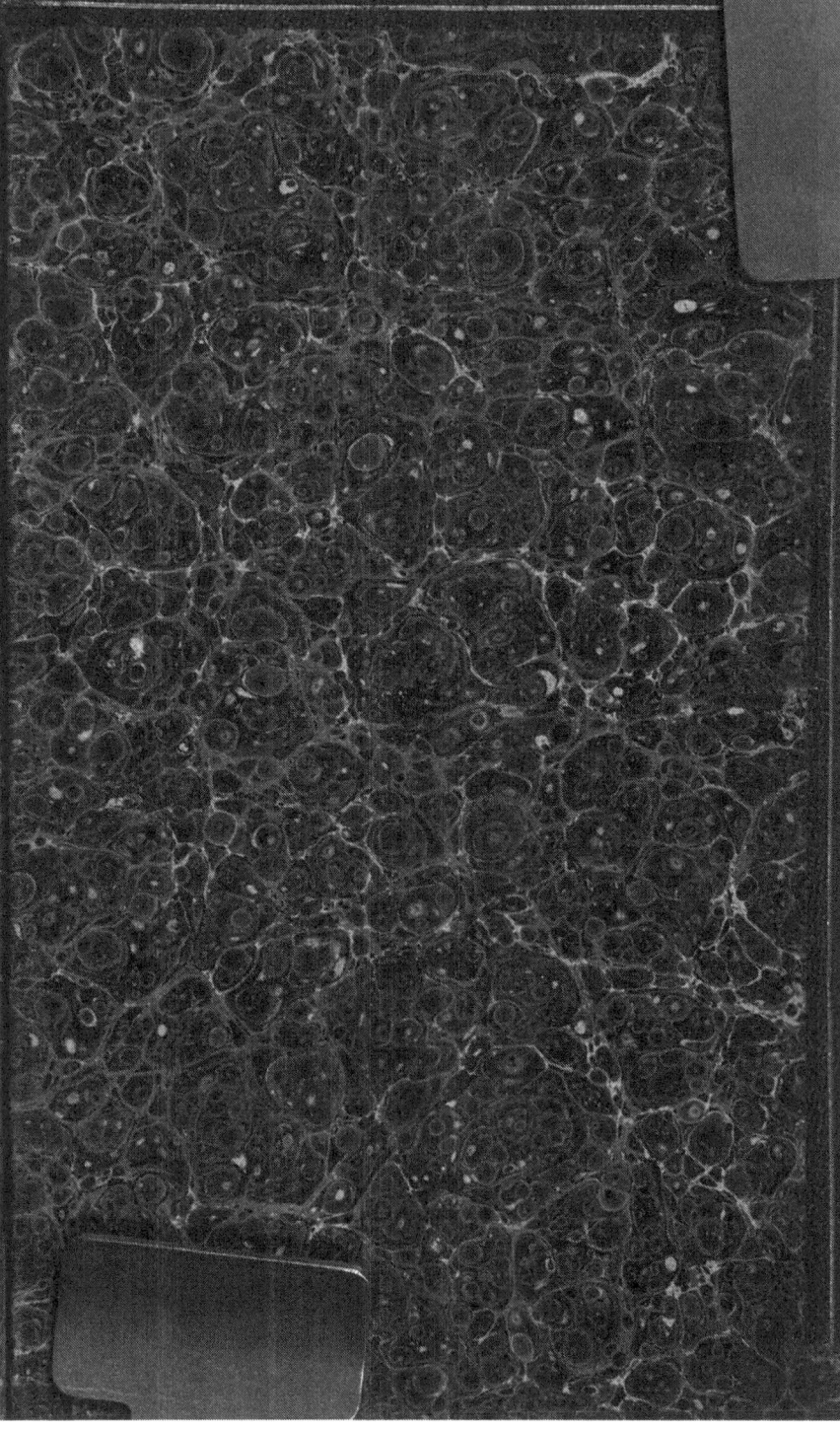

Milton Keynes UK
Ingram Content Group UK Ltd.
UKHW021036031224
452078UK00008B/523